Max Weber

Max Weber

A Critical Introduction

Kieran Allen

Pluto Press

LONDON • ANN ARBOR, MI

First published 2004 by Pluto Press
345 Archway Road, London N6 5AA
and 839 Greene Street, Ann Arbor, MI 48106

www.plutobooks.com

British Library Cataloguing in Publication Data
A catalogue record for this book is available from the British Library

ISBN   0 7453 2239 5 hardback
ISBN   0 7453 2238 7 paperback

Library of Congress Cataloging in Publication Data
Allen, Kieran, 1954–
   Max Weber : a critical introduction / Kieran Allen.
      p. cm.
Includes bibliographical references and index.
   ISBN 0–7453–2239–5 (hardback) — ISBN 0–7453–2238–7 (pbk.)
   1. Weber, Max, 1864–1920. 2. Weber, Max, 1864–1920—Political and
social views. 3. Sociology—History. I. Title.

   HM479.W42A55 2004
   301'.01—dc22

                                                            2003027471

10   9   8   7   6   5   4   3   2   1

Designed and produced for Pluto Press by
Chase Publishing Services, Fortescue, Sidmouth, EX10 9QG, England
Typeset from disk by Stanford DTP Services, Northampton, England
Printed and bound in Canada by Transcontinental Printing

Contents

1
Introduction

We live in a strange world, with inequalities on a scale never dreamt of before. Three billionaires, for example, now own more than the population of sub-Saharan Africa. The small unelected boards of directors of companies such as General Motors control more resources than South Africa or Poland. Virtually every area of life from the human body to sporting activities has been turned into a commodity. And overhanging much of this dismal state of affairs is a new era of global permanent warfare. Under the rubric of an unending 'war against terrorism' the greatest military empire of the world has given itself the right to fight 'preventative' wars in any region of the planet it deems to be harbouring a threat to its interests.

The most elementary question many will ask is: why? Why is our society so violent, unequal and often dehumanised? Each year, thousands not only ask this question but also decide to study how this society functions. They enrol in colleges, for courses in sociology, hoping to get critical insights into how society works – and maybe what can be done to change it. The mere act of wanting to *understand* rather than simply *accept* is often the first incipient sign of a rebellion against social norms. An opening is created for a sense of unease about the world.

To its detractors, sociology is a soppy subject. It has none of the hard and fast mathematical models of economics. Its academic practitioners turn up on televisions to discuss 'trends' in alcohol drinking among teenagers or the relationship between crime and 'family breakdown'. The more serious commentary about the economy or the changes in the political spectrum is left to other 'experts'. Some have claimed that the marginal role of sociology in official society results from it being a left-wing subject. Irving Horowitz, a Hannah Arendt Distinguished Professor of Sociology, has arrived at the startling conclusion that sociology has been taken over by ideologues of the far left and is now 'largely a repository of discontent'.[1] It has changed from being an objective social science to an outpost of political extremism. He claims that in areas like criminology, sociologists are now 'eclipsed by the expertise of police officers, legal and para-legal personnel and so on'.[2] The punishment for the politicisation of the discipline is that funding has been cut and its status has been downgraded. There are, of course, many sociologists who profess sympathy with the left. This is hardly surprising as the task of sociology is, after all, to defend the idea of 'the social' – that we live in a society, and not just an economy. As the global political elite try to turn everyone from hospital patients to students into 'customers', defending the idea of society against notions that we are simply an aggregate of market consumers can radicalise some. One the best representatives of this trend was Pierre Bourdieu. The huge strikes in France in 1995 over pensions and social welfare payments spurred him into an active engagement with workers. He denounced corporate globalisation because 'it is in the name of this model that flexible working, another magic word of neo-liberalism, is imposed meaning night work, weekend work, irregular working hours, things which have always been part of employers' dreams'.[3]

Bourdieu is, however, by no means the norm. For every radical critic of the system, there are scores of others who advocate support for the existing framework of society. The best-known sociologist in the English-speaking world today is probably Anthony Giddens. Many entering sociology courses encounter him through his textbook, titled simply *Sociology*. Giddens alongside his German co-thinker, Ulrick Beck, have become ideologists for Third Way politics. They profess to offer advice to social democratic parties on how best to adapt to the new challenges posed by globalisation. This advice is often quite vague and amounts to accepting corporate globalisation. Third Way politics fits easily with the political outlooks of New Labour in Britain or with that of the former US president Bill Clinton. 'No one has any alternatives to capitalism', Giddens sternly asserts, 'the arguments that remain concern how far and in what ways capitalism should be governed and regulated'.[4]

Sociology is, thus, mainly a site for conflict about interpretations about society. It may profess to be non-political – to focus on wider social trends rather than immediate political issues which people have interests in – but it nevertheless deals with issues that people passionately fight over. Sociologists often adopt a non-political guise because of the pressure of their jobs and careers – even as they make the most outrageously political statements. Many of the disputes within sociology occur at a highly abstract theoretical level, often surrounded by the most forbidding jargon. However, in their complex and confusing ways, they often reflect debates in the wider society about whose interests should be served or which direction society needs to go in.

At the heart of the conflicts there is often a reference back to the argument between Marx and Weber who are described as the founding fathers of the discipline. Their varying interpretations about the origin of capitalism, its nature, the role of class and their ideas on how societies change – or do not change – all impinge on, and re-emerge in, modern debates. The reason for this is that both men provided stunningly comprehensive overviews of modern capitalism.

A study of the writings of both men can be highly rewarding and they cannot simply be dismissed as 'dead white men' with few insights to offer today's society. Marx and Weber wrote in a very different style to present-day sociologists. With the exception of one early work by Weber, they did not carry out detailed quantitative or qualitative studies. They did not confine themselves to simply testing a few isolated and relatively narrow hypotheses. Instead, their work is characterised by a grand sweep that searches for what constitutes the fundamental dynamic of modern society. They were not subject to the now quite rigid divisions between different academic subjects – between history, politics, economics and what is now considered sociology. Instead, they straddled all these areas of inquiry, producing masterpieces which provided interpretations of what was unique about modern capitalism and what were the historical factors which went into its creation. As a result, their writings reach for the totality of experience of life under capitalism.

Moreover, they come at this society as relative strangers. Capitalism was only in its infancy in Germany when Marx wrote and the country had only recently been united when Weber was writing. Sociologists have often stressed that the eye of the 'outsider' can see far more than those who have grown accustomed to their surroundings. Marx and Weber, therefore, had huge advantages when it came to analysing social phenomena such as bureaucracy or the working of the 'free market'. They were not so accustomed to these societies that they regarded them as natural. They did not assume that issues to do with the distribution of income or human freedom had been put beyond argument. Quite the opposite. They subjected the wider social structure to a piercing scrutiny that led, despite their differing perspectives, to quite bleak visions about its future.

Unfortunately, however, students are often introduced to the writings of Marx and Weber in a dry, abstract manner that is shorn of their political contexts. This is more difficult with Marx because of his open advocacy of revolt and his links with the socialist movement. However, if his political activity is recognised, it is then bracketed out again by references to his 'controversial' views and by the suggestion that he was over-focussed on class. Marx is, above all, presented as a reductionist because he stressed the importance of economic factors and outmoded because he failed to see the new complexities that could emerge with a globalised knowledge economy. Thus a recent textbook boldly claims 'analyses of race (and indeed gender) in the contemporary world have pointed to new issues of inequality and power that are not adequately addressed by classical Marxism'.[5]

The winner of the debate within classical sociology is often deemed to be Weber. Of course, few apart from his ardent followers, directly award him plaudits. Weber's main reward comes in the form of a praise of his sophistication. Instead of a crude two-class model of modern society, Weber advocated a complex multi-class model. Instead of Marx's economic determinism, Weber appreciated multi-factoral causation. Instead of naive hopes of a better world, Weber was able to warn of the impending danger of bureaucratisation. He appears in most sociology courses as a well-packaged figure that is the doyen of 'value free' sociology. Whereas Marx advocated revolution, Weber appears detached and engaged with 'complexities' that Marx never considered.

Weber's sociology fits in more easily with a form of academic learning which defines itself as neutral while disguising its own hierarchies and biases. He holds out many intellectual advantages for this tradition. Weberian sociology can recognise the existence of social conflict – but can also imply that there is no need to challenge the wider system. It can provide a powerful appreciation of how social phenomena are historically constructed but deny there are any inherent contradictions within the present society. Weber's overall pessimism, which assumes that domination of human beings by fellow human beings is inevitable, enables sociologists to make a critique of society – but also to imply there is little prospect of overall systemic change. All of this cuts the link between critical knowledge and political action – and that is extremely helpful to a purely career-minded academic.

The great irony, of course, is that Weber was passionately political. His own injunctions about the need for 'value free' sociology were honoured more in the breach than in the observance. Weber was an ardent German nationalist and a free market liberal. His crude endorsement of nationalism offers few attractions for academics of today and so has often been ignored. When Weber, for example, writes at length in his classic book *Economy and Society* about 'the great powers' and the inevitability of imperialist expansion displacing 'pacifist' forms of free trade,[6] many sociologists simply ignore the passage. Their focus is on the more general remarks that apply to many different historical societies rather than concrete stances that Weber took. Weber had a tendency to write in generalities even while promoting the most specific political positions. His overall style indeed lent itself to an apolitical reading of his texts. The problem, though, is that this abstract reading of Weber as the pure academic carries its own undeclared political punch.

The packaging of the academic Weber began after his death and owed much to mainstream American sociology. Weber's influence in Germany was minimal in the years immediately after his death in 1920. Essays and reviews which dealt with his work often appeared in journals that were quite tangential to social science. The major social science journal of the time, *Archiv fur Sozialwissenschaft und Sozialpolitik*, did not review a single book of his.[7] During the period 1922 to 1947, less than 2,000 copies of Weber's *Economy and Society* were sold.[8] Few German sociologists regarded themselves as his followers and so his influence was 'fragmentary and patchy'.[9] With the Nazi seizure of power and the purge of universities, even this was virtually wiped out. His influence grew eventually because of the activities of three key figures.

The first was his wife, Marianne, who helped to construct *Economy and Society* and gathered together four collections of his writings after his death.[10] Marianne Weber's editing of these works reflected some of her personal concerns. In 1926, she also produced the now standard biography from which most subsequent biographies have drawn heavily. Her approach to her husband contains a paradox. She was an active feminist who wrote books on marriage and the women's movement but her biography of Weber is effectively a hagiography. Much is left out and often incidents are referred to only vaguely. The overall aim of the book is clearly to construct a 'great man'. Marianne Weber and her friend Karl Jaspers were part of the Heidelberg Circle in the 1920s. The central belief of this circle was that Max Weber was a personality of outstanding rank who never found the acclaim he deserved among fellow academics or the general public.[11] The aim of Marianne Weber was to correct this alleged wrong.

The second key figure who helped construct the modern Weber was Johannes Ferdinand Winckelmann. This former judge and state official who served the Nazi regime faithfully believed that Weber offered an alternative account of historical development to Marx and so he systematically began to assemble his work after the Second World War. Wincklelmann was, however, quite selective in how the assembly was carried out. He eliminated all polemical writings from the section on government in *Economy and Society* in order to put together a timeless piece of value-free sociology.[12] Weber's description of the enemy armies fighting Germany during the First World War as being 'composed increasingly of barbarians' and ' the flotsam of African and Asiatic savages',[13] for example, disappeared. In a new era after the defeat of the Nazi regime, West Germany took the side of the US during the Cold War. Weber's crude advocacy of German nationalism appeared superfluous and above all unsociological.

The third and by far the most important figure who became a promoter of Weber was Talcott Parsons, the leading theoretician in American sociology in the Cold War era. Parsons has been described as 'the champion of the American version of liberal capitalism'.[14] A Harvard professor, he began his major sociological theorising during the Depression years of the 1930s. He was connected with a group of academics who formed the Pareto circle in the elite university. This was a conservative think-tank that saw Pareto as the 'Marx of the bourgeoisie'.[15] George Homans expressed the ethos of the circle candidly when he remarked that 'as a Republican Bostonian who had not rejected his comparatively wealthy family, I felt during the thirties under personal attack, above all from the Marxists'.[16]

The central concern of Parsons was the problem of how social order was maintained. His sociological writings were developed against a background of mass meetings, marches, union membership drives and widespread unrest in American society. The conservatives felt insecure, threatened and uneasy. As one early critic of Parsons put it, 'the problem of social order is the conservative's way of talking about the conditions when the established elite is unable to rule in traditional ways and when there is a crisis in the master institutions'.[17] Parsons' aim was to construct a 'grand theory' that focussed on how common values and norms helped to generate a stable and ordered society. Through a style of abstract theorising, Parsons sought to develop an alternative approach within American sociology to that of the writings of the Chicago school. This school had grown around a number of brilliant writers who explored the different immigrant communities and subcultures in Chicago. It was often inspired by a vague social reformist politics that expressed a sympathy for the underdog.

The key to the construction of Parsons' grand theories lay in importing some of the themes of classical European sociology into a new intellectual system that defended American values. Parsons saw Weber as the most important figure of the European tradition and the one who was the closest to his own concerns. In one of his final lectures, he stated that Weber 'served in a very real sense, as my teacher'.[18] Parsons did his doctoral thesis at Heidelberg and had become acquainted with an earlier German debate on the origins of capitalism. He translated Weber's work *The Protestant Ethic and the Spirit of Capitalism* into English in 1930.

Parsons' major theoretical book, *The Structure of Social Action*, which was published in 1937, helped place Weber at the head of the sociological canon. Parsons suggested that Weber was 'fighting ... against the positivistic tendencies of Marxian historical materialism'[19] and so Weber's ideas could be regarded as precursors of Parsons' own 'voluntaristic action' theory. This latter theory, it was claimed, had achieved a complex synthesis that integrated the role of values, choices and material situations into a powerful framework of action. *The Structure of Social Action* was subsequently described as 'the American alternative to Marxism'[20] because it offered a grand theory that stressed common values rather than class conflict.

In 1939, Parsons received a letter from Friedrich von Hayek urging him to revise a translation of *Economy and Society*. Von Hayek was the leading free market fundamentalist of his age, opposing not just Marxism but also Keynesian attempts to regulate the economy. He regarded Weber as an important ideological forerunner because, like Hayek himself, he had drawn on the influence of the Austrian school of economics that stressed the role of individual choice in the market place over any form of public regulation. Von Hayek was anxious that Weber's work should receive a large English-speaking audience and so he turned to Parsons for help.[21] Parsons not only obliged in the translation but also wrote an introduction that was designed to further establish Weber's importance.

However, if Parsons established Weber in the canon of American sociology, he also played down his emphasis on power relations. This was exemplified most clearly in his translation of Weber's term

Herrschaft to mean 'leadership' rather than 'domination'.[22] He took up Weber's argument that ideas had significant worldly consequences and could be stimulants to social action. However, he tended to remove some of the bleakness of Weber's vision by stressing how the acting out of conventional ideals led to success. In brief, he Americanised Weber. As Tribe put it,

> There appears to be some justification for concluding that it was the 'agenda setting' activities of Parsons and his associates that played the greatest role in establishing Weber as a classical sociologist, an agenda that was then supplemented by the teachings of émigrés and the appearance of translations. Representing Weber in this way, Parsons set forth in the world a construction that was based on a set of assumptions, which were then employed in the reading of selected 'central' texts.[23]

One of the main effects of Parsons' construction was to create an image of Weber as an architect of a sociological system that was above political conflicts. Weber thus entered the canon of American sociology as a 'value free' sociologist. He became a valuable icon in the Cold War – an intellectual giant who rivalled and surpassed the USSR's championship of Marx. One of Parsons' close collaborators, Edward Shils, for example, described Weber's corpus of work as 'the most fundamental and most learned achievement of sociology'.[24] Shils' praise was by no means disinterested. He strongly disliked the tendency for members of the sociological profession 'to judge their respective societies from the standpoint of a Utopian egalitarian ideal'.[25] He despised the collectivist ethos behind the welfare state and saw Weber as prophetic in warning against bureaucratisation. Shils praised Weber as a classic free market liberal who thought 'rewards should be commensurate with achievement'.[26] In brief, a supporter of the American way before his time.

Shils was linked to the Congress for Cultural Freedom, a CIA sponsored organisation that sought to wage an intellectual struggle for the hearts and minds of left leaning intellectuals. One of the other participants was Daniel Bell. In 1960, Bell produced his famous book *The End of Ideology*, which argued that serious conflicts between social groups with different value systems were over in the industrial societies. The conflicts between left and right would henceforth be replaced by minor tensions within the dominant consensus. Bell's co-thinker and fellow supporter of the Congress for Cultural Freedom,

Seymour Martin Lipset, went further and proclaimed his own 'end of history' thesis. 'Democracy' he argued 'is not only or primarily a means through which different groups can attain their ends or seek the good society; it is the good society itself in operation.'[27]

The inspiration for many of Lipset and Bell's arguments was again to be found in their own particular interpretation of Weber. Bell hailed Weber for having a 'pragmatic view, which seeks reconciliation as its goal'.[28] He used Weber's distinction between 'the ethic of responsibility' which implied an acceptance of the existing framework of society and 'the ethic of conscience' which applied to those who questioned the way society was organised. This latter group had not accepted the permanence of capitalism and so operated as 'pure believers' who ' burn with pure, unquenchable flame and can accept no compromise with faith'.[29] Weber's seemingly reluctant endorsement of capitalism on the pragmatic grounds of realism, efficiency and 'rationality', suited many former left intellectuals such as Bell and Lipset. Weber was thus pressed into service to marginalise the remaining dissenters in Cold War American society as near-religious zealots.

One of the reasons, however, why Weber was such an effective ideological tool was that his influence on American sociology was not just confined to the conservative right. C.W. Mills was the leading dissident in American sociology in the Cold War era. He was also one of the two translators of the classic collection of Weber essays, *From Max Weber: Essays in Sociology*, which popularised Weber's work in America. The introduction to the book helped to establish Weber as the originator of key insights into the system of stratification and domination. Unlike Parsons, it placed Weber in his political context and drew links between this and his sociology. However, it emphasised certain aspects of Weber's writings which made him appear more of a left-wing liberal than he actually was. Weber was presented as moving from an openly imperialist position in his youth to a more democratic position in his later years. He was opposed to the German revolution of 1918 not for class reasons but rather because 'he realized that the revolution could not lead to lasting socialist institutions.'[30] The introduction quotes Marianne Weber at length to indicate that Max had 'sympathy with the struggle of the proletariat for a human and dignified existence'[31] and pondered whether he should join their ranks as a member of the Social Democratic Party. He only rejected this, apparently, because 'one could only be an honest socialist, just like a Christian, if one was ready to share the way of life of the unpropertied'.[32] This Weber could not do because of his health and the fact that 'his scholarship simply depended upon capital rent'.[33]

This relatively sympathetic portrayal of Weber formed the background for a particular presentation of his relationship to Marx. Weber was seen to partake in the 'humanist tradition of liberalism which is concerned with the freedom of the individual to create free institutions'.[34] This led him to try to show how there were different spheres of political and economic power. He was able to incorporate elements of Marx's teaching into his sociology but could also 'round out' his economic materialism. Moreover, whereas Marx had denounced capitalism for being irrational, Weber's liberalism led to a clearer focus on how it was the very embodiment of rationality. This form of rationality was preparing 'man for his absorption in the clattering process of the bureaucratic machinery'.[35] The overall effect of Mills and Gerth's introduction was to present Weber as a more sophisticated sociologist who had corrected Marx's lack of emphasis on human freedom.

The introduction acknowledged that there was certainly a tragic element to Weber's writings because little could be done to arrest the bureaucratic machine – but it was a romanticised tragedy. Thus Gerth and Mills wrote,

> For Weber, capitalism is the embodiment of rational impersonality; the quest for freedom is identified with irrational sentiment and privacy. Freedom is at best a tarrying for loving companionship and for the cathartic experience of art as a this-worldly escape from institutional routines. It is the privilege of the propertied and educated: it is freedom without equality. In this conception of freedom as a historically developed phenomena, now on the defensive against both capitalism and bureaucracy, Weber represents humanist and cultural liberalism rather than economic liberalism.[36]

Weber's deep pessimism about the possibility of changing capitalism and his ambiguous critique of its cold, bureaucratic machinery had a strong appeal to intellectuals such as Mills and many later sociologists. Mills was a fierce critic of the power structure of American society and described himself as a 'plain Marxist'.[37] However, in one key area C.W. Mills was much closer to Weber than Marx: his dismissal of workers as agents of change. Mills saw the main division in society as being between a 'power elite' that grew out of the military industrial complex and a 'mass society', which was firmly controlled and manipulated. Workers were the victims of history with little potential for self-liberation. The awesome power of the cultural apparatus of modern capitalism led to endless possibilities for manipulation. Weber's notion of rationalisiation and bureaucratisation fitted well with Mills' own pessimism. But Mills in turn helped to establish a longer tradition in sociology – which eventually outlived the demise of Parsons' theories – whereby Weber appeared to have a more modern appeal than Marx precisely because he implied that class struggle had no great political potential. As the possibility for fundamental social change was closed down, sociology became at best a source of liberal energies that aimed to create a space for a certain type of freedom – 'freedom without equality'.

Once Weber became dominant in US sociology, concerted attempts were made to re-establish his reputation in Germany. In 1964 Parsons and Reinhard Bendix, an important biographer of Weber, carefully planned and then used the occasion of the German Sociological Association conference to promote Weber's reputation over the growing influence of the Marxist-based Frankfurt School.[38] This occurred against a background of opposition to the nuclear arms race and the Cold War. Afterwards, Guenther Roth gave a flavour of the polemics by claiming that attacks on Weber from 'Marxists and Nazis have been remarkably similar' and that opponents of Weber 'use a sociological approach for political purposes or deny altogether the present rationale of political sociology and to some extent even question the viability of Western pluralist society'.[39] The possibility that those who defended Western capitalism might be equally using sociology for political purposes was discarded. The 'canonisation' of Weber as the main classical sociologist of the free world was complete and he now became 'not the object of scepticism or utility but the object of piety'.[40]

Of course, Weber's reputation was challenged. The student revolt of the 1960s and the huge radicalisation that followed led to a revival of Marxist ideas in some sections of the academy. By the early 1970s, there was virtually no area of sociology without Marxist writers. In many instances, Weber was simply bypassed and a new language of analysis was created. However, there were also direct assaults on his work. A key reference point for a new re-assessment of Weber was Wolfgang Mommsen's book *Max Weber and German Politics* that was completed in 1959 and only translated into English in 1984. It documented the strong German nationalism in Weber's outlook and so shattered some of the make-up that had been applied by right-wing American sociologists. Although Mommsen was eventually to become more sympathetic to Weber, his work had an extraordinary liberating effect. Writers like Paul Hirst were able to challenge the inherent elitism of Weber's critique of popular democracy and attack his arguments that genuine democratic decision-making and popular rule are impossible in all but the most simple of societies.[41] Others like Tom Bottomore could claim that Weber 'remained to the end a fervent nationalist, a half-hearted democrat and an implacable opponent of socialism'.[42]

Nevertheless, the left-wing challenge in sociology was not sustained. When the revolts of the late 1960s subsided there developed a vogue for highly obtuse forms of theory that had no link with actual struggles. Particular variants of Marxism that ultimately looked to China, Russia or particular Third World 'socialisms' for liberation did not help. When many of these regimes collapsed after the fall of the Berlin Wall in 1989, many left academics became convinced there could never be an alternative to capitalism. The only thing that was attainable was a stronger, more pluralistic 'civil society', which became an ethical realm of solidarity held together by moral sentiment and natural affection.[43]

The result has been a resurgence of Weber's popularity in sociology and he has now achieved a near hegemonic status. His work fitted in neatly with the apparent death of the working class. Against the 'reductionist' message of Marxism, Weber's sociology offered a framework for analysing how social groups engage in strategies of exclusion and status-seeking. His work on bureaucracy was taken as almost prophetic after the collapse of the Soviet bloc. His stress on the fragmentation of workers and their inability to advance common political goals is deemed to be more relevant in a post-industrial society. In brief, Weber has become the touchstone for many modern theorists who accept the inevitability of capitalism and the impossibility of change. More than that he has become the fountainhead for the established wisdom of sociology itself. As Hennis put it,

> Never before in the history of the science has an orthodoxy (a 'paradigm') been able to establish itself so powerfully and decisively and yet with minimum of intellectual effort. Seldom today challenged, and certain of its utility, modern social science requires only occasional reference to authority. The greatest, most venerated and silently respected figure of authority is that of Max Weber.

Whoever dares to throw doubt on the legitimacy of established social science must direct himself to that figure.[44]

This book sets out to challenge this state of affairs. Its starting point is that sociology today has lost much of its critical sharpness. The days of the Sociology Liberation Movement when radical sociologists took on establishment figures who worked with governments are long over. The dominant ethos in sociology today is to advocate a mild form of tolerance for multiculturalism and a critique of social hierarchies – but from within a perspective that accepts the status quo. Weber's influence within sociology helps to articulate an overwhelming pessimism about workers' struggles and a dismissal of their significance. His hegemonic status blends in easily with a 'cultural turn' whereby sociologists focus on how reality is constructed through interpretations and meanings – rather than examining the contradictions at the heart of the class structure. This is all the more ironic in a society which is producing inequalities on a scale that has never been dreamed off in previous history. As millions of people look to the wider movement against corporate globalisation, it is vital that this tendency within sociology is challenged.

The book offers both an introduction to Weber and a critique of his ideas. It summarises his argument as accurately as possible for students of sociology and then subjects this argument to critical scrutiny. It places Weber in his political context as a sociologist of empire and shows how his defence of capitalism pervades his writings. It suggests that far from offering an 'objective' value-free account of modern society, Weber's sociology is deeply ideological. It points, for example, to his support for the First World War and his deep hostility to the growth of the revolutionary left in the aftermath of Germany's defeat. It suggests that these political stances were the logical outcome of a type of theorising which advocated an acceptance of capitalism on the grounds of tragic necessity. Such a critique does not deny that Weber provided significant critical insights into the workings of modern society. However, while there are many individual insights to be gained from a close reading of his writings, it is also necessary to identify how his overall framework rested on a belief that capitalism represents the best of all possible worlds.

Our belief is that no value-free sociology is possible in a world where the production of ideas is linked to the dominance of capital. Too often the latent function of the cry that sociologists be value-free is to demand that 'Thou shalt not commit a critical or negative value judgement – especially of one's own society.'[45] By offering an account of Weber which seeks to question his status as the most venerated and silently respected figure of authority, this little book also hopes to help re-open the path for a critical, politically engaged inquiry into modern capitalism.

2
The Sociologist of Empire

Max Weber is conventionally described as a value-free sociologist who rose above politics. His work is assumed to have a timeless quality that is not at all related to the debates within his own society at the time. Textbooks on Weber therefore start with the briefest of biographies which typically emphasise the psychological conflict which arose from his family background and which caused him extreme mental stress. They then move on to his wider sociology. His political interventions are barely mentioned because they are deemed irrelevant to his work. This conventional approach may be useful in creating the myth of a 'great man' who rises above the petty disputes of his day to offer eternal truths. However, it also presents a very partial account of a writer who was torn between his political and academic passions.

If we remove the conventional packaging in which Weber was wrapped and look at his writings in their actual context, we find a concern with three central issues. These emerge in Weber's earliest writings but they continue throughout his life. One was the question of empire: why was imperialism in Germany's interest? The second was the leadership of Germany: after its unification, who was to lead the German nation? Finally, there was the question of class division and the rise of Marxism: how best was Marxism to be combated? We shall start this chapter, however, by giving a brief overview of his life.

AN OVERVIEW OF WEBER'S LIFE

'A class conscious bourgeois' is how Max Weber once described himself in a letter to his friend and fellow sociologist Robert Michels.[1] Seven years previously, he had made a similar reference to his class outlook when he noted that, 'I am a member of the bourgeois class. I feel myself to be a bourgeois and I have been brought up to share their views and ideals.'[2] As a description of his origins, it was accurate.

15

Max Weber was born in Erfurt, Germany in 1864 into a wealthy family. He grew up in a household that was frequented by both the business and academic elite of German liberalism.[3] His father, Max Weber Senior, was a descendant of Westphalian linen merchants who rose from being a salaried city magistrate to becoming a deputy of the National Liberal Party in the Prussian and Imperial parliament. The National Liberals had made their peace with the Bismarck regime and Max Weber Senior was a typical conventional politician who engaged in wheeling and dealing. Weber's mother, Helene, had come from another family of large fortune, the Souchays. She was a deeply religious woman who engaged in philanthropic activity out of an ethical conviction grounded in her Calvinist background. Both parents had descended from Protestant refugees who had faced Catholic persecution.

Much of Weber's younger years were spent in Berlin where he was recognised from an early age as a precocious child. His teenage letters comment on the merits of Goethe, Kant, Hegel and Spinoza. Just before his fourteenth birthday, he wrote an essay about the course of German history and one on Roman Imperial history after Constantine. While attending his school, he secretly read all 40 volumes of Goethe during his class hours. Of his own accord, he learnt Hebrew in order to study the Old Testament in the original.

At the heart of the Weber household was a deep-seated psychological conflict that was to have a lasting effect on Max. His father ruled with a heavy authoritarian hand inside the home but outside lived the life of a carefree pleasure-seeking man about town. He did not seem to share his wife's grief over the loss of Anna, one of their children who died as an infant. He maintained a tight control of the family budget and ceded little autonomy to his wife. Overall his pleasure-seeking ways clashed fundamentally with his wife's deep sense of Calvinist morality.

At first Max leaned towards the lifestyle of his father. While at University in Heidelberg, he joined his father's duelling fraternity and consumed enormous quantities of beer. He also followed his father's footsteps in studying law. However, when he left Heidelberg for military service in Strasbourg, he stayed at the house of Hermann Baumgarten and his wife, Ida, Helene Weber's sister, and both were to have important influences on him. Hermann Baumgarten was a liberal like Weber's father but he never reconciled himself to Bismarck and left Weber with an abiding dislike of Bismarck's legacy. Ida shared the religious convictions of Weber's mother but was much more forceful and introduced him to her favourite theologian, William Ellery Channing. Although Weber never shared the Christian beliefs, the Baumgarten household left him with a lifelong respect for Protestant virtues.

One immediate result was a new identification with his mother's values when he moved back into the family home in 1886, becoming her confidant. He stayed there for the next eight years and became increasingly alienated from his father activities. As a student, he was forced into a prolonged financial dependence on his father, which he deeply resented. For a period, however, the smouldering psychic conflict was put aside. Weber was a brilliant student who completed his post-doctoral dissertation on 'Roman Agrarian History' in 1891. Thereafter he began to move away from legal studies to what is now referred to as sociology. He undertook a research assignment for the Verein fur Sozialpolitik into the conditions of agrarian workers by administering a questionnaire to landowners. The result was an 891-page book titled *The Conditions of Farm Workers in East Elbian Germany*.

His research on the 'social question' brought him into the orbit of organisations that offered an alternative to the growing influence of the Marxist Social Democratic Party (SPD). One of these was the Evangelical Social Congress that had been founded by Adolf Stoecker in 1890. Stoecker was a former court preacher who held deep anti-Semitic views and wished to build a workers party that was pro-monarchy and based on conservative social Christian principles. Weber did not share Stoecker's anti-Semitism nor his support for the Prussian aristocracy but he was interested in ways in which Protestant morality could help overcome the growing social divide in Germany. In particular, he shared the aim of the Evangelical Social Congress 'to make the classes conscious of their social obligations toward one another and get them to fulfil them, and in particular to make employers acknowledge the morally equal value of labour'.[4] Through the Evangelical Social Congress, Weber came into contact with Friedrich Naumann, who was at the time a chaplain and known as the 'poor people's pastor'.[5] Nauman had originally considered joining the SPD to move it away from Marxism by working from within. But later he sought to develop a social Christian party that would offer an alternative to the SPD. Naumann became Weber's closest political collaborator as they both shared a strong conviction in remedying the defects of capitalism from within and winning the workers movement to liberal imperialism.

The other organisation that Weber joined in 1893 was the Pan German League, which one writer has described as 'the voice of Germany's most vicious nationalism, well endowed with money and media influence'.[6] He was an enthusiastic advocate of a social imperialist outlook. According to his wife, Weber believed that 'the preservation and advancement of Germany's position as a great power was not only a duty dictated by the past but also a pre-requisite for a decent life for the masses'.[7] He remained a member of the League until 1899 and left because it was too close to conservative agricultural interests and would not pursue a campaign to close the borders to Polish immigrants enthusiastically enough. He nevertheless acknowledged that his resignation 'did not prevent him from a lively sympathy for the league's efforts.'[8] It was only later that he distanced himself from the Pan German League's rabid anti-Semitism and its lack of a strategy for expanding Germany as a great power.

By the mid 1890s, Weber had become relatively well known in both academic and political circles. In 1893 he married Marianne Schnitger who would be his companion until his death. He was appointed to the chair of economics in Freiburg University in 1895 and delivered an impassioned nationalist inaugural address on 'The National State and Economic Policy'. A year later, his growing reputation meant he was invited to take up the post of Professor of Economics in Heidelberg University. However, suddenly the bright career seemed to come to an abrupt end. In 1897, he had a violent clash with his father over the way he treated his mother and told him to leave the family home. The father died a month later and shortly afterwards Max Weber suffered a nervous breakdown from which he did not recover for more than five years. He resigned his chair in Heidelberg, travelled and visited a sanatorium but he was not to resume teaching until 1918.

In 1903, he showed the first signs of recovery when he agreed to become an editor of the *Archiv fur Socialwissenschaft*, which soon became the main German journal of social science. The following year he visited America and was deeply impressed by the dynamism of that society and the role of Protestant sects in its creation. His famous work *The Protestant Ethic and the Spirit of Capitalism* appeared soon after his return in 1905. In 1904 he wrote his important essay on 'The Objectivity of Knowledge in Social Sciences'. Nine years later in 1913 he intervened in a wider debate to produce *The Meaning of Value Neutrality in the Sociological and Economic Sciences*. Together these became the core of the posthumously published *Max Weber on the Methodology of the Social Sciences*. With some exceptions, Weber's work in this period is extremely difficult. Nevertheless there are also rare moments of lucid political engagement. In 1905, for example, after the first Russian Revolution broke out, Weber wrote a number of important studies on the role of Russian liberalism. In 1910, he became a co-founder of the German Sociological Society. The difficult and spasmodic nature of Weber's work during this period has meant that commentators have traditionally focussed on the growth of an 'intellectual circle' around the Weber household. This intellectual circle extended from the future Hungarian Marxist Georg Lukács to the psychiatrist–philosopher Karl Jaspers.

A new phase opened up in 1914 with the outbreak of the First World War, which Weber welcomed. On a personal level it also seemed to restore his productive intellectual capacity. In September 1915, for example, he began his series of articles on *The Economic Ethic of World Religions*. Throughout the course of the war, Weber also wrote a number of articles on policy, mainly to defend the strategy of the German Prime Minister Bethmann Hollweg. His central argument was that Germany needed clear strategic goals to achieve its war aims rather than rhetorical bombast that might easily slide towards despair. After the war, Weber resumed teaching and pushed himself to the fore as a strong opponent of the revolutionary left in German society. In a series of articles including 'Politics as a Vocation' he combined a pessimistic vision about the realities of mass politics with a pragmatism that advocated working within the status quo.

Throughout his life Weber saw himself as a 'bourgeois scholar'[9] with a sense of mission. He wanted Germany to be a great power and his writing involved a combination of sociology and political commentary. The political commentary was more evident in his earlier and later years. Nevertheless there were a number of central interests and concerns which underlay much of his writing.

GERMANY'S INTEREST IN IMPERIALISM

The last quarter of the nineteenth century witnessed the redivision of the world between the big industrial powers. Germany was a major player in this expansion and its overseas empire encompassed 900,000 square miles.[10] The old restraints imposed by Bismarck of avoiding African colonies were removed. Germany demanded 'its place in the sun', as the foreign secretary Bernhard von Bulow put it in 1897.[11] Alongside its direct colonial possessions, Germany was also vying for domination of central Europe.

This imperialist outlook made a huge mark on the contemporary bourgeois mind. According to Blackbourn, 'the membership of the Colonial Association' read like a 'Who's Who of prominent figures in German business'.[12] Millions of middle-class Germans participated in foreign policy pressure groups such as the Flottenverein – the Naval League.[13] The Flottenverein was a huge propaganda machine that was secretly funded by the naval ministry. Admiral von Tirpitz, the head of this ministry, also paid journalists to sing the praises of imperialism and professors to give *Weltpolitik* their academic blessing. Little boys and girls from well-to-do families wore sailor suits as their Sunday best and there was not a family photo from those days where a naval uniform did not feature. Weber's ideas developed out of this colonial culture but he gave it a sharp and distinctive edge by asserting that power struggles, particularly between nations, were part of the eternal conditions of life.

Weber's imperialism was militant, direct and above all 'realistic'. He assumed that Africans were 'kulturlos' and could be legitimately colonised.[14] He criticised Bismarck's 'accommodating policy' of forging diplomatic alliances because it was 'disinclined to all thoughts of overseas expansion'.[15] He supported von Tirpitz's plans to break from the traditional Prussian restraint on naval matters and develop a battle fleet that could challenge Britain's.[16] Attempts to expand Germany's navy triggered off an arms race as Britain replied with the development of the dreadnought battleship and Germany responded in turn with the torpedo boat and the U-boat. Weber, however, believed that imperialism was in the direct interest of German industry. He claimed that the expansion of trade 'must now once more lead to a situation in which power alone will have a decisive influence on the extent to which individual nations will share in economic control of the world'.[17] He persuaded his close associate Friedrich Naumann to move from a Christian socialist outlook to one that embraced national power politics and imperialism.[18] In a speech in 1896 on unemployment, Weber spelled out explicitly his rationale:

> We need more room externally, we need an extension of economic opportunities through our expansion of our markets … and that is nowadays in the long run absolutely dependent upon expansion of our political power abroad. A dozen ships on the East African Coast are at certain moments of more value than a dozen trade

agreements which can be terminated ... It is a vital matter for us that the broad masses of our people should become aware that the expansion of Germany's power is the only thing which can ensure for them a permanent livelihood at home and the possibility of progressive improvement.[19]

Weber linked an imperialist foreign policy with the need to promote industry above agriculture. In a key debate in 1897, he challenged the arguments of the economist Karl Oldenburg who proposed an artificial halt to Germany's development as an industrial state. Oldenberg had claimed that the growth of industry and trade involved greater dependence on foreigners and called instead for more emphasis on agriculture and self-sufficiency. Weber countered that the capitalist development of Germany was 'unavoidable and it is only possible to economically influence the course which it takes'.[20] Any attempt to restrict industrial expansion would lead to a stagnant form of capitalism based on 'lazy rentiers and a dull traditional mass'.[21] This 'peculiarly conservative domestic capitalism ... in economic terms promotes class struggle from above and in political terms sees its deadly enemy to be the rise of the working class and free institutions in the land'.[22] Weber acknowledged that a pro-industry policy was more risky as it depended on export markets. However, he argued that 'we are not pursuing a policy of national *comfort* but rather one of *greatness*, hence we must take this burden upon our shoulders if we wish to have a national existence other than that of Switzerland, for example'.[23]

However, promoting industry did not mean that Weber ignored developments in agriculture. His first main study on *The Conditions of Agricultural Workers in East Elbian Germany* showed Weber's sharp ability to assess the consequences of economic changes for German nationalism. Weber argued that a community of interest had originally existed between the Prussian estate owners – the Junkers – and the Instman, peasants who were provided with a house and a small plot of land and received a share of the crop. This relationship meant that East Elbian estates were not 'merely economic units, but local political *centres of domination*'[24] and ultimately they helped Prussia provide a leadership for Germany as a whole. However, towards the end of the nineteenth century the large estates were threatened by international competition in grain. Many of the peasantry began to migrate to the towns in search of a better life and greater freedom.

Polish seasonal migrants who were paid in money rather than in kind increasingly took their place.

Weber claimed that his analysis of these changes was not guided by questions such as 'is the worker doing well or badly, how can he be helped' because his sole concern was the interest of the nation state.[25] Prussia was the heartland of German nationalism and the influx of Polish workers into this region could only weaken the wider state. He referred to the Polish workers as 'animals'[26] and attacked 'a Slavic invasion which would mean a cultural regression of major proportions'.[27] His racist remarks were connected to his belief that central Europe was a region to be dominated by Germany. In the meantime, the German state had to resettle German peasants in the area:

> We want to fetter them to the soil of their fatherland, not with legal, but rather with psychological chains. We wish, we say it quite openly – to make use of their hunger for land to bind them to their homeland, and even if we have to hammer a generation to the land to secure its future, so we should assume this responsibility.[28]

Weber recognized that this policy ran counter to short-term market interests of the landlords. However the interests of the German nation had to take precedence over the needs of the Junker class for obtaining cheap labour.

Weber's imperialism was not simply a product of his youth. Throughout his life, he engaged in a cold calculation about what was necessary for Germany to become a great power. He had little time for bragging and bluster and sought a shrewdly realistic foreign policy. This realism led him tactically to disagree with other German nationalists because he wanted to avoid a life and death struggle with England. He found the speeches and behaviour of the German Kaiser irresponsible in this regard.[29] The weakness of the monarchy led Weber to favour a system of parliamentary democracy as the best method of building the internal resources required to establish Germany as a power state. Weber's support for democracy was, however, subordinate to his aim of expanding Germany's sphere of influence. He saw the parliament primarily as an institution that was best suited to fulfilling the function of training a leadership that could avoid the irresponsibility and capriciousness of the German monarchy. It could also provide a mechanism to conciliate the working class and win them to an imperialist outlook. A parliament would produce a 'political maturity' that united the nation and rendered it capable of domination. As he wrote later in his classic *Parliament and Government in Germany*,

> Only a politically mature people is a nation of masters (Herrenvolk) ... Only a nation of masters are called upon to thrust their hands into the spokes of the world's development. If nations who do not have this quality attempt to do so, then not only will the sure instincts of other nations rebel, but they will also fail inwardly in the attempt.[30]

THE LEADERSHIP OF GERMANY

The future of Germany as a great power was linked to the second central question for Weber: which class could provide the leadership for Germany? Unlike France or England, the leading political force in bringing about an end to feudalism did not come from the bourgeoisie. During the revolution of 1848, the liberal movement in Germany had an opportunity to unite Germany, extend democracy and forge conditions favourable to industrialisation. However, it failed to carry through a decisive transformation. It was much more fearful of radical movements from below than it was determined to abolish feudalism. As Marx put it,

> The German bourgeois developed so sluggishly, timidly and slowly that at the moment when it menacingly confronted feudalism and absolutism, it saw menacingly confronting it the proletariat and all sections of the middle class whose interests were related to those of the proletariat.[31]

The result was that Germany did not unite as a republic in 1848 but as an empire in 1871. As with the Risorgimento in Italy or the Meiji Restoration in Japan, modernisation came through 'a revolution from above'.[32] The key social force dominating society was the Junkers – the Prussian landowners whose large estates were increasingly producing for wider markets. After the failed revolution of 1848, Bismarck emerged as a Caesar-like figure to unite Germany under Prussian domination. He constructed a massive state bureaucracy that was dominated by the Prussian landowners but into which the big industrial bourgeoisie was integrated. An alliance was forged between heavy industry and agrarian interests in which the latter were dominant politically.

Weber was acutely conscious of the limitations for Germany's future. He argued that Bismarck's coalition had led to a 'feudalization of the bourgeois capital'[33] so that German politics placed an undue emphasis on the preservation of the Junker estates. This in turn led to the political immaturity of the bourgeoisie. Culturally, they aped the German aristocracy by engaging in duels or buying land in the hope of winning a noble title. Politically, they failed to develop leadership skills and allowed themselves to be smothered by a state bureaucracy that assisted in the creation of cartels. Weber wanted the bourgeoisie to 'free itself from its *unnatural* association' with the Junkers and 'return to the self-conscious cultivation of its own ideals'.[34] This meant challenging the comforting notion that the massive bureaucracy which Bismarck had created stood above society and expressed its interests in a rational way.

Many of Weber's ideas on the leadership of Germany came into public view when he was appointed Professor of Economics in Freiburg in 1895, taking up the chair of one of the founders of the German Historical School, Karl Knies. The Historical School had distinguished itself from Adam Smith's classical school of economics by opposing its cosmopolitanism and abstract theorising. In its place, it stressed national peculiarities and the role of cultural values in economic development.[35] It advocated protectionism and saw economics as linked to state policy. As the new professor in Freiburg, Weber defined himself as part of this school but also added his own innovations.[36] His inaugural address as professor, 'The National State and Economic Policy', contained probably the clearest programmatic statement on both his political views and his conception of academic inquiry.

The inaugural address resonated with a sense of the precariousness of Germany's position in the world order and Weber's own mission to combat any comforting notions that might hinder its struggle for power. Its central theme was that national greatness had to be fought for rather than assumed. Generalising from the imperialist culture of his age, Weber assumed that the struggle between peoples was the key feature of human life. The population problem, he argued, 'prevents us from imagining that peace and happiness lie hidden in the lap of the future, it prevents us from believing that elbow room in this earthly existence can be won in any other way than through the hard struggle of human beings with each other'.[37]

He had few illusions that trade and economic progress would do away with the need for struggle. Quite the reverse; they would only intensify it:

> We do not have peace and human happiness to bequeath to our posterity but rather the *eternal* struggle for the maintenance and improvement by careful cultivation of our national character ... Our successors will not hold us responsible before history for the kind of economic organization we hand over to them, but rather for the amount of elbow room we conquer for them in the world and leave behind us. Processes of economic development are in the final analysis also *power struggles*.[38]

Weber's aggressive nationalism did not blind him to the sources of German weakness. There was, he claimed, smugness and a lack or urgency about winning the battle for power. One source of this complacency was an older social Darwinist ideology that assumed that 'superior' human beings were automatically better able to adapt to their environment. Drawing on his research on Prussian agriculture, he claimed that there could be forms of negative selection because he had seen the Polish peasant gaining 'not *despite* but *on account of* the low level of his physical and intellectual habits of life'.[39] He warned that 'human history does not lack examples of the victory of less developed types of humanity and the extinction of the fine flowers of intellectual and emotional life'.[40] There was little doubt about whom he was referring to as the 'fine flowers'.

The critical issue in power struggles was national leadership and the problem was that German political leadership lay in the hands of the Junkers. Weber expressed his admiration for their political instincts but recognised that in unifying the country they had 'done their work now, and today are in the throes of an economic death struggle'.[41] The key issue was whether the bourgeoisie could replace them as a leading class and there was nothing at all inevitable about this. Historians, who had a mechanical notion of human progress, he claimed, often '*forget that economic power and the vocation for political leadership of the nation do not always co-incide*'.[42] The very success of Bismarck created a situation where the German bourgeoisie suffered from an 'unpolitical mood' and were 'drunk as it was with success and thirsty for peace. German history appeared to have come to an end.'[43] In brief, they lacked the political vitality that the Junkers had. This was all the more dangerous, he argued, because nationalist sentiments were not carried primarily by the masses. It was rather that the 'specific function of the economically and politically leading strata is to be the repositories of political understanding'.[44]

The inaugural address pointed to key concerns in Weber's sociology. His advocacy of German imperial greatness led him to focus on leadership and power as his dominant concepts. But for all his elitism about the historic role of bourgeois elites, his subtlety and realism led him to identify the peculiar weakness of his own class. His brilliance was that he could focus on disjunctures – between economic resources and political will, between the stability guaranteed by bureaucracy and the need for leadership to overcome its inertia, between the grandeur and bluster of empire and the need for sharp, realistic assessment of how to win. While the inaugural address did not offer an answer to the problem of national leadership, it suggested that academic science had a role to play in providing the bourgeoisie with a sense of their own historic mission. Like his forerunners in the German Historical School, Weber was not interested in a form of economics that used abstract standards of technical productivity or even social justice. Behind all human sciences there were value judgements and these judgements were 'bound up with the distinct imprint of humanity we find in our own nature'.[45] Or put even more crudely, 'The economic policy of a German state, and the standard of value adopted by a German economic theorist, can therefore be nothing other than a German policy and a German standard.'[46]

This peculiar view of science – where value judgements are placed beyond criticism and assumed to be a 'distinct imprint' of particular nations – forges a link between academic study and state interest. Weber made no bones about his view of academic science: 'The ultimate goal of our science must remain that of co-operating in the political education of our nation.'[47] By political education he meant a mission to lead the German empire.

COMBATING THE INFLUENCE OF MARXISM

This leads, finally, to the third central issue that Weber faced – the influence of Marxism in the German working class. Formed in 1875, the German Social Democratic Party was the first mass Marxist party in the world. To counter its influence Bismarck introduced anti-socialist laws in 1878. Fifteen hundred people were imprisoned and many others driven into exile before these laws lapsed in 1890. The strategy failed and after the party was legalised again, it went from strength to strength. In 1893, it won 11 per cent of the vote; in 1898, 14 per cent and in 1903, 20 per cent.[48] In 1891, the SPD adopted the Erfurt Programme, which combined a call for the socialisation of industry with immediate demands for the democratisation of Germany and the betterment of workers.[49] Its intransigent opposition to the political establishment meant that the SPD drew its mass membership into a virtual 'society within a society'.

The politics of the SPD were shaped by Karl Kautsky, who was described as the Pope of Marxism. Kautsky's particular interpretation of Marxism was highly mechanical and stressed the 'inevitability' of socialism. This led to an extreme passivity when it came to struggle. The level of strike activity was quite low in Germany and there was often a far higher level of struggle in other countries, which had weaker Marxist parties. The SPD saw its main function as the production of general socialist propaganda as it waited for its votes to mount higher and higher. Despite all this, the SPD prided itself on its Marxist orthodoxy and deviations were quickly dealt with. One such deviation was the small revisionist wing of Eduard Bernstein who advocated an openly reformist rather than a revolutionary agenda. Bernstein's ideas were officially discarded and the SPD continued to present itself as a rigorous Marxist party until the crisis of 1914.

Weber's attitude to the SPD and its particular brand of Marxism played a decisive influence on his sociology. He had no sympathy with the SPD's goal of socialism and saw the advocacy of an equal society as utopian. 'Such notions as "will of the people" and "genuine will of the people" have long since ceased to exist for me; they are fictitious notions', he told his friend Robert Michels, who was then a socialist.[50] More than that, Weber regarded any sort of independent working-class politics with suspicion. He believed that workers would always be submissive to demagogic leaders and so real decision-making rested with a small number of people. He believed in the 'principle of the small number, that is, the superior political power of manoeuvre of *small* leading groups always governs political action'.[51] Militant action by the working class moreover undermined progress because it frightened sections of the elite and pushed them in reactionary directions. A very considerable proportion of strikes, he declared, 'achieve the opposite of their desired effect not only in the unions (this you would not mind) but on every kind of progress within the working-class movement which they set back by years if not by decades'.[52]

It is interesting to compare Weber here with one of his contempories, the Russian revolutionary Leon Trotsky who came to prominence in the 1905 revolution. Trotsky built on Marx's experience of the 1848 revolution to argue that once the working class appeared, the bourgeoisie ceased to be revolutionary and sought alliance with the old feudal aristocracy. His theory of 'permanent revolution' asserted that workers even in underdeveloped countries should not confine themselves solely to supporting democratic revolutions but should fight for socialism.[53] As we have seen, Weber agreed with some elements of Trotsky's diagnosis. His concept of the 'feudalisation' of the bourgeoisie points to a similar phenomenon that Trotsky alluded to – the integration of industrialists into political structures created by the old feudal elite. Trotsky and Weber, however, drew entirely opposite conclusions. For Weber, independent working-class activity not only scared the bourgeoisie but also strengthened the old regime. 'Because Social Democracy has set itself against the bourgeoisie, it has smoothed the path of reaction' he claimed in Germany in 1896.[54] Less than a decade later when writing about the Russian Revolution of 1905, he also attacked,

> the small-minded attitude of 'the professional socialists' who urged their supporters to attack bourgeois democratic parties, 'competing' with them and thus gave vent to their need to hurl insults, a need, as we in Germany well know, is politically impotent and above all destructive of political education.[55]

There was thus a clear tension in Weber's view about working-class struggles. On the one hand, he recognised the reality of conflicting interests within modern capitalism but, on the other, he argued that once labour asserted itself with any degree of militancy or political independence it was hindering progress. His main goal was to see a 'politically mature workers' movement co-operating positively to achieve Germany's greatness'[56] and his model for this was the English labour movement. The English working class showed little antagonism to business interests and had forged an alliance with its more far-sighted representatives in the Liberal Party. Weber attributed this to 'the reverberation of a world power position' on class-consciousness.[57] In other words, Britain's colonies paved the way for class compromise at home and this, in turn, helped to strengthen the colonial mission abroad. Infusing the working class with an imperialist outlook so that it moderated its class outlook was central to his project. He argued that 'only if we succeed in creating a labour aristocracy of the kind we now miss in the workers' movement',[58] could the burden of leading the German nation be shared with workers.

As an acute observer of the political scene Weber believed he detected some possibilities in this regard. He attended the Social Democratic Party convention in Mannheim in 1906 where the SPD accepted a separation between political activity and economic activity by ruling out the possibility of political strikes. The previous year the party had passed a resolution advocating mass strikes but at this conference the party leaders capitulated to the union leaders who were frightened of this prospect. Weber was struck by the number of times the SPD leaders referred to their own weakness and concluded that 'these gentlemen don't frighten anyone any more'.[59] The fear of the 'Red Peril' that often haunted the German bourgeoisie was virtually without foundation. Perceptively, Weber thought that the growing bureaucracy within the SPD offered a bulwark against any serious attempt to overthrow the system. Behind the SPD's radical rhetoric, Weber detected a desire for accommodation with official society. He sought to remove the 'bourgeois fear complex'[60] of his own class and get them to reach out to the SPD. He also repeatedly made approaches to revisionist leader Eduard Bernstein, although little appeared to come from this.[61] Nevertheless, Weber was unique in being one the few commentators outside the ranks of the far left who saw the tendencies that would led to the SPD's integration into German society in the war years.

Weber, however, believed that the promotion of a labour aristocracy and its conciliation with the business elite, had to be fought for. In particular, a polemic was needed against the ideas of Marxism, which represented an obstacle to these developments. By the 1890s, it was clear that Bismarck's 'carrot and stick' approach of a paternalistic state and repression had failed to curb the growth of Marxist influence. Bismarck had wanted a state of emergency to crush the strike of 150,000 miners in Silesia and the Ruhr in 1889 for higher wages and better accident protection. However, even the Kaiser baulked at the possible consequences, later declaring that 'I do not wish to stain my reign with the blood of my subjects.'[62] Not only were the membership and votes of the SPD increasing, but there was even a growing resonance for left-wing ideas inside the academia. In 1895, Volume 3 of *Capital* was published and in the same year Engels' classic on *The Origin of the Family, and Private Property and State* appeared, both receiving a growing audience among intellectuals.

Weber undertook to counter this influence by tackling the arguments of Marxism at their very roots. Occasionally, he lashed out calling the *Communist Manifesto*, for example, a prophecy.[63] However, generally he chose to attack Marxism implicitly rather than explicitly. Typically, he sought to develop alternative theoretical accounts while making oblique references to some central Marxist tenets. One example may help to illustrate his method. In his *General Economic History*, which was published posthumously based on lecture notes by students, Weber attacked the idea that men and women ever lived in non-monogamous relations or that in early society descent was ever reckoned through the 'mother right'. Instead he claimed that private property and individual family relationships existed from the start of human society. Weber's target was, of course, Engels' book on *The Origin of the Family, Private Property and State* – but nowhere in his account is this explicitly mentioned. The method was to present Marxist ideas implicitly as crude, one-sided and lacking the sophistication necessary to analyse complex societies. But the central thrust of Weber's own sophistication was, as Lukács put it,

> aimed – but never explicitly – at arguing the case for capitalism as a necessary, no longer essentially changeable system and at exposing the purported internal economic and social contradictions which, it was claimed, made the realization of socialism impossible in theory as in practice.[64]

CONCLUSION

Giddens has argued that Weber's political writings provide 'an essential source of illumination of the continuity and coherence of his thought'.[65] They are not an extra, a supplement to his otherwise neutral and value-free research. Quite the opposite: the central themes of sociology are closely linked to his own value concerns. His sociological writings focus on the origins and workings of modern capitalism. They contain a desire to convey to the bourgeoisie a sense of its historical mission and to counter Marx's account of the possibility of an alternative to their society. Whereas earlier writers from the German Historical School effectively celebrated the bureaucratic state that Bismarck had created, Weber's realism led him to look at its weakness. If it was to advance, Germany needed leadership from industrialists who were committed to a free market and to an expanding empire. Not surprisingly, his sociological writings are full of gloomy warnings about bureaucracy but he also saw the domination of human beings by human beings as an eternal feature of life. There was no alternative to bureaucracy other than more dynamic and 'charismatic' forms of leadership. Weber could recognise the inhumanity of late capitalism, accurately describing its cold, calculating culture, while still supporting it. His justification for capitalism was that alternatives end up as worse bureaucratic nightmares. However, his dismissal of any alternative to the present system was by no means disinterested. Weber aimed to enhance the power of his own class and his empire. While he defended the use of scientific and academic methods, his sociology generalises out from the political polemics he was engaged in. Sometimes his sociological writings may appear timeless and devoid of context. Sociological textbooks and standard sociological courses have often confined themselves to this formal aspect of his work. However, it is time to move beyond this to see Weber in his full political context.

3
The Spirit of Capitalism

Weber's most famous book is *The Protestant Ethic and the Spirit of Capitalism*. It is regarded by many sociologists as one of the key texts in their discipline. Its central question is: why did capitalism begin in Western Europe rather than in Asia? Weber's answer focussed on religion – in particular, the Protestant Reformation.

The book is important because it moved sociology from a concern with general evolutionary patterns to a comparative approach. Writers such as Auguste Comte had devised a universal scheme whereby societies moved through a series of stages. His three main stages were the 'theological', where religious belief was dominant; the 'metaphysical', where the language of human rights became more prevalent; and finally the 'positivist' stage, where conflicts were resolved by a scientific elite who understood social laws. Marx had questioned this broad schema, which was based on abstract systematising. However, it was Weber who shifted the focus to a comparative analysis, attempting to identify what was unique and different about particular societies.

Weber's method was to focus on internal cultural factors as the key determinants of development or non-development. This helped to shape future approaches in the sociology of development. After Weber became influential, sociologists who were known as 'modernisation theorists' argued that underdeveloped countries were as they were as a result of their internal value systems. By contrast, countries which were industrialised owed their success to a culture which promoted entrepreneurship.

Before Weber's book was published in 1904, there was already a debate in Germany over how the capitalist system began. The late development of Germany created the stimuli for this debate. Weber's friend Friedrich Naumann wrote, 'Just as the French have their theme: what was the great Revolution? So our national destiny has given us our theme ... what is capitalism?[1] The debate was dominated by a search for the 'spirit' or the 'motive complexes' that helped to set the system going. Writers such as Werner Sombart had argued that the Jewish population had played the key role in developing the spirit from which modern capitalism sprang.[2] Weber's personal background inclined him to look in a different direction.

Reared in a strong Protestant household, Weber had supported Bismarck's anti-Catholic campaign, the Kulturkampf, that had sought to identify Germany as a Protestant nation.[3] In 1904 he travelled to the United States and was impressed by the 'life-forming effect of [Protestant] religious sects'.[4] His wife describes how he was treated as 'equal among equals, a "brother"' and how he in turn 'quickly won their hearts with his beautiful "Nigger-English" [sic] and his stories'.[5] All condescending attitudes aside, the direct result of this journey was an essay titled 'The Protestant Sects and the Spirit of Capitalism'. A more substantial work that discussed a similar theme was *The Protestant Ethic and the Spirit of Capitalism*.

In this chapter, we shall outline Weber's definition of capitalism, his discussion of how the Protestant Reformation played a crucial role in its origin, and his argument for why Protestantism produced a form of asceticism, which was vital for the entrepreneurial spirit. We shall then outline a number of criticisms of his thesis, which question his lack of explanation for how the Reformation became successful, his standardisation of Protestantism around a particular ideal model of belief and his reading off of social action from religious texts. Our overall argument is that Weber's explanation tends to romanticise the origins of the present system.

WHAT IS CAPITALISM ?

The Protestant Ethic and the Spirit of Capitalism began with an extraordinary problem: why was it only the culture of Western civilisation which became universally significant? A quick summary of the deficiencies of the culture of the Orient followed – the Orient had no valid science; it had no systematic theology; its astronomy lacked a mathematical foundation; the historical writing of China did not match that of the Greek historian Thucydides; Oriental art lacked perspective; Oriental music missed out on harmony, sonatas and even the violin! Not only had the present-day Orient fallen behind Western Europe in industrial development, its culture lacked a rationality that made the West successful. It was a classic statement of what Edward Said called the discourse of Orientalism, which assumed the superiority of Western civilisation.[6] However, the crucial point of Weber's argument was that Western Europe was unique in giving birth to modern capitalism. This then framed the question that forms the core of the book: how did this unique development occur? In asking this particular question Weber, however, avoided another: what did the West do to the Orient to stifle its development? Little justification was offered about why one question was favoured over another. Western rationality and, implicitly, its superiority were taken for granted and an account of their uniqueness was therefore demanded.

A similar elision occurred when Weber defined capitalism. 'The impulse to acquisition, pursuit of gain, of money, of the greatest possible amount of money', Weber wrote 'has in itself nothing to do with capitalism'.[7] Many people might, on the contrary, think that these features have everything to do with capitalism. If you remove the catchall phrase 'in itself' the sentence would appear truly extraordinary. However, Weber's argument was that the impulse to pursue money is common to all people in all times and so is not unique to capitalism. Definitions have to focus on what is unique and essential and so Weber claimed that the essential feature of capitalism is its pursuit of '*renewed* profit, by means of continuous rational ... enterprise'.[8] Formally, he defined capitalist action as 'one which rests on the expectation of profit by the utilization of opportunities for exchange, that is on (formally) peaceful chances of profit'.[9]

This is quite a selective definition. Weber's original assumption that the impulse to pursue money is a natural one is questionable. The claim that a trait such as moneymaking is part of human nature can be the result of reading back features of his own society to a dim and distant past. Removing the element of avaricious moneymaking from a definition of capitalism may therefore bias the research question.

Moreover, if capitalism is primarily based on peaceful, rational calculating enterprise then other features such as 'unlimited greed for gain' or 'acquisition by force' are defined in advance as extraneous and accidental. However, some of the largest companies in Weber's day and in modern capitalism have worked closely with their respective states to derive gains from armed force. Thus one of the leading entrepreneurs in Germany, Walter Rathenau, could make an easy transition from running the giant AEG firm to becoming the chief organiser of Germany's war industries during the First World War. One key US commentator has summed up the relationship between the market and armed power in more recent times as follows:

> Markets function and flourish only when property rights are secured and can be enforced which, in turn, requires a political framework protected and backed by military power ... Indeed,

McDonalds cannot function without McDonald Douglas, the designer of the US Air Force F-15. And the hidden fist that keeps the world safe for Silicon Valley's technologies to flourish is called the US Army, Air Force, Navy, and Marine Corps.[10]

Having highlighted Weber's key assumptions, let's return to the structure of his argument. Like Marx, he notes that rational capitalism rests on 'formally free labour'.[11] This is labour which is bought and sold on the market place like any other commodity. For this system to emerge there had to be a number of preconditions in place. One was a rational structure of law that lent stability and certainty to the calculations about moneymaking. Another was an administration based on trained officials who did not rely on tax collection to line their own pockets. Still another precondition was the development of technology. Technology here is understood not simply as machinery but also as forms of knowledge such as bookkeeping, which paved the way for a more calculating culture. These preconditions helped to promote a culture of 'economic rationalism' but they were in turn dependent on the removal of spiritual obstacles to the pursuit of rational conduct. When discussing why this rationality did not develop in the Orient, Weber admits an attraction to ideas about 'biological heredity' but he concedes that 'racial neurology and psychology' would have to develop further before they could throw any light on the issue.[12]

THE PROTESTANT SPIRIT

After this brief suggestive flirtation, Weber turns to his central analysis. There is some evidence, he claims, to suggest a prima facie case for a link between the Protestant religion and capitalism. Business leaders in Germany tend to be Protestant; districts with the highest level of economic development are Protestant; Protestant students tend to study technical and scientific subjects while Catholics choose more 'humanistic' ones.[13]

He then returns to the object of his study which is the capitalist spirit. This can be summarised in its 'almost classic purity' by means of a piece of writing by Benjamin Franklin. Franklin writes that 'time is money'; that the upright person should pay their debts on time and be in good credit; that anyone who 'murders a crown, destroys all that it might have produced, even scores of pounds'.[14] Franklin argues each individual has a *duty* to increase his or her capital and this should be seen as an end in itself. The spirit of capitalism then is 'the earning of more and more money, combined with the strict avoidance of all spontaneous enjoyment of life'.[15] This spirit led to the formation of a sober, industrious bourgeois class but it was also necessary for the creation of a modern working class. Capitalism needed constantly to increase productivity but it could only do so when workers did not look for 'the maximum of comfort and the minimum of exertion' and instead performed labour as if it were an 'absolute end in itself, a calling'.[16]

Where did this new capitalist spirit come from? After all, moneymaking went against the dominant culture of medieval times. According to Thomas Aquinas, moneymaking was a *'turpitudo'* – it was dirty, and sinful. Money was a 'filthy lucre' and painters such as Pieter Bruegel often depicted money as faeces. An individual could not make the breakthrough against this culture. The spirit of capitalism had to come from a way of life that was common to whole groups. Possible candidates were traders or pirates who engaged in moneymaking, despite the dominant culture. Weber, however, rules them out as originators of the new society because they were not engaged in *regular, systematic accumulation of capital*. They went for a series of one off gains or displayed an uncontrolled impulse of greed. Traditionalist opposition to moneymaking could only be shaken by a profound culture change and this is precisely what occurred in the Reformation. The psychological impact of the Reformation allowed Protestants both to adopt an enterprising, rational spirit and to look on work as a duty. The teachings of Luther and Calvin were decisive.

Prior to Luther, the Catholic Church drew a sharp distinction between the moral codes that applied to the laity and secular clergy on the one hand and religious orders on the other. The religious orders were obliged to follow the higher morality of the gospels, especially expressed in vows of obedience, poverty and chastity. This moral code was seen as impossible to fulfil in a secular life and so holiness was defined as a withdrawal from the world. Luther changed all this when he introduced the concept that every person had a 'calling' or a 'vocation' given to him or her by God. Weber claims that Luther's translation of the Bible shifted the meaning of a key term so that labour in everyday life was seen as a God appointed task. Withdrawal from the world into monasteries was deemed a form of selfish idleness; true holiness meant fulfilling your worldly duties so as to glorify God.

This was potentially a revolutionary doctrine but Luther still gave it a traditional twist. Under the impact of the Peasant War in Germany – where Luther turned on many of his own radical supporters – he stressed how individuals needed to adapt themselves to the *particular* calling chosen for them by God. If a peasant's lot was to farm barren land while the lord lived off his taxes, then each had simply to accept those positions as their calling.

It fell to Calvin to draw out the more radical elements of the Reformation. Calvin returned to the traditional dilemma that all Christians face – if God is all-powerful, then how can individuals have a genuinely free choice? Logically there was no scope for autonomous human decision-making if God was so powerful that he had created the future in advance. Calvin, therefore, adopted the famous doctrine of predestination whereby God had preordained who was going to heaven and hell. The effect of this doctrine was to produce an intense, lonely form of anxiety, which cut each individual off from other human beings.

Consider for a moment what was involved. If it was preordained that only a small number of students – the elect – would pass exams and the rest would be thrown out of college, think of the high levels of anxiety this would cause. However, in the sixteenth century, we are not considering relatively trivial matters such as careers but the whole of one's eternal life. One result of this anxiety was that it led people desperately to search to see if they were part of the elect. The Calvinist sects, who were communities of true believers, taught that it was one's 'absolute duty to consider oneself chosen, to combat all doubts as temptations of the devil'.[17] In order to attain this self-confidence, intense worldly activity was recommended. Success in one's calling alone dispersed religious doubts and gave certainty of grace. Calvinism therefore led to a highly individualistic desire for achievement as a means of counteracting religious anxiety.

ASCETICISM

Weber refers to the psychological state whereby people removed everything from their life that interfered with their calling as a 'worldly asceticism'. Protestant beliefs encouraged people to bring their actions under constant self-control. They could not turn to a priest or the confessional to relieve sins and anxiety. Their only way of relieving anxiety was 'not single good works but a life of good works combined into a unified system'.[18] Idleness and wasting of time became the greatest sins. Everything had to be put into a methodical pursuit of a calling. In this way, the asceticism of the monastery was brought out into the marketplace. Calvinism 'substituted for the spiritual aristocracy of monks outside of and above the world, the spiritual aristocracy of the predestined saints of God within the world'.[19] Unlike Luther's interpretation, the doctrine of the calling did not imply an acceptance of one's lot but rather an injunction to work hard, to make money in order to glorify God. It condemned idle 'spontaneous enjoyment of possessions',[20]dishonesty and impulsive avarice but still promoted wealth as a means of showing the individual that they had a sign of God's blessing.

All of this was part of the unintended consequences of the Reformation. Nobody became a Protestant in order to become a capitalist but the psychological effects of the actual doctrine were highly significant, in their unanticipated consequences. It led to 'the accumulation of capital through ascetic compulsion to save'.[21] Religious asceticism also provided employers 'with sober, conscientious and unusually industrious workmen, who clung to their work as to a life purpose willed by Gods'.[22] Above all the ideal of methodical self-control led to the 'ethos of rational organisation of capital and labour'.[23] Against Sombart, Weber claims that Judaism led 'to the politically and speculatively orientated adventurous capitalism'[24] whereas Puritanism promoted a rational sober bourgeois life that restrained the consumption of wealth and so increased productive investment of capital.

The Protestant Ethic and the Spirit of Capitalism provides a heroic account of the rise of capitalism. Or rather, the capitalist appears as the modern anti-hero whose great qualities consist in his modesty, dourness and determination. There can be little doubt of Weber's admiration for these qualities. After all, capitalism was established by moral men with a mission. The shorter essay 'The Protestant Sects and the Spirit of Capitalism' is even more explicit about the moral quality of early capitalists. Weber argues that the American sects were voluntary communities of religious believers who only accepted into membership those whose conduct made them appear morally qualified. Unlike in the established churches into which one was born, in sects 'membership meant a certificate of moral qualification and especially of business morals for the individual'.[25] This in turn meant access to credit and purchases from their stores because members were regarded as trustworthy. The sect member also had to prove repeatedly to their fellow members that they were endowed with these moral qualities. This type of open presentation of oneself to one's peers bred a trait of ethical discipline and so the Protestant sects were highly successful in diffusing the sober bourgeois message that 'the gods bless with riches the man who pleases them'.[26]

Weber did not argue that Protestantism was necessary for the functioning of modern capitalism. He assumed that once the system got going, it developed an economic logic of its own which forced individual capitalists to accumulate. His focus was exclusively on its origins and was designed to show that even where material factors are in place for economic 'take-off', there was a need for a catalyst to produce the 'spirit' of capitalism. Protestantism had operated as that catalyst in Western Europe and so provided a positive example of how ideas and culture played a key role in changing the course of history. Asia provided a negative example of where religion could operate as a block on economic development. Weber's writings on Asia are contained in *The Religion of India* and *The Religion of China* and also in important passages of *Economy and Society* and we shall discuss these in the next chapter.

THE REFORMATION AND CAPITALISM

The Protestant Ethic blends together two of Weber's central themes. It provides an account of the rise of the bourgeoisie that gives it a sense of historic mission and a positively charged moral strength. It also offers a method of interpreting history that counteracts Marx's historical materialism. Throughout the book, Marxism is presented as mono-causal and less complex than Weber's own approach. Weber attacks the assumption of the 'more naïve historical materialism', that ideas 'originate as a reflection or superstructure of economic situations'.[27] He takes the high ground by claiming that his aim is not to substitute an equally 'one-sided spiritualistic causal interpretation'[28] for a one-sided materialism. The effect, it is implied, is to both subsume and improve on Marx. Thus, Anthony Giddens claimed that Weber 'partly vindicates Marx against his own professed disciples'.[29]

However, this is to misread Weber's intentions. His aim was to assume the mantle of complexity but to emphasise the primacy of ideas. Thus he writes explicitly that his study is designed to show how 'ideas become effective forces in history'.[30] Although he refers to material factors, there is, as even Parsons acknowledges 'no systematic account of the other side with respect to this specific empirical subject matter'.[31] As Kolko points out,

The Protestant Ethic serves as the equivalent of a historic prime mover, a Geist, similar in function to those deeply embedded in the German philosophical tradition. For all intent and purposes, the development of Calvinism is marked off by Weber as the beginning of a new historical epoch. Yet if we ask rather simplistically what preceded and caused the Ethic we find no plausible answer in Weber's writings ... the whole concept of the Ethic is developed in an unreal historical vacuum.[32]

Weber was correct to stress the affinity between Protestantism and the rising capitalist class. His exact empirical arguments about the co-relation between Protestant regions and capitalist development are not the key issue and criticisms of him on this regard miss the point.[33] Overall, the Reformation was seen as a revolt against the Catholic Church, which was directly tied to the feudal order and the aristocracy. It found an echo in many social classes – disgruntled German princes, peasants but particularly in the case of Calvinism among 'the small manufacturers, lesser merchants and craftsmen who constituted its rank and file'.[34] Nor is there any need to argue that Protestantism was simply a 'reflection' of bourgeois class position. Clearly, the religious ideas themselves played a huge role in stimulating the *revolt* of capitalist forces.

WHY DID LUTHER GET A HEARING?

Weber's implicit polemic against Marxism, however, means that he gets the exact role of these religious ideas wrong. He offers no explanation for the reception that Luther received. Previous heretical movements such as the Hussites in Bohemia had offered ideas that were similar to Luther's but were crushed. Luther's reformation, however, overwhelmed Germany. Four years after Luther posted his 95 theses in Wittenberg in 1517, the papal nuncio declared that 'All of Germany is in open revolt. Nine tenths cry out "Luther!". And as for the remaining tenth, in so far as they are not bothered about Luther, they see the solution in the slogan "death to the Roman (papal) court".[35] One explanation for his popularity is print technology and Luther's use of the vernacular. However, while these may serve as explanation for how widely his ideas were disseminated they do not answer the question about the reception of his ideas.

It is difficult to explain the audience for Luther's religious ideas without examining the high level of social unrest which prevailed.

Luther himself acknowledged this high level of social suffering in his 'Address to the Christian Nobility of the German Nation'. There he referred to 'the burdens of pain and oppression weighing on all classes in Christendom, which have moved not me alone, but indeed all men, to give vent to their cries of outrage and pleas for redress'.[36]

European society was characterised by a form of 'market feudalism' at the time. The market was making greater and greater intrusions into people's lives. Cities were expanding and were being organised on different principles. In 1200, there were 50 towns and cities in Europe but by 1500 there were 4,000.[37] Originally, the cities were organised as communes that were governed by guild representatives and others for the common good. However, the growth of the market made it easier for a wealthier class to free themselves from guild restrictions. They demanded the right to hire rural labour, to dispense with notions of a 'customary price', to impose a new division of labour on their journeymen. The instability created by the growing market also forced the feudal orders and the church to increase the pressure on the peasantry for more taxes and tithes. Money increasingly invaded the church as families like the Medici in Florence bought their way into the papacy.

The Reformation received huge support precisely because it was seen as addressing these issues. It was not simply an abstract, theological corpus as Weber presents it, but a movement that fused religious, social and political demands. The Evangelical leaders got a hearing 'because they offered answers to long posed questions and they sowed seed on long prepared soil'.[38] Luther, for example, asserted the right of Christian assemblies to appoint, install and dismiss their spiritual teachers. This was but the corollary to the 'communal principle' of self-government in the secular sphere. Luther denounced usury and speculation; monopolistic business practices; the displacement of local customs by Roman laws; the draining of Germany's wealth into a grasping and wasteful church. His doctrine about the priesthood of all believers provided a powerful theological justification for removing the privileges of the clergy and subjecting them to taxes.

Anyone who doubts the social impact of the Reformation might simply consider the agreement reached between the Erfurt town council and the clergy in July 1521. After a set of riots, the clergy committed themselves to

1. Reveal to the worthy council whatever goods we have inside and
    outside Erfurt ... We will submit such goods to taxation and pay
    one per cent wealth tax and the assessment, the same as other
    citizens.
2. We will allow secular properties we have acquired from citizens
    to be returned to them whenever they so request, for the price
    we paid for them.
3. We will take no more than four per cent interest on all annuities
    in the town and the council's territories.
4. We will acquire no secular properties from the citizens or subjects
    of the council by purchase, brokerage or in other ways without
    the permission of the council.
5. We will wholly refrain from malting and brewing.
    [...]
7. We will not sell, serve or exchange our wine in secret, so that
    the council loses excise.
    [...]
9. We will pay the excise on slaughtering as completely as citizens,
    and will not import meat secretly.
    [...]
11. We will not evade the poll tax on our servants.[39]

WEBER'S MODEL OF PROTESTANTISM

Weber discards entirely these social dimensions to the Reformation
and concentrates instead on its theological essence. In his desire to
show psychological effects that led directly from the theology of
Protestantism to the 'spirit' of capitalism, he has to standardise this
theology around his own particular logic. He assumes that Calvinists
of the time were all motivated by the belief that an all-powerful God
meant predestination, which produced anxiety, which led to worldly
asceticism. Yet even in the case of Calvinism, these themes may not
have been picked up with the same emphasis by all social classes.
There are some indications, for example, to show that Weber played
down the more revolutionary aspects of Protestant theology.

Christopher Hill has advanced an alternative account of Protestant
theology which stresses its objection to mechanical religious actions
which do not involve the heart; its emphasis on morality being self-
imposed rather than coming from obedience to priests; its stress on
preaching rather than prayer and sacraments; its use of a vernacular
Bible and Prayer Book. He argues that,

The appeal to inner conviction and the rejection of the routine of ceremonies through which the priesthood imposed its authority could have liberating effects on any society. The hold over men's minds of an established doctrinal system had to be broken before the political and social order sanctified by those doctrines could be challenged ... Since opposition to the Roman Church in 16th and 17th century Europe drew its main strength from big cities, protestantism could be developed in ways, which favoured the rise of capitalism. But there is nothing in protestantism which leads automatically to capitalism. Its importance was rather that it undermined obstacles which the more rigid institutions and ceremonies of Catholicism imposed.[40]

Protestantism like any complex ideology had mixed themes, which appealed differently to social classes. It can therefore be argued that Weber *selected elements* of Protestant theology and read off a psychological impact from them while he discarded other elements of the theology in order to facilitate his argument about the internal logic of the religion leading to capitalism. As Walker puts it, Weber's method 'is constitutionally incapable of taking account of the *variety* of the Reformation'.[41] Hyma has shown that in Holland, Calvinists used their theology to exclude bankers and their wives from services.[42] Similarly, Catherine and Katherine George examine many Protestant texts in England and conclude that there were 'attacks from many angles (on) any orientation of life toward the increase of wealth'.[43] Hill's own book, *The World Turned Upside Down*, shows a clear link between the ideas of some Protestant sects and a demand for 'a levelling' and a sharing of common land.[44] It is difficult to disagree with Tawney's assertion that 'both an intense individualism and a rigorous Christian Socialism could be deduced from Calvin's doctrine. Which of them pre-dominated depended on differences of political environment and of social class.'[45]

THEOLOGY AND SOCIAL ACTION

Even if we assumed that Weber's non-revolutionary model of Protestant theology is correct historically, it does not follow that humans necessarily live by an official theology that is prescribed by their leaders. So Luther may have preached obedience to secular authority but this did not prevent a peasants' revolt that used some of his doctrines as its justification. (Luther's inability to comprehend this elementary paradox led him to write a tract 'Against the Murdering Thieving Hordes of Peasants' which called for the theologically misguided to be 'knocked to pieces, strangled and stabbed ... just as one would kill a mad dog'.)[46]

Benjamin Franklin, whose writings were held up by Weber as an exemplar of the link between Puritanism and the capitalist spirit, did not live by his own words. 'He did not save money like a true Puritan but rather spent evenings in such notably ascetic activities as theatres, sports, drink and women.'[47] Far from pursuing his duty to accumulate capital he retired from business at the age of 42. Nor was this simply an individual failing. According to the Puritan leader James Truslow Adams 'throughout all the colonies (of America) drunkenness was a prevailing vice and nearly every event ... was frequently made the occasion of scandalous intemperance'.[48]

The weakness of Weber's explanation of *how* the affinity between Protestantism and capitalism worked is shown in the inadequate chronological order in *The Protestant Ethic and the Spirit of Capitalism*. The book relies heavily on later Protestant writers such as Baxter who wrote his *Christian Directory* in 1673 and Franklin who wrote his *Advice to a Young Tradesman* in 1748 to draw out the connection between doctrines such as 'the calling' and the capitalist spirit. However, even if Weber is correctly describing the meaning of the doctrine for these periods, it does not follow that Protestantism had the same meaning in the sixteenth century when the Reformation occurred. Robertson has pointed out that 'owing to this unhistorical treatment he has not noticed the change in the conception of the "calling" from an antidote against covetous ambition to a comfortable doctrine for a commercial people'.[49] The lack of a proper chronology means that there is a missing century between the start of the Reformation in 1517 and the seventeenth century. As Weber provides no account of the economic changes that occurred in the intervening period, we are left with impression that capitalism flowed from the internal logic of Protestantism.

Yet there is every indication that capitalism had begun to expand inside the framework of feudalism before the seventeenth century. Only Weber's self-imposed definition of capitalism as exclusively about 'renewed profit, by means of continuous rational ... enterprise' could allow us to avoid seeing this. Marx argued that the capitalist era began in the sixteenth century in two main ways. In the first 'really revolutionary way' direct producers who were guild members accumulated capital, broke free of guild restrictions, and began to trade. In the second, some of the existing merchant class began to take direct possession of production.[50] Financiers like the Fugger family, who Weber argues were lacking the capitalist spirit, were already establishing mines in Germany and Bohemia based on wage labour. It is precisely because capitalism and the market had begun to spread under feudalism, that the content of ideas such as 'the calling' took on a new meaning for the urban classes that were the active participants of the Reformation. As Hill put it, 'there was no inherent theological reason for the Protestant emphasis on frugality, hard work, accumulation but that emphasis was a natural consequence of the religion of the heart in a society where capitalist industry was developing'.[51]

SPIRITUALISING CAPITALISM

Lukács has argued that the overall effect of Weber's account was to 'de-economise' and 'spiritualise' the nature of capitalism.[52] In other words, capitalism is presented as a by-product of rationalising forces, which grew out of moral duties, imposed by religion. The account leaves out the brutal role of force in accumulating capital, in imposing new disciplines on labour and in subjecting the colonies to the economic needs of the metropolitan countries. In doing so, it romanticises the origins of capitalism.

Weber provides no satisfactory explanation for how the early sums of capital were accumulated. He claims that the question of 'motive forces' in the expansion of capitalism 'is not in the first instance a question of the origin of the capital sums' but above all it is about the spirit.[53] As a result the question of the original accumulation of capital is ignored throughout the work. In a revealing aside, however, Weber retails the hoary old myth that in several cases known to him 'the revolutionary process was set in motion with a few thousands of capital borrowed from relatives'.[54] Commenting on such explanations, Marx has compared them to 'nursery tales' which tell how a diligent, intelligent, frugal elite broke free from the other lazy rascals to save up their money. These nursery tales play the same role as the doctrine of original sin in theology – they explain nothing. The real story of capital accumulation is one about

> The spoliation of the Church's property, the fraudulent alienation of the state domains, the theft of common lands, the usurpation of feudal and clan property and its transformation into modern private

property under circumstances of ruthless terrorism, all these things were just so many idyllic methods of productive accumulation. They conquered the field for capitalist agriculture, incorporated the soil into capital and created for the urban industries the necessary supplies of free and rightless proletarians.[55]

A similar romanticism surrounds Weber's explanation of how workers acquired the labour discipline required for raising productivity. According to Weber, religious convictions led employees to regard work as a 'calling'. This again conveniently ignores how brute force was used to terrorise the early working class into accepting the routines of time-managed work. The passing of the Vagrancy Acts, the licensing and whipping of unlicensed beggars, the use of work fines, legal terrorism to enforce an idea about not touching the property of masters – these were just some of the methods used to get people to accept the discipline of wage labour.[56] Even after capitalism was well established, workers did not simply accept wage labour as a 'calling' but rebelled in all manner of ways – attempting to hold on to a Saint Monday as a day of rest, for example.[57] Yet all this sordid history of brutality is obscured by an image of workers spiritually accepting the need for 'sober, industrious ways'.

CONCLUSION

As a writer who brings out the early affinity between capitalism and the Protestant ethic, Weber has much to say that is of interest. Undoubtedly, his theory makes an important contribution to understanding the unintended links that flow between religion and economic life. However, these insights are marred by his attempt to find a heroic role for the bourgeoisie and win a polemic against Marxism. The result is to standardise the varieties of the Reformation around a particular theology which he constructs. He then assumes that the psychology of masses of people was directly affected by this version of Protestantism. He plays down the revolutionary elements in Protestantism and projects a necessary, logical support for capitalism. By ignoring the material conditions that gave rise to capitalism, he writes off the brutal realities of colonialism, expropriation and the role of political and economic terror in imposing new work disciplines.

4
Why Didn't Asia Develop?

Why did capitalism develop in Europe rather than Asia? Weber's comparative approach eventually led him back to this question. He had isolated the Protestant Reformation as playing a crucial role in promoting capitalist entrepreneurship in Western Europe. He then turned the issue on its head and asked: what was it about the religions of India and China which had hindered development there?

In one sense, Weber had hit on an important problem. Asia had at different points in its history been more advanced than Europe. Culturally it showed considerable development in the arts, sciences and mathematics. J. Pirenne in his *History of the Universe*, which was published in Paris in 1950, noted that in the middle of the seventeenth century Asia was a far more important place than Europe. He claimed

> The riches of Asia were incomparably greater than those of the European states. Her industrial technique showed a subtlety and a tradition that the European handicrafts did not possess. And there was nothing in the more modern methods used by the traders of the Western countries that Asian trade had to envy. In matters of credit, transfer of funds, insurance and cartels, neither India, Persia nor China had anything to learn from Europe.[1]

Yet by the nineteenth century these countries were reduced to colonies of the Western powers. Their economies stagnated and they became suppliers of primary produce for the factories of Europe. Weber believed that religion prevented the emergence of native capitalism in India and China. Just as Protestantism acted as the trigger to industrial development in the West, so did Hinduism and Confucianism operate as blockages to capitalism in the East.

Weber developed his ideas in this area in two key texts, *The Religion of India* and *The Religion of China*, which were part of his overall series on the sociology of religion, written during the First World War. In this chapter, we will first look at his arguments on how Hinduism, the caste system and the doctrines of samsara and karma held back Indian society. We will offer an assessment of these arguments in terms of Weber's colonial outlook. We will also summarise his arguments on the social structure of China and the link between Confucianism and bureaucracy before claiming that his understanding of Chinese society was limited.

ASIAN RELIGIONS AND EUROPEAN RELIGIONS

All religions contain elements of superstition, blind faith and devotion to religious hierarchies. They promise an escape from human suffering and even liberation from the cares of this world. However, for Weber, the central issue was not what they had in common but rather how they differed. Each was associated with a different social psychology that led to quite specific economic orientations. As Hans Gerth and Don Martindale put it, Weber 'isolated the religious institutions and the key social strata which mediate them to the wider society as crucial … for receptivity or resistance to industrialisation'.[2]

In *Economy and Society*, Weber drew a sharp distinction between the religions of Asia and those of Europe. Asiatic religions usually led to contemplation whereas European religion – especially after the Protestant Reformation – placed 'a primary preference upon some type of active conduct'.[3] In Europe, there was a belief in an all-powerful God who was outside of the world and this meant that 'the road was closed to self deification and to any genuinely mystical possession of God'.[4] By contrast in Asia a 'flight from the world'[5] and a mystical union with God was deemed desirable. In Europe, the idea of a personal God led to a 'sort of legally definable relationship of subjection' and, thanks to the influence of the Romans and the Jews, a 'methodical procedure for attaining salvation'.[6] In Asia, by contrast, there was no such methodical procedure and the influence of the Indians and Persians led to 'orgiastic, spiritualistic and contemplative characteristics'.[7]

This contrast had major implications for economic development of the respective continents. The 'spirit' of European religion led to an active orientation to the world, one that sought to dominate it. This yearning for mastery was closely tied to systematic, methodical forms of behaviour. The 'spirit' of Asian religion, by contrast, led to passivity and a desire for escape from the world. Instead of activity, there was contemplation. Instead of method, there was an all-engrossing loss of self in orgies or contemplation. Weber's vocabulary may on occasion have been dense and idiosyncratic but his meaning was perfectly clear: the mindset of Europe was naturally domineering; that of Asia fatalistic and passive. Weber's colonial imagery breaks through with full force in his writings on India and China.

HINDUISM AND THE CASTE SYSTEM

Weber's book on *The Religion of India* begins with a description of the Hindu social system. Weber acknowledges some of the main achievements of Indian society briefly, noting that it originated the rational number system; it developed numerous philosophical schools; it had a legal system that could have served capitalist purposes; it had a sophisticated trading system and strong handcraft system. However, even though 'the acquisitiveness of all Indian strata was highly developed' capitalism did not develop there indigenously.[8] It had to be taken over 'as a finished artefact without autonomous beginnings'.[9]

Why this occurred is the central problematic of Weber's book. His focus is on Hinduism and its influence on the social structure. The term 'Hindu' was first used by the Muslim invaders to describe unconverted native Indians and later became the official term used in the British census. The central feature of Hindu life is the caste system. A caste differs from other social categories such as a tribe, a guild or a social class. Unlike a tribe, it is not based on a local territory. Whereas members of a tribe can follow different occupations, caste rules specify which occupations are legitimate and which are not.

Further, the caste system differs from the medieval guild system of Western Europe because it is hereditary and surrounded with ritual barriers which go well beyond defending opportunities for income. The caste system precludes the type of fraternisation between guilds, which occurred in European cities, and so blocks the very idea of citizenship. Weber saw religious belief as the crucial factor in the presence or absence of ritual barriers. So, he claims, St Paul's break from Judaism to promote a universal pattern of Christian freedom led to the abolition of ritual barriers to taking communion together. This in turn played a central role in the development of the concept of citizenship. 'For without commensalism in Christian terms, without the Lord's Supper – no outbound fraternity and no medieval urban citizenry would have been possible'.[10]

Caste is, in fact, a special case of a status group. Whereas a social class describes people who share a similar economic position, status groups refer to social honour and rank and are associated with different lifestyles. A caste is a closed status group because all the barriers to membership that might exist in other status groups are intensified to an unusual degree. Not only are there bars on intermarriage between castes but there are also rules on who eats together, from whose hand might one be served and what type of diet is appropriate.

There are four main caste orders from the classical learning of Hinduism. The Brahmans developed from the small group who played the chief role in Hindu cult practices in the Ancient Vedic period. They displaced the knights and warriors at the top of the social hierarchy and so the 'social and economic privileges of the Brahmans are unsurpassed by any other priesthood'.[11] The Kshatriyas were originally charged with warfare and defence and later became the equivalents of knights and nobles. The Vaishyas had a comparable status to the free commoners of Europe. They lacked the socio-economic privileges of the higher castes but they had the right to own land and engaged in money lending and trade. Finally there were the Shudras who were composed primarily of artisans and workers who had no right to the land.

Weber describes how there are complicated subdivisions within this overall caste system. He acknowledges that there are social struggles between rival groups to improve their caste position. However, the central feature of the caste system is *dharma* – each caste is supposed to live by a set of ritualistic duties that are inherited from a sacred tradition. The individual Hindu is heavily socialised into accepting these caste duties because of two other dogmas of the religion.

SAMSARA AND KARMA

The doctrine of *samsara* is a belief in the transmigration of souls. An individual who dies can be reborn continually in a variety of other living forms, primarily of animals. Weber clearly finds this idea of transmigration far odder than the notion that a soul might live forever in a paradise surrounded by white-feathered angels or in a furnace with dark-skinned creatures and explains it in racist terms. Apparently, when the Aryan folk of Northern India encountered the more dark-skinned Dravidians of Southern India they concluded that 'apes and men were thought to look alike'.[12] This in turn facilitated the idea that souls might pass from a human form to an animal form in the afterlife!

The other key belief of Hinduism was the doctrine of *karma* – the idea of compensation for ethically relevant actions. Every good or bad deed – and this includes the fulfilment or non-fulfilment of caste duties – had inevitable consequences for the fate of the actor. It was as if a ledger of accounts was opened about the merits and faults of each individual – and the accounts had to be balanced in the next life after rebirth. According to Weber, a Hindu is 'bound in an endless sequence of ever new lives and deaths and he determines his own fate solely by his deeds – this was the most consistent form of the karma doctrine'.[13] There was no notion of an 'accident of birth' – a concept which could lead to a critique of the existing social order through the questioning of why some get to the top while others are condemned to a life of misery. Instead, there was a strong tendency to believe that the social standing of any individual was directly related to the doctrine of *karma*.

> An orthodox Hindu confronted with a deplorable situation of a member of an impure caste would only think that he has a great many sins to redeem from his prior existence. The reverse of this is that a member of an impure caste thinks primarily of how to better his future social opportunity at rebirth by leading an exemplary life according to caste ritual.[14]

This produced a profound conservatism at the heart of Hinduism – a 'dread of the magical evil of innovation'.[15] It placed a huge premium on adherence to caste duties and ritual traditions. The stakes for adherence or non-adherence were particularly high because rebirth might 'drag man down into the life of a "worm in the intestine of a dog", but according to his conduct, it might raise and place him into the womb of a queen and Brahman's daughter'.[16]

REVOLTS AGAINST HINDUISM

Throughout Indian history there were numerous revolts against the rigid hierarchies of Hinduism. One such was Jainism, which followed the doctrines of Mahavira, a Kshatriya noble who died in 600 BC. He rejected the ritual commandments and sought freedom from endless rebirth through a detachment from the world of imperfection. Jainism sought a form of 'spiritual homelessness' through renouncing the needs of the body. It stressed ascetic practices such as fasting and opposed all forms of deception and dishonesty. According to Weber, it grew primarily among the trading classes of the city as its emphasis on asceticism fitted in with their need for compulsory savings. Jainist believers were, however, confined to commercial capitalism because they were ritualistically excluded from industry.

The greatest revolt against Hinduism came with Buddhism. Buddhism saw salvation as a purely personal act. It believed that it was senseless to have hopes or desires connected to this life – or to otherworldly lives. Against the Brahmans it stressed that it was not birth but right living which held the key to holiness. Its challenge to the ritualistic knowledge and practices of the Brahmans made many princes sympathetic to it. Buddhism, however, represented a more democratic outlook than Hinduism.

Hinduism was able effectively to oppose these challenges because it offered ruling elites a powerful source of legitimation. It spread into other 'barbarian' communities because

Integration into the Hindu community provided such religious legitimation for the ruling stratum. It not only endowed the ruling stratum of the barbarians with recognised rank in the cultural world of Hinduism, but also, through their transformation into castes, secured their superiority over the subject classes with an efficiency unsurpassed by any other religion.[17]

Moreover, the worldly indifference of Buddhism meant that, in its purest form, it remained a religion of genteel intellectuals. As Hinduism adapted and incorporated magical elements and developed a cult of gurus, it stymied and eventually repelled Buddhism from India from 1000 AD onwards.

The primary cause of the underdevelopment of India was, thus, Hindu religious culture. The stability of the caste order blocked 'technological change and occupational mobility, which from the point of view of the caste were objectionable and ritually dangerous'.[18] Certain occupations became the preserve of particular caste groupings and this prevented free market competition. The rigid rules about segregation between castes made modern factory discipline difficult. The whole 'spirit' of Hinduism cut across the spirit of capitalism because,

A ritual law in which every change of occupation, every change in work technique, may result in ritual degradation is certainly not capable of giving birth to economic and technical revolutions within itself or even of facilitating the first germination of capitalism in its midst.[19]

The doctrine of endless rebirths also led to a devaluation of the world. There was no space to seek economic success as a sign of grace. There was no need to master the world by rational techniques. The purpose of Asiatic knowledge was not developing empirical sciences, which made possible a rational domination of nature and human beings, but rather reaching a 'mystical and magical domination over the self and the world: gnosis'.[20] Later Hinduism incorporated strong elements of magic – particularly for the masses – and offered all sorts of spells. This element of magic was also very much at odds with the spirit of modern capitalism. According to Weber 'a rational practical ethic and life methodology did not emerge from this magical garden which transformed all the life within the world'.[21]

THE COLONIAL VISION

If *The Religion of India* was studied as a text that revealed the prejudices of an early-twentieth-century German gentleman, it might have considerable merit. Unfortunately, however, it is still taught for the insights it gives on why some societies develop and others do not. Modern sociology students still learn about how the Protestant ethic was linked to the rise of capitalism and how, unluckily for the Indians, Hinduism blocked its development. Few are encouraged to read Weber's book in the original because is often difficult and rambling. Instead a brief, packaged summary of *The Religion of India* is provided to illustrate that Weber anticipated 'modernisation theory' by several decades. His focus on the internal value system to explain the slowness of industrial development is taken up by later sociologists such Rostow in his theory of 'stages of growth'[22] and so the great 'debate' between modernisation theory and 'dependency theory' is set up.

Weber's book, however, is deeply condescending and offensive to the people of India because its tone is that of a shrill confident European imperialist. Extraordinary caricatures are presented of Indian practices. We are told, for example, that 'no correct Hindu will bypass a urinating cow without putting his hand into the stream and wetting his forehead, garments etc with it as does the Catholic with holy water'.[23] And that the 'excrement of the Brahman could have religious meaning' for the Indians. Such exotic title-tattle about the Orient did the rounds of many dinner parties during Weber's time and, no doubt, many a host could regale his table with such stories.

Closely linked to these tall tales is an interest in 'racial matters'. Although he avoided the cruder forms of racism which were common at the time, Weber sometimes used 'racial differences' to explain Indian practices. He was strongly influenced by that arch-categoriser of Indian society H.H. Risley whose work *The People of India* set out to classify Indian 'races'. Risley used India as a laboratory to test many of the claims about race and the human species that had been developed in Europe.[24] He claimed that the encounter between the lighter-skinned 'Aryans' and darker-skinned 'Dravidians' gave rise to notions of caste: 'By the stress of that contact, caste was evolved ... and the whole fantastic structure of orthodox ritual and usage was built up.'[25] As we have seen, Weber gave considerable credence to this theory, explaining the doctrine of *samsara* by contact between white-skinned Northerners and dark-skinned more 'ape'-like Southern Indians. In an echo of Risley he claimed that 'the juxtaposition of racial differences and – this is sociologically decisive – of externally striking different racial types has been quite important for the development of the caste order in India'.[26]

Weber's overall view of the Indian 'character' was distorted by colonial imagery. The stereotype of the shifty Oriental appears when he states that 'the unrestricted lust for gain of the Asiatics ... is notoriously unequalled in the world'.[27] He repeats the common claim that Indian society needed imperialism to attain peace and that, left by itself, it could have become a chaotic mass of tribal conflicts:

> It is still possible for some eminent English students of the land to argue on good grounds that the removal of the thin conquering strata of Europeans and the Pax Britannica enforced by them would open wide the life and death struggle of inimical castes, confession and tribes.[28]

Indians, it seems, like other Asiatics were not capable of developing a sense of nationality because 'the character of the Asiatic intellectual strata had in essentials hindered the emergence of a "national" political form of the type developed in the West'.[29] One reason apparently was their lack of a 'speech community' and the reliance of their cultural language on sacred and literary forms.[30]

THE ABSENCE OF AN ECONOMIC ANALYSIS

This imperialist outlook led to a rather peculiar approach to solving the problem of why capitalism did not develop in India. Oddly, *The Religion of India* is virtually devoid of any sustained analysis of the economic structure of India. There is barely any discussion of its pattern of foreign trade; the geographical dispersal of industry; the nature of its credit system or the interrelationship between the accumulation of capital in land and its transfer into cities. There is virtually no discussion on the political structures of India or the wider socio-economic effects of the Mughal invasion and its subsequent disintegration. Instead the key to the secret of India is to be found in religious texts. If such an approach had been applied to why Germany, for example, established its industrial base later than Britain this would have been astounding.

As in *The Protestant Ethic and the Spirit of Capitalism*, Weber tends to 'read off' social behaviours from a number of religious dogmas. However, while he had a deep and intimate knowledge of Protestantism, it is by no means clear that his description of Hindu belief systems is always correct. So, for example, Dumont criticises him for asserting that transmigration was a 'dogmatic belief' which had implications outside the field of religion.[31] More fundamentally, Weber's textualism belonged to a long tradition of Indology, which was closely linked to colonial rule.

As early as 1774, Warren Hastings, the first governor general of India, argued that the British would understand India once they gained access to the elaborate system of law which had been passed down from ancient times. Hastings claimed that the Hindus 'had been in possession of laws which remained unchanged from remotest antiquity' and these were known to the Brahmans who received 'a degree of personal respect amounting almost to idolatry'.[32] These laws were codified in classic texts and it was necessary to understand them in order to rule the colony. This approach was taken up by Sir William Jones, an official of the British East India Company who founded the Asiatic Society of Bengal in 1784 with a view to mastering Indian society for the empire.[33] Jones was the principal founder of Indology, a discourse with a number of themes, which Ronald Inden has summarised as follows:

> Indological discourse, I argue, holds (or simply assumes) that the essence of Indian civilization is just the opposite of the West's. It

is the irrational (but rationalizable) institution of 'caste' and the Indological religion that accompanies it, Hinduism. Human agency in India is displaced by Indological discourse not onto a reified State or Market but onto a substantialized Caste. This has entailed several consequences for the Indological construction of India. It necessitated a wholesale dismissal of Indian political institutions, and especially of kinship. To give this construct of India credibility, the depiction of Indian thought as inherently symbolic and mythical rather than rational and logical has been required. Finally, it has been necessary for Brahmanism or Hinduism, the religion considered to be the justification of caste, to be characterised as essentially idealistic (i.e. apolitical).[34]

This discourse was particularly prevalent in Germany at the time that Weber was writing. The German state invested more in Indological studies throughout the nineteenth century than the rest of Europe and America combined.[35] Beginning with Frederick von Schlegel, there was a fascination with Sanskrit, the ancient language of the Aryans. The romantic search for identity led to a focus on this language, which, it was claimed, yielded evidence of a highly developed historical culture with a deep spiritual meaning. The implication was that the early Aryan ancestors of Germany had a strong culture, which was independent of Latin or Roman culture. The price, however, was that Indian society was set in stone – wedded to holy scripts that offered insights into the childhood of humanity.

Weber's book *The Religion of India* provides a classic example of what later came to be referred to as an Orientalist discourse. Malek has outlined three fundamental features of the discourse which are evident in the book. There is, first, a problematic where the essence of people of the Orient differs from the essence of Westerners in being passive. This 'essence' is both 'historical since it goes back to the dawn of history and "ahistorical" since it transfixes the being, the object of study within its alienable and non-evolutive specifity'.[36] Second, the method of study focuses on the past, which is in turn studied in its cultural aspects, particularly religion, detached from social evolution. Third, the sources for the study are drawn from colonial administrators, missionaries and travel description.

More recent research on India, which was not hidebound by this Orientalist perspective, has cast considerable doubt on Weber's argument about the absence of an entrepreneurial spirit. Thus Gillion has described how there was a corporate tradition of a hereditary bourgeois elite, and a history of indigenous financial, commercial activity in Almedabad.[37] Bayley's study of Benares shows that the 'burgher city' that existed there in the late eighteenth century had 'forms of arbitration, market control, brokerage, neighbourhood communities, and above all conception of mercantile honour and credit, which breached caste boundaries'.[38] Prakash has shown that there was a thriving merchant class in Gujarat in the sixteenth century who used the manufacturing base in their hinterland to export cotton goods, silk and indigo.[39] Habib and Raychaudhuri have claimed that Indian merchants, principally Gujarati merchants, dominated trade in the Indian Ocean in textiles, raw cotton, silks, pepper and common foodstuffs until the seventeenth century.[40] Overall, writers such as Malik have argued the course of Indian development stemmed from a complex interplay of religious belief, state formation and economic developments.[41]

INDIA AND BRITAIN

The most glaring omission from a book which discusses the lack of capitalist development is the impact of colonialism. Nowhere does Weber examine how the colonisation of India by Britain might have retarded India's development. He provides no rationale for why his study should focus on Indian religion rather than the destructive impact of colonisation. As Madan has pointed out, he 'completely ignored the political situation in the country at that time when modern capitalism was developing in the West'.[42] It is as if capitalism develops autonomously through a free market and a cultural 'spirit' which motivates it. This liberal myth conveniently ignores how the nation state played a central role in the development of capitalism in countries as diverse as Germany and Japan.

After the battle of Plassey in 1757, India was run by a private company – the East India Company. This was a trading monopoly which took on itself the right to make peace or war with any prince or people according to its pleasure and to place the pecuniary interests of a few stockholders above the rights of millions of Indians. The military power of the company was used to destroy the factories of its rivals, to force Indian weavers to work for it for pitiful wages. The company enjoyed duty-free trading passes while its Indian rivals were subject to numerous tolls and customs duties.[43] Yet despite this immense power, there is not a single reference throughout the whole of Weber's book to the company which has been described as 'a modern capitalist corporation of an advanced bourgeois nation (which) entrenched itself like a parasite in the agrarian state dominated by a decaying military feudal regime'.[44]

Nor is there any discussion in Weber's book about the wider relationship between India and Britain at this time. If such a discussion had occurred, then Weber might have been forced to ask more questions about the blockages to capitalist development in India. Two areas in particular might have stood out: the fate of the Indian textile industry and the transfer of capital from India to Britain.

Up to the first two decades of the nineteenth century, Indian woven cotton was competitive with British machine cloth but suffered from the discriminatory practices of the British state.[45] Later, the industry was decimated, as India became the largest market for British export of cotton goods – the largest single item of British exports at the end of the nineteenth century. Weber's failure to analyse the fate of the textile industry in this context is astounding. So too is his total neglect of the wider plunder of Indian society. Only a small amount of capital was transferred from Britain to India through the celebrated expansion of the railway network. However, even this only took place because the British government guaranteed a minimum rate of return of 5 per cent on shareholders' investment at a time when the average rate of return was 3 per cent in Britain.[46] This subsidy was borne by Indian society. Beyond that, Indian society was forced to pay high Home Charges to the empire – often raised through land taxes on over-priced land – and to devote nearly one quarter of its national expenditure to sustaining an army. How Weber could conclude that this level of plunder might not be of some relevance to capitalist development is simply extraordinary.

Mike Davis has aptly summarised the effect of colonialism on Indian society by pointing out that from 1872 to 1921, the life expectancy of ordinary Indians fell by a staggering 20 per cent, a deterioration in human health without precedent in the subcontinent's long history of war and invasion.[47] Weber did not appreciate the devastating effects of colonialism because he wrote from the mindset of a European gentleman. As we have seen, one of his main concerns was simply that Germany got its share of the colonial plunder of the day.

WAS THE CASTE SYSTEM ALWAYS STATIC?

It is not simply a matter of showing that Weber neglected the economic aspects of colonialism. His argument that the caste system caused a fundamental block to development only makes sense if this is analysed in isolation from the structures of colonial rule. However, there is considerable evidence that the caste system, which Weber took as a traditional aspect of Indian life stemming from sacred texts, was profoundly influenced by a colonial intervention.

Prior to colonial rule, Hinduism did not represent the same set of dogmatic beliefs that it assumed afterwards. According to Metcalf, for example, the British gave Hinduism a degree of coherence it had not possessed before and 'by imposing their "knowledge", the British made of Hinduism, previously a loosely integrated collection of sects, something resembling a religion'.[48] Similarly Dirks has argued that the modern phenomenon of caste was the product of an encounter between India and Western rule in the sense that 'caste' became a single term capable of expressing, organising and above all 'systematising India's diverse forms of social identity, community and organisation'.[49] The *varna* system with its four main orders of caste with the Brahman at the apex of the hierarchy only developed fully under British rule. The Laws of Manu (Manu Dharma Sastras), which are the standard source of authority for this division, only achieved their special legal status under British rule after William Jones translated them in 1794. The particular hierarchy of the caste order was also re-enforced by a number of British colonial practices. From 1881, the British census organised the population according to large caste blocks. Inside the Indian army, the philosophy was to put 'the races into watertight compartments'[50] so that different caste groups were assigned to different regiments.

Prior to colonisation, it appears caste was much more flexible and fluid. Under Mughal rule the most salient titles conferring status signified a relationship to the court. Caste was certainly there but not in the fixed, important form with a religious hierarchy at the top. In his study of the Pudukkottai state in Tamil Nadu, Dirks has shown that it was the king and not the Brahman who was at the apex of the hierarchy and that caste relations were not simply religious but reflected a system of social relations that was ordered by the king.[51]

The British Empire had a direct interest in creating an image of India as a caste-ridden society with a Brahman hierarchy. It played down the role of native political structures and, in particular, local kings. It allowed the colonial authority to align itself with 'non-political' hierarchies to legitimate its own rule. It fed into an idea – shared by Weber – that the Indian population was so divided that they were incapable of developing the idea of nationality. A few years after the formation of the Indian National Congress, for example, J.A. Baines, the census commissioner for 1891, justified his distribution of the population on caste lines, by stating that it was necessary to clear 'out of the way the notion that in the Indian population there is any cohesive element that is implied in the term nationality'.[52] Finally, the caste system gave the colonial administrator the illusion of knowing people. He did not have to differentiate among individuals but simply recognise how a Brahman or a Shudra had certain characteristics that were 'well known' in the folklore of the colonialists.[53]

Weber assumed that the colonial order was natural and inevitable – even to the extent of barely mentioning it in his account of India. He was therefore in no position to assess how apparently 'traditional' India might have been a social construct. Europe was defined primarily as the modernising force – and India was mired in backwardness until colonialism arrived. The mere possibility that colonisation had a direct interest in the domination of a particular form of 'traditionalism' was not even considered. What emerges therefore as an explanation of Indian underdevelopment is deeply flawed.

CHINA'S SOCIAL STRUCTURE

Weber's book *The Religion of China* raises similar themes to his discussion on India. The author makes, however, a more determined attempt to link material and spiritual factors into a comprehensive explanation. Thus, the first third of the book looks at wider sociological obstacles to capitalism in China rather than simply the religious factors. Weber notes that in the sixteenth century there was an increase in the use of precious metals and the money economy. This combined with the enormous growth of the population could have shattered traditionalism and allowed the seeds of capitalism to grow – but they did not. The reasons for the failure are the central themes in the book.

One factor was that the cities of China – like in the Orient generally – lacked political autonomy. The 'fetters of the sib were never shattered'[54] and an urban citizenry never materialised. (The term sib might possibly be translated as 'clan' and one of Weber's central points was that this form of localised, blood-based social organisation was particularly strong in China.) There was no oath-bound political association which transcended sib ties and established a set of legal rights which guaranteed the city a degree of autonomy allowing capitalism to flourish.

Related to this was the power of a bureaucratic, patrimonial state in the Chinese empire. China was unusual in that the unification of the vast empire proceeded, with only minor interruptions, from the third century BC onwards. This removed 'legitimate opportunities for internal war' and defence against barbarian invasions became largely a 'police duty'.[55] Two important effects emerged from the early unification and growth of state power in China. The first was that the social hierarchy of Chinese society was not fragmented through feudal status. Authority did not rest with lords and knights who established a degree of independence through their ability to raise armies, but rather in the hands of high provincial officials. The central state maintained enormous control over these officials by assigning them short terms of office, by moving them regularly and by not employing them in their home states.

Ironically, the very measures used to strengthen central control over the individual officials weakened their base and made them dependent on local unofficial subordinates who were drawn from the key sibs. The power of the sibs meant there could not be a free market in land. The sibs offered a powerful form of solidarity that cut across the free market selection of labour and the imposition of work discipline. They also offered a huge counterweight to power of the state officials and Chinese history, therefore, is often characterised by an attempt to extend the power of the state beyond the cities. According to Weber, 'a "city" was the seat of the mandarin and was not self governing; a "village" was a self governing settlement without a mandarin'.[56] China, therefore, combined a concentrated form of bureaucracy with traditionalist sib ties.

BUREAUCRACY AND CONFUCIANISM

The second major social effect of a long stable empire was the unification of spiritual and temporal power. According to Weber, 'the unshaken order of internal political and social life, with thousands of years behind it, was placed under divine tutelage and then considered as the revelation of the divine'.[57] The emperor was supposed to have charismatic powers which could in turn be bestowed on his officials. The unification of spiritual and temporal power led to a lack of criticism and served as another reinforcement of traditionalism. One result was that 'Chinese intellectual life remained completely static and despite favourable conditions, modern capitalist developments simply did not appear.'[58]

At times Weber's description of Chinese social structures reads like a morality tale about the danger of bureaucracy and centralised power. Bureaucracy was twinned with a 'pacifistic' ethos, which in turn led to stagnation. Weber's central argument was that China's relatively peaceful development became a millstone around its neck because in the absence of war and conflict there was no innovation.

> Modern Europe ... is the great historic exception ... because, above all, pacification of a unified empire was lacking. .... Just as competition for markets compelled the rationalization of private enterprise, so competition for political power compelled the rationalization of the state economy and economic policy both in the Occident and in the China of the Warring states. In the private economy, cartelization weakens rational calculation, which is the soul of capitalism; among states, power monopoly prostrates rational management in administration, finance and economic policy.[59]

The religion of the literati who ran China's bureaucracy was Confucianism. For more than 2,000 years the prestige of the literati was derived from knowledge of writing and of literature. They were trained in ritual and were primarily orientated towards problems of internal administration. Their culture was that of 'old men' who held pacifist values rather than the heroic values of war and bravery. Confucianism was a highly appropriate vehicle for conveying a bureaucratic ethos. According to Weber, 'the traditional view held by Confucius is that caution is the better part of valour and that it ill behoves the wise man to risk his own life inappropriately'.[60] Confucianism placed a high premium on education and had no beliefs about innate evil – only a lack of education prevented the individual adapting to the world around them. The form of education that was valued was a broad humanist one, which Weber rather disparagingly described as 'a highly exclusive and bookish literary education'.[61]

The Confucian ideal was a gentleman who ensured that within his character there were 'no disturbances caused by the restless spirits of nature or of men'.[62] Above all, Confucianism promoted propriety and adjustment to the world. There was no yearning for an afterlife or an anxious desire to be saved. The aim was rather a happy tranquillity in this life and so Confucianism was only interested in the affairs of this world. Self-control was considered essential – but control in the sense of an absolute acceptance of conventional society. The revolutionary force of other religions with their powerful criticisms of this world in the name of God or the spirit kingdom was quite simply lacking. As Weber put it cryptically, 'the Chinese "soul" has never been revolutionized by a prophet'.[63]

Weber believed that entrepreneurship arose from a high moral tension, which was both part of this world but also fought against in it. Its psychological mainspring was a self-directed methodical lifestyle which sought higher ends. The spirit of Confucianism was, however, diametrically opposed to this capitalist ethos. It suppressed any impulse to break the bonds of traditionalism and advocated an adjustment to the conventions. Confucianism faced a rival religious force in Taoism. However, Taoism tended to stress more magical elements and had degenerated into an irrational outlook. Overall, Confucianism was the dominant religion of China and the principal force in counteracting the possibility of capitalist development.

WEBER'S RACISM

Weber's analysis of Chinese society is again marked by an extraordinary sense of European superiority. Chinese society is derided for its pacifism that produced a stagnant bureaucracy whereas Europe's history of war and conflict is credited with development and dynamism. *The Religion of China*, which was undertaken during Weber's enthusiasm for the First World War, offers a thinly disguised vision of war as the progressive motor of history.

Weber's account is also marred because his vision of Chinese society is drawn uncritically from the literature of missionaries, which he describes as 'the most authentic' on offer.[64] The missionaries' racist stereotypes of the 'Chinese character' are not only accepted at face value but amplified. Weber accepts missionary observations about the Chinese capacity for 'absolute insensitivity to monotony'.[65] He notes the Chinese 'slowness in reacting to unusual stimuli, especially in the intellectual sphere'.[66] He claims there is a 'typical distrust of the Chinese for one another' and casually refers to their 'incomparable dishonesty'.[67] His own more 'educated' speculations about Chinese culture are even worse than the casual racism of the missionaries. He claims that the 'peculiarity' of the Chinese script and the particular nature of Chinese speech patterns meant that 'the Chinese tongue was unable to offer its services to poetry or to systematic thinking'.[68]

In case his meaning is not clear, Weber spells it out: 'In spite of the logical qualities of the language, Chinese thought has remained rather stuck in the pictorial and the descriptive. The power of *logos*, of defining and reasoning, has not been accessible to the Chinese.'[69] And again ... 'The very concept of logic remained absolutely alien to Chinese philosophy, which was bound to script, was not dialectical, and remained orientated to purely practical problems as well as to the status interests of the patrimonial bureaucracy.'[70]

WAS CHINA SO STAGNANT?

In some ways, the fundamental problem with Weber's book is not the absurd casual racism, which is easily dismissed by the modern reader. It is rather the more abiding image of China as a stagnant society that is stuck in time because of its religious culture. In fact, there was considerable commercial development in Southern China in the period of the Sung dynasty from 960 to 1279. Hangchow, the capital of Southern Sung, had a population of more than 1 million; the then leading European city of Venice had a population of 50,000. Cast iron output in China produced in blast furnaces reached a level that England did not reach until the late eighteenth century. Trade relations with Japan developed rapidly and eleven large Japanese trade missions were recorded arriving in China between 1433 and 1549.[71] By the start of the seventeenth century, new centres of industrial activity had appeared at Soochow for silk textiles, Sungkiang for cotton goods and Chingtechen for porcelain. By 1621, Shanghai and its surrounding administrative area was estimated to have had 200,000 looms operating.[72] Far from the Chinese language limiting new forms of thought, Gernet notes that,

> The end of the 16th century and the first half of the 17th century were marked by the remarkable development of the theatre, the short story and the novel, and by the upsurge of a semi learned, semi popular culture. It was the culture of an urban middle class eager for reading matter and entertainment ... Never had the book industry been so prosperous or its products of such good quality.[73]

By the 1640s at the end of the Ming dynasty, however, China did enter a period of stagnation even before the colonial powers arrived. The question of why Chinese development was halted is an interesting one but Weber's approach is marred by his textualism. His method is to assume that people live according to the precepts of the official religion. Life, however, is far more varied. Patricia Ebrey, for example, has shown that a widely circulated book for gentlemen in Sung China contradicted many of the tenets of Confucianism. Yuan Ts'ai's *Precepts for Social Life* 'assumed that one's goal in business was profit' and expressed 'business like attitudes'.[74]

Instead of assuming China suffered from a primordial defect in its religious culture, it might be more useful to see stagnation as a feature of many diverse societies. Some more recent writers have, for example, compared this period in China's history to the crisis of Western feudalism in the seventeenth century.[75] Looked at from this perspective, other reasons for China's decline become available – such as the relative power of rival social classes at the time. In Europe, the crisis of feudalism was overcome by the rise of the bourgeoisie, by revolutionary means in the case of England and Holland. In China, however, the aristocracy was more successful in imposing much greater control over the merchants and prevented any breakthrough from below. The Ming dynasty ended the naval voyages to India and Africa and sought to stop overseas trade. It was hostile to the merchant class because it saw them disturbing the basis for its rule. When this dynasty collapsed in the face of a peasant rebellion, the majority of the gentry transferred their allegiance to the Manchu dynasty.

COLONIALISM

While Weber explores a number of aspects of China's social structure, he provides little specific historical analysis. He focuses on eternal aspects of culture or legal forms rather than specifically examining changes in economic conditions. As with India, there is a complete blind spot on colonialism, with no discussion, for example, on the effects of the Opium Wars. Yet, under the Treaty of Nanking in 1841, Britain not only won the right to flood the country with opium – insisting for example that the Chinese authorities pay compensation for seizures from drug dealers – but also effectively took control over tariff policy for decades. Only a thoroughgoing liberal who denied the role of state policy in economic development could argue that the inability of a state to set its own tariffs on imports did not affect the development of capitalism.

Similarly, the focus on theology also led Weber to misrepresent important opposition movements. He treats the Taiping Rebellion primarily as a religious peculiarity that was 'stimulated in part through the influence of Protestant missions and the Bible'.[76] The ideology of the Taiping movement certainly contained elements of Christianity mixed in with concepts derived from the classical Chinese tradition. However, far more important than its specific theological mix was its social base among the peasantry. The Taiping Rebellion was quite simply the greatest peasant rebellion in Chinese history and, as Rodzinski puts it, 'its fundamental purport was the mission to create a Heavenly Kingdom in China, in which all men would be brothers'.[77] Describing the movement fundamentally in religious terms misses out on this important social reality.

CONCLUSION

Weber's ultimate purpose in *The Religion of China* and in *The Religion of India* was to use both countries as counterfactual arguments for his central thesis about the role of Protestantism in giving birth to the capitalist spirit. As we have seen, this meant ignoring important aspects of social life in these colonised countries. However, equally it meant painting the capitalist spirit in extraordinarily positive terms. At the end of *The Religion of China* there is a passage which purports to describe the essential features of the modern entrepreneur:

> The indispensable ethical qualities of the modern capitalist entrepreneur were: radical concentration on God-ordained purposes; the relentless and practical rationalism of the asceticist ethic; a methodological conception of matter-of-factness in business management; a horror of illegal, political, colonial, booty and monopoly types of capitalism which depended on the favour of princes and men as against the sober, strict legality and the harnessed rational energy of the routine enterprise ... This must be added to the pious worker's special will to work.[78]

A horror of illegal booty and monopolies ... strict legality ... and pious workers with a special desire for work ... can this really be a serious description of capitalism as it really operated? Weber has romanticised capitalism and painted India and China in dark colours to create a shining ideological image. He presents an image of stagnant, passive societies by often ignoring their long history of economic development. He constructs an image of 'traditional' India and China by mainly reading off their social structure from religious texts. He ignores the impact of colonialism on their development and so effectively blames their religion for their stagnation. In brief, both books display an imperialist disposition that was common in many German gentlemen who wished to justify the creation of an empire.

5
Methodology

Early sociology tried to model itself on the natural sciences and sought to import their methods into the study of society. The positivist school of Auguste Comte was the most ambitious in this regard. It believed that the process of observation and comparison of social phenomena would eventually yield evidence of social laws. These in turn would enable the sociologist to predict future behaviour and so develop a certain power to control events.

The positivist approach put primary emphasis on observable human behaviour. But soon questions emerged. What if our observations were biased by our culture, language or the peculiar features of our mind? In addition, where did mental activity, which was unobservable, fit into this? What role did interpretation and choice play in constructing the social order?

Weber's sociology became part of the revolt against positivism. Philosophically, he was influenced by German idealism, which assigned a huge role to the human mind in actively constructing the observable world. Ideologically, he was deeply committed to what might be now termed a neo-liberal concept of 'free choice', which grew out of his support for market-based economics. Both these strands led him to a series of writings on methodology which has had enormous influence on subsequent sociologists.

Weber's writings on methodology were published posthumously in *Max Weber on the Methodology of the Social Sciences*. This contains articles on whether knowledge about society can be objective or whether it is relative. It also contains Weber's argument on why sociology had to be 'value free'. In this chapter, we shall first indicate philosophical and economic influences on Weber. We shall then outline his methodological individualism, his advocacy of value-free research and his use of ideal types. Finally, we shall offer a critical assessment which argues that Weber smuggled the methods of conventional economics in to sociology.

BETWEEN GERMAN IDEALISM AND AUSTRIAN ECONOMICS

Discussions on methodology played an important role in German academic life at the start of the twentieth century. One common theme was that there was a fundamental divide between the natural sciences and the social sciences. Wilhelm Dilthey argued that the 'humanistic sciences' – history and the social sciences – did not seek regularities or 'laws' in the same way the natural sciences did. Instead they dealt primarily with the human mind and Spirit (*Geist*) and these could only be understood 'from the inside' in terms of intentions and beliefs. Heinrich Rickert argued for a similar distinction but in a slightly different way. The natural sciences, he claimed, broke objects down into their elementary constituents in order to establish their general properties. The aim was to arrive at abstract, generalising laws that were valid throughout space and time. The historical sciences, however, examined their subject matter in all its individual and concrete forms. They focused on unique events, individuals or collections of unique individuals that the researcher selected as valuable for analysis.[1]

One of the major influences in this discussion was the philosophy of Immanuel Kant. Kant opposed the idea that our minds passively registered information received from our senses. Sense data only gave us a mass of chaotic images which had to be organised by the mind. The mind used categories such as Space, Time and Causation in order to organise this data but these categories did not come from the world itself. They were, rather, like internal filters in the brain. All of this meant that 'things in themselves' were unknowable and that the mind had an active role in processing knowledge. Kant's philosophy belonged to a peculiarly German tradition of focussing on the *Geist* or Spirit as the active element in reality. This tradition stressed how all knowledge was the result of a process of selection according to values. In complex ways, this outlook, which was broadly known as German idealism, was subsequently linked to a revolt against modernity and the philosophies linked with it. Modern society was seen to be materialistic and built on a mechanical culture which stressed how individuals were like machines determined by forces outside themselves. Against the 'English' emphasis on the free market and happiness for the greatest number, the German mandarins promoted 'culture', 'the national cause' and 'values'.[2]

One area where the tension between modernity and German idealism was most evident was in Weber's first discipline of economics. Originally, Weber supported the German Historical School, which opposed the idea of abstract economic laws and instead looked at the role of national spirit and culture in shaping an economy. His own focus on the Protestant Ethic as the trigger for capitalism derived from this approach. However, Weber was also aware that the theories of the Historical School could also lead to sentimental support for weak economic practices. Figures such as Gustav Smoller, for example, supported the patriarchal relations that prevailed in agriculture. The Historical School had originated in opposition to the English philosophy of free trade and demanded protectionism. However, its avoidance of a more abstract and general approach to economics became an intellectual disadvantage once Germany became an industrial power on the global stage.

The main rival to the German Historical School was the Austrian school of marginalist economics. This was the school which eventually became dominant in most modern conventional economics. Unlike the Historical School, it used abstract concepts and aimed at establishing general laws. In one sense this represented a return to the earlier school of classic economics of Adam Smith and David Ricardo. However the marginalists differed from the classical school because they opposed the notion of an objective measure of value. Value, they believed, came from a subjective estimation by individuals of the 'utility' they got from every extra amount (marginal increment) of any commodity. In 1883, Carl Menger set off a debate with the Historical School when he defended the use of abstract ideal types as the only way to scientific knowledge in natural sciences and economics. The debate itself reflected, in complex ways, the divergent pulls of German nationalism with its traditional embrace of idealist philosophy and the demands for modernisation that came with becoming an industrial power.

Weber was torn both ways in this debate and in many ways his intellectual concerns reflected both his vibrant German nationalism and his belief that his country had to 'de-feudalise' in order to advance. He wanted to retain the emphasis on values and a sense of uniqueness of the social and cultural spheres. However, he also wanted access to the more 'scientific' formulations, which the marginalists promised, as a way of building up an industrial culture in Germany. He was also attracted to the marginalists because of their focus on the individual and, crucially, their seemingly rigorous theoretical alternative to Marxism.[3] His complex writings on methodology can only be understood if this background is noted.

A METHOLOGICAL INDIVIDUALIST

Weber's sociology is based on a methodological individualism which seeks to break down collectivities such as 'classes' or 'nations' or 'the family' in order to see them as the outcome of social actions of individual persons. He wrote that

> If I have become a sociologist (according to my letter of accreditation) it is mainly to exorcise the spectre of collective conceptions which still lingers among us. In other words, sociology itself can only proceed from the action of one or more separate individuals and must therefore adopt strictly individualistic methods.[4]

Marx, by contrast, argued that one only became an individual in, and through, society. According to Marx, social relations are formed prior to the individual and help to forge his or her identity. In other words, individuals do not simply choose, but live in a class-bound society where the framework of their lives is structured beforehand.

For Weber, however, choice plays a huge role in society and, therefore, in the methodology of disciplines that study it. The subject matter of sociology, he argued, was social action. Action occurs when 'the acting individual attaches a subjective meaning to his behavior – be it overt or covert, omission or acquiescence'.[5] In other words, the individual interprets, chooses, and evaluates what they are doing, according to their own distinct mental life. Action is social when the meaning given by the individual 'takes account of the behavior of others and is thereby orientated in its course'.[6] Society is formed by individuals choosing, interpreting and acting in ways that take account of the fact that other individuals are doing likewise.

This focus on individual choice meant that values and motives were hugely important in Weber's sociology and he wrote in considerable complexity about their role. He adopted quite an extreme version of Kantianism by claiming that all knowledge of reality is structured by the particular point of view that the actor brings to bear on it. Reality is a chaotic mass of sense experiences, which our perceptions actively structure: 'Empirical reality becomes "culture" to us because and insofar as we relate it to value ideas. It includes those segments and only those segments of reality, which have become significant to us because of their value relevance.'[7] But if this is the case, how does one arbitrate between these values? How does one know which value system provides a closer approximation towards the truth? If the value system of a socialist leads them to focus on particular activities on Wall Street and see them as greedy and chaotic and a stockbroker selects others and sees them as a model of efficiency, how are we to assess whose view is correct?

It is at this point that a strong element of relativism appears in Weber's work. His emphasis on the inevitability of power struggles led him to argue that value systems cannot be assessed objectively. 'Scientific' pleading (between the different stands) is meaningless in principle because the various value spheres of the world stand in irreconcilable conflict with each other' he noted in his speech delivered at Munich University in 1918 and later printed as 'Science as a Vocation'.[8] More stridently, in 'The Meaning of Ethical Neutrality in Sociology and Economics' written in 1917, as the drums of war roared in the background, Weber wrote that 'It is really a question not only of alternatives between values but of an irreconcilable death struggle like that between "God" and "the Devil". Between these, neither relativization nor compromise is possible'.[9]

VERSTEHEN METHOD

A number of complex conclusions followed from this particular view of the social world. The first was the famous *Verstehen* method. Following the wider German idealist tradition Weber denied that the discovery of general laws added anything to our understanding of 'why' humans acted as they did. Even if there was strictly statistical evidence to show that all men who had been placed in a particular situation invariably reacted in a certain way, all this would show would be that their actions were calculable. Such a demonstration, he argued, would 'contribute absolutely nothing to the project of "understanding" "why" this reaction ever occurred and, moreover, "why" it invariably occurs in the same way'.[10] What was needed instead was a method of *Verstehen* or understanding, which would allow us to get into the inner sense of how individuals subjectively interpreted and chose what they were doing. In Weber's own words, the *Verstehen* method means,

> to identify a concrete 'motive' or complex of motives 'reproducible in inner experience', a motive to which we can attribute the conduct in question with a degree of precision that is dependent upon our source material. In other words because of its susceptibility to a meaningful *interpretation* ... individual conduct is in principle intrinsically less 'irrational' than the individual natural event.[11]

There are two types of *Verstehen*. One is a direct observational understanding where we grasp what is really going on merely through noticing facial expressions or outward behaviour. Another type is explanatory understanding where we place the action in a 'sequence of motivation' and so work out why it is occurring. In both cases sociology is primarily about putting oneself in another's mind. By using precise methods to access the motives of other people we are able to understand why they acted as they did. From this point of view, the behaviour of someone you truly know is far more predictable than the weather. Notice here the implicit promise that Weber is holding out: it is possible to focus on *Geist* or culture or motives and still be as 'scientific' as the natural sciences. His aim was to rid the *Verstehen* method of a lazy, intuitive approach, which simply assumed there was a natural empathy between individuals. He wanted to lend it instead a 'scientific' rigour. Or, to put it in a broader context, to link the German idealist tradition to the motor of modernity.

VALUE-FREE SOCIOLOGY

This rigorous approach to *Verstehen* demanded a trade-off from the sociologists – they would have to be 'value free'. As conflicting values reflected power struggles in society, the sociologist had to put aside their own values when engaged in research. In order to access the mind of others who might have opposing values it was necessary to temporarily put one's own values aside. It should be clear 'exactly at which point the scientific investigator becomes silent and the evaluating and acting person begins to speak'.[12] Another reason for the strict injunction about value freedom was that Weber believed that there was an unbridgeable gap between the world of 'what is' and 'what should be'. Empirical research could not lead to any conclusions about values because 'to *judge* the *validity* of such values is a matter of *faith*'.[13] There were also, however, more pragmatic reasons for advocating 'value freedom'.

German universities at the time faced considerable interference from the state authorities and the Prussian authorities in particular. In one famous case, Ludwig Bernhard was directly appointed to a professorship by the Prussian Ministry of Education without any consultation with the university faculty. One of Weber's own students, Robert Michels, was denied a PhD by virtue of his membership of the Marxist SPD. Brilliant academics such as George Simmel were not given permanent posts because of the culture of anti-Semitism. In addition to these problems, academics who were '*privatdozenten*' were paid according to the number of pupils who attended their lectures.

This put a premium on developing a populist style to attract students and some academics turned their lecterns into soapboxes. One in particular, Heinrich von Treitschke, won large numbers with his anti-Semitism and his promotion of a cult of Bismarck. Weber believed that this type of demagogic nationalism was a block on learning and led students to a 'fantastic ignorance of the history of this century'.[14] Ignorance cultivated by populist rhetoric, albeit nationalist rhetoric, would in the long run hold Germany back.

Weber therefore proposed a direct trade-off. The state should not seek to enforce standards of political obedience or loyalty in universities but should allow academic freedom. If it did not do this, he claimed, 'the interest of science and scholarship are no better and indeed in many respects, are worse served than they were in the earlier condition of dependence on the church'.[15] The universities could only contribute to character building if they gave individual students responsibility for developing their own values. But on the other hand, academics had to show severe restraint in promoting their values. The university could only develop a culture of consensus and freedom 'if one put aside the idea of any sort of instruction in ultimate values and beliefs' and if the university lecturer was 'under sternest obligation to avoid proposing his own position in the struggle of ideals'.[16]

Weber's aim was both to safeguard the freedom of the state to promote German national policy and to defend the university as the seat of Western rationality. However, as Gouldner has pointed out, the implication was that academics were not entitled to freedom from state control in matters of value since they had no specialised qualification in these areas.[17] Weber's liberalism has therefore often been misunderstood. He was not mainly concerned to limit the power of the state and defend individual liberties. His primary aim was to ensure that the German state was able to develop modern rational methods.

There were further complexities involved in Weber's notion of value freedom. On the one hand, the injunction about 'value freedom' demanded of researchers that they set aside their own values when engaged in research and teaching. However, Weber also argued that the social scientist had to study unique events and phenomena and this in turn demanded some form of selection as the items for study had to be hewn out from an infinite number of possible areas. This process of selection involved value judgements. Weber therefore noted that there can be no, 'absolutely "objective" analysis of culture

– or ... "social phenomena" independent of special and "one-sided" viewpoints according to which – expressly or tacitly, consciously or unconsciously – they are selected, analyzed and organized for expository purposes'.[18] Items of study were selected according to the relevant value system of the researcher. One had to distinguish therefore between *value freedom* and *value relevance*. *Value freedom* represented a severe injunction to put aside all value judgements when engaged in the process of analysis. However *value relevance* implied that particular research problems were chosen by the researcher because of their own value-related interest. These same cultural interests also 'give purely empirical scientific work its direction'.[19] In other words, the researcher's values – which were not amenable to rational argument – shaped the way in which investigators went about providing answers to the problems they chose. One might suggest that Weber's book on *The Protestant Ethic* provides a good example. His value system selected the problem – how did Western capitalism begin? In addition his cultural background led him to look in a particular 'direction' – towards the role of Protestantism.

Weber appears to be on very slippery ice here and much of his writing on methodology is torturously complex as he tries to navigate the rapids between the traditional German idealist emphasis on the active mind creating reality and the requirements of modern research. One way he tried to solve this conundrum was by drawing a distinction between 'ends' and 'means'. All human conduct, he claimed, is orientated to particular ends. We desire something for its own sake or as a means to something that is more desirable. The social scientist has little say to say about those ends other then to suggest whether they are internally consistent, whether they are feasible in terms of the present society or whether they represent 'absolutist' ends. So Weber claimed, for example, that the ends of syndicalists – militant advocates of a general strike – were 'doomed in advance to absolute failure' and belonged in the realm of 'absolute values'. They were like those of religious sects – 'not of this world'.[20]

Social scientists also needed to assess how people used the scarce means that were available to achieve their ends. They could 'scientifically' draw out the implications of the pursuit of certain values and illustrate to people the actual means that would be required to achieve them. They could do this even while opposed to their value system. The social scientist could select a problem for investigation and have the direction of the investigation kick-started by their own value system – but once underway, he or she needed to suspend their own values and adopt the most rigorous scientific methods. The following is probably is the clearest summary of Weber's complex argument:

[1]   The choice of the object of investigation ... [is] determined by the evaluative ideas which dominate the investigator and his age.

[2]   In the *method* of investigation, the guiding 'point of view' [of the researcher] is of great importance for the *construction* of the conceptual schema which will be used in the investigation.

[3]   [BUT] in the mode of their use [i.e. the conceptual schema] the investigator is bound by the [scientific] norms of our thought just as much here as elsewhere. For scientific truth is precisely what is *valid* for all who *seek* the truth.[21]

ECONOMIC METHODS AND IDEAL TYPES

Weber added one more element to his attempt to marry a subjective focus on values with his desire for objective methodological rigour. This was the *ideal type*, which Weber believed was 'heuristically indispensable' for sociological and historical research.[22] To understand it we need again to return to the old debate between the Historical School of Economics and the Austrian marginalist school.

The Austrian school sought to eliminate all discussion of particular national cultures from the workings of each economy. Their analysis started out from an economic man who existed as an isolated atom. The marginalists placed this imaginary man in particular situations of scarcity, or in situations with different balances between supply and demand. From these scenarios, they devised general laws of the economy that could be stated with quite mathematical precision. One of their number, Stanley Jevons, stated that 'the general form of the laws of economy is the same in the case of individuals and nations'.[23] This level of formal equivalence could only occur because the economic man they started out from was shorn of his particular histories, foibles, and cultures – he was an abstract model or 'ideal type', which functioned as a sort of thought experiment. Weber summarised the underlying philosophy of the marginalist school by saying that it examined what course a 'given type of human action would take if it were strictly rational, unaffected by errors or emotional factors and if, furthermore, it were completely and unequivocally directed to a single end, the maximization of economic advantage'.[24]

Weber wanted to import the methodology of the ideal type into the wider field of social science because he believed it would impose an intellectual discipline on the researcher who was using the *Verstehen* method. The sociologist, he argued, had to follow the economist in constructing an ideal type that highlighted certain aspects of reality. The ideal type was not meant as a description but was a 'one-sided *accentuation* of one or more points of view' and a 'synthesis of a great many diffuse, discrete ... *concrete individual* phenomena, which are arranged according to those one-sidedly emphasized viewpoints into a unified *analytical* construct'.[25] It was therefore a model that was based on pure elements that represented people's motive and culture. So, for example, the researcher could develop an ideal type of a Puritan by assembling together the pure motives that followed from their religious beliefs. Or in a more complex fashion, he or she could develop an ideal type of the 'handicraft' economy in order to contrast it with 'industrial capitalism'. Ideal types were models for highlighting contrasts and comparisons between different societies. They also allowed connections to be drawn between different spheres of society, between, say, religious beliefs and economic action. These were known as elective affinities.

Weber was keen to stress that the ideal types were only explanatory devices which helped to bring out the significance and meanings that humans bestow on their actions. The criterion of their success was whether they revealed 'concrete culture phenomena in their interdependence, their causal conditions and their significance'.[26] The crucial issue was that they did not represent forces that existed in reality. Marxism, Weber claimed, operated with a number of ideal types, using, for instance, specific 'relations of productions' as an explanatory variable, but it failed to see that these ideal types were only one among many possible other ideal types. Its fatal flaw was to believe that its own models existed in reality. By contrast Weber argued that anyone who could 'perceive the fundamental ideas of modern epistemology which ultimately derive from Kant' would have no difficulty accepting that they were 'primarily analytic instruments for the intellectual mastery of empirical data and can only be that'.[27]

The ideal types were related to the four main categories of social action. These were:

- *Traditional action*, which was a form of ingrained habit – you do something because it was always done like that;

- *Affective action*, which is based on emotional feeling – you do something because of love for, say, a brother or sister;
- *Value rational action*, where actions are undertaken for some ethical or religious ideal and there is no consideration of its prospect of success – you do something for God or 'the cause';
- *Instrumentally rational action*, which is based on rational calculation about the specific means of achieving definite ends – you do something because it is the most effective means of achieving a specific goal.

Weber believed that the first two were very 'close to the borderline of what can justifiably be called meaningful orientated action'.[28] In other words, these categories did not embrace the main activities in modern society. That left, therefore, a division of social action between actions undertaken for absolutist, utopian goals and actions carried out by a calculating variant of 'economic man'.

ASSESSMENT

Behind this rather complex discussion, Weber was smuggling the bias of conventional economics into sociology. His writings repeatedly used economic examples and his own methodology borrowed from the 'economic principle' which assumed that actors have full knowledge of their future needs and resources available.[29] In his refutation of Rudolf Stammler's account of Marx's theory of historical materialism, for example, he claimed that the standards of marginal utility theory should be used as a 'way of determining how [an actor's] actual conduct "measures up"'.[30] Sociologists had to operate as if the social actor in modern society fully knew their present and future needs and also knew the exact resources that were available to them. Just like the 'rational' economic man, the social actor had perfect knowledge of their ends and calculated precisely how to use the scarce resources available to them. Their ends were pure choices, which only they as an atomised individual decided on. But once an end was chosen, they would behave like a sober bourgeois, calculating a profit and loss account on how to get there.

Weber was aware that this was a pure idea – a utopia. However, just as conventional economics proceeded from this model, he still argued that the sociologist had to start by attributing a 'right rationality' to the actor and then examining where this would take them. Only after sociologists had done this, could they build in a calculation of incorrect assessments made by the social actors or deviations from the norm of rationality.[31]

All of this raises serious problems with Weber's methodology. The cornerstone of his entire approach is that values are arbitrary entities that are freely chosen by individuals and so cannot be subject to scientific analysis. Researchers can only accept the values of those they study as an irrational given for which there is no explanation. It seems that any inquiry into the value system of the individuals is an infringement on their freedom of choice. However, one can equally ask, why should inquiries be restricted in this fashion? Why put arbitrary limitations on research inquiries, asserting that one can only start from the effects of values and one cannot analyse why values arose? As Hirst puts it, 'the effect of ... the unquestionable priority of human freedom ... is to limit the explanatory power of discourse, to close and to silence areas of problems and avenues of theorisation'.[32]

There are also practical problems with Weber's methods. Even if we were to assume that an individual's values existed prior to, and independently of, society, how can we be sure that we have understood them. What if they are living in a different culture to our own? Weber's own immersion in the imperialist culture casts considerable doubts about his own abilities to engage in *Verstehen*. He states, for example, that 'our ability to share the feeling of primitive men is not very much greater' than our ability to know 'the subjective state of mind of an animal.'[33] More generally, his method of assuming that actors are typically aware of the motives for their action is questionable. Individuals can make mistakes and lie to themselves and others about their motives. Their motives can be confused, vague and contradictory. There may also be rationalisation for the pressures which society places upon them. Many women stayed at home in the 1950s believing that this was part of their motherly duty. It just so happened that this was part of an ideology about the natural roles of women that was propagated by a powerful Catholic Church and by a media who popularised the 'maternal deprivation' thesis of John Bowlby. It is now clear that this ideology was used against the interests of most women.

Weber's argument that ideal types are purely analytic devices with no relationship to reality means that he cannot show causal links. The ideal types become, instead, entirely formal categories around which large segments of history are grouped. As there is often no reference to the specific content of particular societies, Weber can make links between very diverse activities under the one rubric. So Ancient Egypt and socialism are linked together under the term bureaucracy. Or the ideal type of 'charisma' connects revolutionary leaders and Hindu shamans. The overall effect is that Weber substitutes the drawing up of typologies for real explanations of how societies change.[34] This method can sometimes illuminate interesting possible connections. However, there is also a profound agnosticism attached to the whole procedure as Weber explicitly states that alternative, equally valid ideal types could always have been used. The result can be a very formalistic sociology. The focus on how history changes is replaced by a desire to 'set up typologies and arrange historical phenomena in this typology'.[35]

CONCLUSION

Behind all of Weber's relativism there is, therefore, a systematic bias. He claims that values cannot be scientifically assessed or subject to discussion. However, if values cannot be critiqued, then the dominant values of the present system emerge unscathed from serious challenge. This is particularly useful for the elite. Moreover, Weber's calculating rational man who pursues randomly chosen values, is by no means a neutral figure. His very individualism, his assertion that his choices cannot be subjected to rational inquiry, his notion of a profit and loss account, mean that he acts according to the abstractly 'formulated psychology of the calculating individual agent of capitalism'.[36] Where, as the example on the syndicalists showed, people do not follow this calculating culture, Weber steps down from his academic chair, to pronounce that they are 'not of this world'. In other words, the psychology of the sober bourgeois is the norm – all else is interesting but entirely ineffective.

6
Class, Status and Party

Inequality is growing in the modern world. One might therefore think that discussion of the class system should form a central part of sociology. Not always, however. The British sociologist John Westergaard has pointed to an extraordinary puzzle: as inequalities widened in the 1980s, fashionable theories arrived to dismiss the relevance of class.[1]

The context was the Reagan–Thatcher era when the offensive against left-wing ideas was intense. Within the discipline of sociology, the notion that there was a 'death of class' won a considerable following. When the Berlin Wall collapsed, the argument gained further momentum as it was claimed that Marxism had died. 'Class as a concept is ceasing to do any useful work for sociology'[2] asserted one writer while others dismissively asserted that class consciousness in any strong sense is 'an increasingly redundant issue'.[3] In 1996, Jan Pakulski and Malcom Waters published a book entitled *The Death of Class* that claimed that there was a wide redistribution of property and so 'classes are dissolving and that the most advanced societies are no longer class societies'.[4] Class was, apparently, being replaced by the individualisation of society and social division was marked by different lifestyles among a contented majority and persistent failure among the 'underclass'.

Max Weber never had the slightest doubt about the importance of class in his era. His cold realism led him to focus on power struggles at the centre of social life. The growth of the unions and the SPD in Germany testified to the importance of working-class organisation. The influence of Marxist ideas also meant that Weber was less confident about challenging them on their home ground. One therefore finds that some of Weber's comments on class read like an echo of Marx. He had few illusions about the nature of the modern wage contract, for example:

> The formal right of a worker to enter into any contract whatsoever with any employer does not in practice represent for the employment seeker even the slightest freedom in the determination of his own

conditions of work, and it does not guarantee him any influence in this process. It rather means ... that the powerful party in the market i.e. normally the employer, has the possibility to set the terms, to offer the job, 'take it or leave', and, given the normally more pressing economic need of the worker, to impose his own terms upon him.[5]

However, while recognising the reality of class conflict, Weber denied there was any link between this conflict and any possible overthrow of capitalism. He stressed the fragmentation of the two main classes of workers and capitalists and denied there was a necessary antagonism between them. Crucially, he also stressed how 'status' divisions often cut through class conflict.

Weber's writings on the subject were, however, quite fragmentary. Rather confusingly they consist of two fairly brief sections in different volumes of *Economy and Society*. There he analysed social division according to his three main categories of class, status and party. However, as Parkin points out, he failed to relate this classification to some of his central concerns with power and bureaucracy.[6] The brief and fragmentary nature of Weber's analysis has meant that his followers have had to 'add on' new concepts to his ideas to build them up as worthy alternatives to Marx. What appears as Weber's analysis of the 'stratification system' is sometimes a hybrid of both Weber's own writings and those of modern Weberian sociologists. We shall, therefore, divide this chapter into two sections. The first will look at Weber's own writings on class, status and party. We will then critically assess the Weberian legacy as it has been constructed subsequently. We shall discuss the issue of white-collar employees as a litmus test for the alternative approaches of Marxism and Weberian sociology.

CLASS AND THE MARKET

Weber's analysis of social division started from a discussion of power – rather than economic inequality. Power was seen as all-pervasive, like a nebulous energy that runs through the social system. 'Man' according to Weber 'does not strive for power only in order to enrich himself economically. Power, including economic power, may be valued for its own sake.'[7] Weber defined power as the chance to realise one's will even against the resistance of others. All of this reflected Weber's wider metaphysical view, drawn from Nietzsche, that struggle for power is at the heart of human life. Class and status group conflict are therefore just one expression of this general distribution of power.

Classes, according to Weber, emerged in commodity or labour markets. They represented categories of people who shared similar life chances and, crucially, a 'specific causal component',[8] which determined how they got those life chances. This causal component was primarily based on 'the possession of goods and opportunities for income'.[9] Crucially, it was the manner in which material property was distributed which affected people's life chances. '"Property" and the "lack of property" are therefore the basic categories of all class situations.'[10]

An obvious question arises from these simple truths: how did some people get significantly more property than others? Weber, however, avoided this issue and started from the fact that *in the market place* the wealthy are able to use their position to 'increase their power in the price struggle with those who being propertyless, have nothing to offer but their labour or the resulting products'.[11] This is certainly true but it tells us little about how they managed to accumulate their wealth in the first place. The source of wealth has always been an embarrassment for conventional sociology and economics because any examination of this mystery must look at what happens in the sphere of production where labour power is exchanged for wages. As we saw above, Weber himself recognised that the formal equality of the wage contract was a sham but he did not want to draw the conclusion that profit arose from systematic exploitation. He therefore started out from the second rather than the first rung of the analytic ladder – what happens in the market place rather than at the heart of the production system itself.

This leads to one distinctly odd conclusion about people who do not produce for a market. 'Those men whose fate is not determined by the chance of using goods or services for themselves on the market e.g. slaves are not, however, a class in the technical sense of the term.'[12] Now this is an extraordinary claim. There is an ongoing controversy in the study of classical civilisation about whether slavery was the essential element of Ancient Greece and Rome or whether small independent or dependent producers were more central.[13] Whatever the controversy about numbers, however, it is difficult to deny Ste Croix's assertion that slavery 'was an essential pre-condition of the magnificent achievements of Classical civilisation'.[14] How else could the wealthy patricians who owned large estates gain a surplus if it were not for the unpaid labour of slaves? Surely, then, all slaves had an interest in gaining not only their freedom but also payment for the full value of their labour. In other words, slaves had common interests that were opposed to those of their masters. Weber's notion that classes could only be linked to a market thus leads to dogmatic assertions.

A MULTI-CLASS WORLD

The dogmatism arose primarily because Weber wanted to recognise class conflict but to stress its fragmentary nature. By focussing on divisions created in the market rather than the common interests that are formed in production, he was able to do this. In brief, he had picked up on one element of the dialectic involved.

Rather confusingly he discussed three main types of class: a 'property class'; a 'commercial class' and a 'social class'.[15] The first two were then subdivided into 'positively privileged' and 'negatively privileged'. The 'positively privileged property class' were defined primarily by their ability to achieve a monopoly of high-price goods, loan capital and status privileges. Weber stated that this group were typically 'rentiers'. This was a term that was particularly popular in the early twentieth century to describe those who derived their wealth from finance. The 'positively privileged commercial class' were primarily entrepreneurs who managed their business interests and sought to influence the economic policy of political organisations. Weber also briefly mentioned the 'negatively privileged property class' who were mainly paupers and 'negatively privileged commercial class' who were primarily labourers. The 'social class' was supposed to consist of primarily the working class as a whole, the petty bourgeoisie, and white-collar employees.

The schema is confusing but the central point comes through clearly, namely that there is neither a unified ruling class nor a unified working class. So Weber drew a distinction between the rentier and the manufacturing capitalist proper and suggested that workers may be misplaced in targeting their immediate employer:

> It is not the rentier, the shareholder, and the banker who suffer the ill will of the worker but almost exclusively the manufacturer and the business executives who are the direct opponents of workers in wage conflicts. This is so in spite of the fact that it is precisely the cash boxes of the rentier, the shareholder, and the banker into

which the more or less unearned gains flow rather than into the pockets of the manufacturers or of business executives.[16]

There are, of course, different fractions in the capitalist class. However, the distinction between financiers and manufacturers has never been as absolute as Weber claimed. There was a high level of integration between banks and manufacturing cartels in Weber's Germany; indeed, it has been held up as the example of 'organised capitalism' for precisely this reason.[17] Weber, though, was drawing on a populist discourse that made a distinction between the unhealthy, parasitic 'rentiers' and the healthy, productive capitalists who were their victims. However, even though he took a populist swipe against the rentiers, he did not believe in curbing their activities. He opposed the state regulation of the stock exchange arguing that

> A strong stock exchange cannot be a mere club for 'ethical culture' and the funds of the great banks are no more a 'charitable device' than are rifles and cannons. From the point of view of a national economic policy aimed at *this-worldly* goals, they could only be one thing – a weapon for achieving power in that economic struggle. If it can also achieve what is right and proper from an 'ethical' point of view in regard to these institutions, well and good; but it has a duty in the last resort to guard against the disarmament of its own nation by the fanatical interest groups or the unworldly apostles of economic peace.[18]

Weber's economic liberalism and his great power nationalism could not have been more clearly expressed.

If the capitalist class is divided, the working class is, according to Weber, fragmented between the skilled and unskilled. He argued that 'a *uniform* class situation prevails only when completely unskilled and propertyless persons are dependent on irregular employment'.[19] However, this is less and less the case in modern capitalism. Once there were opportunities for regular income, social mobility and differences in qualifications these broke up the unity between workers. Weber was not referring to white-collar employees at this stage since he assumed they were not part of the working class. He was rather pointing to the conflicting interests that skilled and unskilled manual workers developed.

Weber's overall argument then was that capital and labour were not the main protagonists within the present system. Each side was internally fragmented and 'class conflict' took place between a variety of groups, which were formed in the market place. Workers had few common interests since the focus was on the market rather than exploitation in the sphere of production. As Parkin puts it, 'what is portrayed instead is a Hobbesian war of all against all as each group fights its own corner in the anarchy of the market place'.[20] As a result, there was little theoretical space in Weber to explain why workers might spontaneously identify with their class. His wider sociology assumed that only individuals were real and 'ideal types' concepts such as social class might not have an actual reality in society. As Brennan has pointed out, Weber could not theoretically explain how shared economic interest of workers gave rise to class conscious organisations so 'workers' resistance has no theoretical foundation in Weber's sociology of action'.[21]

STATUS

Overlaid on class structure is another crucial source of division based on status. Status refers to one's place in the hierarchy of prestige or honour. A brain surgeon, for example, ranks high on many lists of 'respected' jobs. Unfortunately, bus drivers usually get a rank lower even though they are probably responsible for the care of many more lives than the brain surgeons. Status privileges can co-exist with wealth but there can also be important discrepancies. Casino owners may have amassed considerable wealth but generally have a low status while religious ministers have a high status but may have little wealth.

Weber suggested that people form themselves into status groups to protect their privileges. The hierarchy that is formed cuts across the ethos of modern economies because 'status groups hinder the strict carrying through of the sheer market principle'.[22] The reason is that 'the status order would be threatened at its very root if mere economic acquisition and naked economic power' prevailed.[23] Status groups try to gain a monopoly of certain privileges whereas the market is a great leveller that reduces everything to money.

Parkin, for example, has developed the concept of status and given it a more modern expression by linking it to Weber's concept of closure. Status groups, Parkin argues, seek to monopolise certain resources by erecting barriers to outsiders and are organised to exclude other groups that might encroach on their areas. Teachers, for example, often stress their educational qualifications to argue that classroom assistants should not be allowed to assume direct teaching duties. Parkin adds that these tactics can produce a countervailing pressure that 'seeks to bite into the privileges of legally defined superiors'.[24] Developing Weber, he thus claims there are two sorts of closure. One is 'exclusion' whereby one group erects barriers to maintain its privileges against lower status competitors. Another is 'usurption' whereby a lower group seeks to move upward by undermining these barriers. Subsequently, the concepts of closure, exclusion and usurpation have commonly been applied in study of race and ethnicity. Different ethnic groups are supposed to be fighting over monopoly of privileges in ways that cut across the class divide.

STATUS IN MODERN AND PRE-MODERN SOCIETIES

All of this is a perfectly valid way of developing Weber's ideas. However, it is equally important to recognise a confusion at the heart of Weber's concept of status as it may have an influence on subsequent theorising. Two very different views of status were, in fact, present in his work and, unfortunately, often were mixed up. One is the notion of status being predominant in pre-capitalist societies. It should be remembered that the German term that Weber used was *Stand*, which could be translated either as 'estate' or 'status'. Feudal societies were ranked according to different 'estates' – ranks of people who claimed different legal rights and privileges. Weber tended to see status as mainly emerging in feudal societies and as carrying over into capitalist societies. So he explicitly stated that 'Commercial classes arise in a market-orientated economy but status groups arise within the framework of organisations which satisfy their wants through monopolistic liturgies or in feudal or in *standisch-*patrimonial fashion.'[25] There was thus a strong suggestion that, as the tempo of economic change picked up, status groups gave way to class division.

His second less common usage made reference to the status of modern 'educated' classes. So he wrote that

> Present day society is stratified in classes, and to an especially high degree in income classes. But in the special *status* prestige of the 'educated' strata, our society contains a very tangible element of stratification by status. Externally, this status factor is most obviously represented by economic monopolies and the preferential social opportunities of holders of degrees.[26]

By 'educated' classes, Weber was referring to what we might call white-collar employees today who gain employment on the basis of their educational qualifications and receive a salary rather than a wage. Weber assumed that this group was not part of the wider working class but belonged to the bureaucracy. In 1918, in an address to army officers in Vienna, one of his main arguments against the possibility of socialism was the growth of a new layer of white-collar officials. He described these office workers as 'the bureaucrats of the private enterprise system' whose 'interests clearly do not by any means lie in the direction of proletarian dictatorship'.[27] White-collar employees used their position in the private sector and public sector bureaucracy to erect status barriers, which guaranteed them privileges.

Weber had a general tendency to skip between vastly different historical periods. As Cox pointed out, he seems to 'range over different social systems in an unsystematic way, with illustrations derived practically at convenience'.[28] However, the use of the concept of status to describe both the activities of white-collar employees and feudal estates such as courtly knights has left a legacy of confusion. The status barriers that protected courtly knights in feudal society were much more permanent and rigid than the relatively precarious 'status' situation of official and white-collar employees in modern capitalism. The knight may be impoverished but still expect privileges as of right. However, no matter how high an opinion they have of themselves, the office employee can be sacked, harassed by their boss or have their salary cut.

The discrepancy between the two notions of status comes out most clearly in Weber's claim that 'a specific *style of life*'[29] is expected of those who belong to a status group. As an example of this 'style of life' he mentioned 'restrictions on social intercourse'[30] and rules to confine marriage within the status group. One could certainly acknowledge that this applies to courtly knights in sixteenth-century Germany but it had limited relevance for the low-paid civil servant in Berlin even in Weber's time. Later in the twentieth century, it became entirely irrelevant. However, Weber's legacy has often led sociologists to see rigid, lasting barriers between white-collar employees and manual workers at precisely the point they are disappearing.

STATUS AND ETHNICITY

Similar problems attend Weber's discussion of status in connection with ethnic groups. He argued that over time status groups can evolve into a closed caste with rules about social intercourse and exogamous marriage when there are ethnic differences. The Jewish people were held up as a primary example.[31] More generally a belief in ethnic affinity arises because people often identify themselves by different styles of housing, dress and eating, stressing their unique customs as against other groups. The sense of what is 'correct and proper' is linked to an individual's sense of 'honour and dignity'.[32] In other words, not only do people seek to preserve their own customs, they assume that these customs are better than others. This sense of 'ethnic honour' is therefore closely related to the formation of status groups because the latter are ranks on a wider scale of social honour. 'The conviction of the excellence of one's own customs and the inferiority of alien ones, a conviction which sustains the sense of ethnic honour, is actually quite analogous to the sense of honour of distinctive status groups.'[33]

This analysis rests on a major assumption that is part of Weber's implicit world outlook – that there is a natural tendency for masses of people to seek a 'sense of ethnic honour' and to hold the notion of [themselves as a] 'chosen people''. Consequently 'ethnic repulsion may take hold of all conceivable differences among notions of propriety and transform them into "ethnic conventions"'. [34] Weber argued that when ethnically homogeneous groups come into contact with others through migration or expansion 'the obvious contrast usually evokes on both sides, the idea of blood disaffinity, regardless of the objective state of affairs'.[35] When differences of hairdo or beards are added to this, 'there is an ethnically repulsive effect, because they are thought of as symbols of ethnic membership'.[36] As further evidence, he argued that in the colonies, the 'attachment to the colonists' homeland'[37] remains no matter how much social mixing occurs with the natives.

The latter example is particularly illuminating. Writing from an explicitly imperialist outlook in early-twentieth-century Germany, Weber was 'naturalising' the outlook of his contemporaries. He assumed there was a natural propensity for ethnic repulsion precisely because the bourgeois outlook at the time needed to justify its conquest. The mere idea that future young white German teenagers might actually be attracted to the pulsating rhythms of black music was literally off his radar screen. Moreover, if conflicts over 'ethnic honour' were natural, then the problem of racism was played down. If all groups wanted their status honour, then why focus on how dominant identities were used to marginalise and ghettoise oppressed groups? If the Jews were so focussed on ethnic honour that they had evolved into a caste, then why focus on the role of anti-Semitism? Thus, Weber explained the segregation of Jews as follows:

> Towards the outside world, Jewry increasingly assumed the type of a ritualistically segregated guest people (pariah people). And indeed Jewry did this voluntarily and not under pressure of external rejection. The general diffusion of 'antisemitism' in Antiquity is a fact. Likewise, this only slowly increasing rejection of the Jews precisely kept step with the increasingly rigid rejection of community with non-Jews by the Jews themselves.[38]

The legacy of Weber's argument about an eternal conflict over 'ethnic honour' is the notion that racism transcends the structures of capitalism and imperialism. For the convinced Weberian any discussion on the link between capitalism and racism is in danger of being 'reductionist'. One of Weber's central assertions was that 'any cultural trait, no matter how superficial, can serve as a starting point for the familiar tendency to monopolistic closure'.[39] In other words, as the struggle between social groups is eternal, it is relatively accidental which visible trait is used for discriminatory practices. However, this is quite a sweeping assertion. There are few recorded moments in history when status groups based on brown-eyed peoples or baggy trousered groups united to discriminate against blue-eyed straight-laced types. There is no known recorded instance in modern society of status conflicts between people with and without glasses. These absurd examples only beg the question: why do other equally insignificant and superficial human features such as skin colour become *significant*, cultural traits. If one leaves aside the assumption of a natural, ahistoric basis for racism, one is surely forced to conclude that the history of imperialism helped to construct racial features as a marker of inferiority or superiority. Weber could not draw this conclusion, however, because of his own embrace of imperialism.

POLITICAL PARTIES AND STRATIFICATION

The final element of Weber's threefold division of power can be dealt with much more briefly because the third category of party is, as Parkin points out, 'very much the odd man out'.[40] Parties are geared to the acquisition of social power. Unlike the categories of class and status, they are formed through an organised association that directs itself to acquiring power. In modern societies, their focus is on attaining state power. However, in his discussion in *Economy and Society*, Weber ranges from parties in ancient and medieval times to modern mass political parties. His essential point is that since 'a party always struggles for political control its organisation too is frequently strict and "authoritarian"'.[41]

In a later article on 'Parliament and Government in Germany', Weber is much more specific in his analysis. In the modern period, parties are based on two different principles. One is where they are open machines for gaining patronage in office. This is the case in the US after the end of the great conflicts about the constitution. Alternatively, they can be parties with a world outlook where they seek the victory of substantive political ideas. The SPD in Germany belonged to the latter type before it became bureaucratised.[42] However, the distinction between the principles underlying both parties is by no means absolute because the latter type of party also wants patronage in office. Weber plays down the importance of political ideology and stresses the organisational needs of party staff. No matter what their ideology, party functionaries need material rewards to sustain themselves. This leads to bureaucracy and authoritarian patterns of command in the SPD and in parties such as the Democratic Party in the US.

Overall, however, Weber's main categories of social division are class and status. His fundamental argument is that 'classes are not communities'[43] and so the basis for collective class action is fairly minimal. Classes are riven by divisions created by the market and, contrary to Marx's notion of two polar classes at either end of the mode of production, there are many different classes. Conflicts occur but they are not built around fundamental contradictions or exploitation. Criss-crossed onto this fragmented class struggle is a conflict between status groups. Although Weber slips between pre-capitalist and modern societies, one is left with the distinct impression that status groups form the real communities – particularly if they are forged through 'ethnic honour' or 'educational credentials'. Status groups cut against the logic of the market by using closure strategies. Sections of workers often try to do this and so operate as a status group rather than a class.[44] The dissolution of the wider working class into a myriad of subgroups that mirror the market and social rank means that there is little prospect of changing the world. Marx could issue the ringing call 'workers of the world unite' in the hope of winning socialism. But an equivalent call from Weber, let's say, 'dentists of the world unite' could only elicit the question – so what?

THE LEGACY

In the late 1950s and early 1960s, Weberian sociology arose to challenge the dominant American school of functionalism that had played down class conflict. Two prominent representatives of the latter school, Kingsley Davis and Wilbert Moore, had argued that inequality was functional because it was a device by which 'societies insure that the most important positions are conscientiously filled by the most qualified persons'.[45] Weberian sociology became popular in Britain from the 1950s because it tied in with a social democratic attitude that criticised inequality and accepted the reality of class conflict within certain limits. However, the leading exponents of Weberian sociology also wanted to offer a more sophisticated challenge to Marxism. Thus Reinhard Bendix, the author of a key intellectual biography of Weber, claimed that Marx had been proved wrong because the growth of a middle class had brought an end to laissez-faire capitalism and established social rights.[46] This emphasis on a contented middle class composed mainly of white-collar employees became an important part of the repackaged Weberian sociology.

The legacy is particularly evident amongst a number of influential British writers on stratification. In 1958, David Lockwood produced his celebrated book *The Blackcoated Worker* which claimed to offer an account of 'a socio-economic group that had long been a discomfort to Marxist theory: the growing mass of lower non-manual or white-collar employees'.[47] Lockwood also worked with Goldthorpe on a classic study of British car workers where they argued that even a section of the highly paid manual workers were becoming 'embourgeoisied' or, more simply, middle class.[48] The era of the high-paid British car workers did not last long and writers in the Weberian tradition, such as Frank Parkin, for example, argued that the crucial break in the class hierarchy was between manual and non-manual occupational groups. The dominant class in modern society consisted of an elite who formed an alliance with non-manual employees. Outside of this was a lower class of manual workers.[49]

The most sophisticated variant of these stratification studies has come from Goldthorpe who developed Lockwood's earlier ideas to produce a multi-class model which drew distinctions between a higher and lower 'service class' made up mainly of professionals; a white-collar labour force, made up of routine white-collar employees; a skilled and unskilled manual working class.[50] Under Goldthorpe's schema, class analysis was a matter of grouping particular occupations according to both their 'market situation' and 'work situation'. Even while defending this approach against those who claimed that 'class was dead', Goldthorpe and his co-thinker Marshall have been at pains to attack the Marxist notion that social class was linked to a theory of exploitation.[51]

WHITE-COLLAR EMPLOYEES

In the early part of the twentieth century, it was understandable that Weber could focus on the differences between clerks and manual workers and assume that the former belonged to a class of their own. Clerical employees at the time often hired domestic servants. They worked in small offices with their employer and lived in the better parts of town. The clerk was regarded as an 'honoured employee', as Corey put it, 'his position was a confidential one, the employer discussed affairs with him and relied on his judgement; he might and often did, become a partner and marry the employer's daughter'.[52] These differences meant that even in the late 1920s in Germany a high proportion of office employees looked to Nazi-led unions in contrast to manual workers who stayed loyal to socialist unions.[53]

The legacy of Weber's sociology, however, has been to focus on status perceptions and differences in work situations and to ignore the wider changes that have been forced on employees by the nature of capitalism. The theory has not been sensitive to how the search for ever higher rates of profit has transformed the lives of white-collar, 'middle-class' employees. Yet, the changes have been quite dramatic. In the period after Weber's death, managerial functions were separated off from clerical work and the office became subject to the same process of rationalisation as the factory. Instead of seeing the clerk as an ally, employers sought to raise his or her productivity levels and cut back on costs. Braverman drew out the implications of this process of proletarianisation:

> The labour market for the two chief varieties of worker, factory and office, begins to lose some of its distinctions of social stratification, education, family and the like. Not only do clerical workers come increasingly from families of factory background, and vice versa, but also increasingly, they are merged within the same living

family. The chief remaining distinction seems to be a division along the lines of sex.[54]

Lockwood's own criteria on the primary differences between white-collar and blue-collar employees are useful benchmarks to show what has changed. His benchmarks were wages, job security and promotion.

First, wages. Traditionally office employees were supposed to earn more than their manual counterparts. However, the wages of skilled manual workers overtook those of routine white-collar employees in the mid 1930s and by the 1960s, a factory worker was on average earning more than a routine office worker. By 1971, Braverman has shown for the US, the median wage of white-collar employees was lower than the wage for every type of so-called blue-collar work.

Second, office employees were supposed to have greater job security. Yet, the security of white-collar employees has clearly diminished. 'Temps', short-term contracts and 'the contingent worker' have all invaded the white-collar sector. Thirteen per cent of the EU workforce is presently on fixed-term contracts and many are white-collar employees.[55] In the US, Manpower Temporary Services rivals Wal-Mart as the largest private employer. Klein estimates that the real number of temporary employees in the US and the EU is 36 million.[56]

Third, white-collar employees were supposed to have greater prospects for promotion. Today, however, promotion varies for different categories of white-collar employee. A small number of these employees occupy what the American Marxist Eric Olin Wright called 'contradictory class locations'.[57] They operate mainly as semi-autonomous employees who are not subject to the discipline imposed by the dictates of capital and are normally involved in organising the exploitation of other white-collar employees. Many of these can make rapid jumps up the managerial hierarchy. However, for the mass of routine white-collar employees, there is often a ceiling put on promotions. Promotion tends to be into higher grades rather than into managerial positions. With the feminisation of white-collar employment, this tendency has become even more pronounced. Very few female white-collar employees can now hope to be promoted to managerial grades that have substantial decision-making powers.

In brief, there is considerable evidence to suggest that the majority of the much-vaunted 'middle class' is being proletarianised. Not in the sense of wearing overalls and looking like the stereotypical proletarian of previous years but rather in facing the same pressures to raise productivity, to show 'flexibility' and to reduce unit costs as their manual counterparts. 'Stress' has become almost a universal feature of work and the 'social rights' that Bendix referred to in the 1950s are being torn away. The number of office employees who can expect a proper pension scheme, for example, is diminishing. All of this explains why the largest number of recruits to trade unions is coming from white-collar employees. Strikes by teachers or nurses are now probably more common than strikes by miners and dockworkers.

CONCLUSION

Weber's sociology had the merit of recognising the existence of class conflict. Weber would have been unlikely to fall for some of the more recent claims about the 'death of social class'. However, he tended to see social class as simply a category of measurement. It was formed in the market place rather than in the sphere of production. This meant that classes could not unite around common interests but would be forever fragmented. This approach, however, only made sense if the relationship between employers and workers was not based on exploitation. As a class conscious bourgeois, Weber had no option but to deny this feature of social life. A less partial vision, however, would suggest that the concentration of wealth in a few hands could only arise if there was exploitation.

Weber's emphasis on status groups having different lifestyles and abstaining from social intercourse with each other has been toned down by his followers. Subsequent Weberian sociologists have effectively discarded his notion that status groups arose in pre-capitalist societies and were carried over to modern society. However, they have retained Weber's passionate belief that exploitation is not the central fulcrum on which the class structure rests. Instead, they have seen a multitude of different occupations in conflict with a fragmented ruling elite – and with each other. They have not seen a common interest between those who sell their labour and those who have their labour controlled by others. Ultimately this has led to a focus on occupational typologies while ignoring the very real process of proletarianisation that has been under way among white-collar employees.

Moreover, when nurses or teachers have gone on strike, Weberian sociologists have often only seen a 'contented middle class' defending their status privileges. There has been little understanding that a defence of the sectional interests by white-collar trade unionists might be linked to wider questions over the distribution of power and resources in a capitalist society. In brief, they have only seen industrial relations 'problems' rather than revolts against the logic of capital.

7
Domination and Bureaucracy

Weber provided subsequent sociologists with a wealth of concepts that became their toolbox for generating new theories. He liked to draw up a set of typologies to categorise different forms of social action. One of the most famous of these is the different categories of domination which have been exercised in society. Weber argued that there were three main forms of domination – traditional, charismatic and rational legal.

The writings on these forms of domination are to be found in *Economy and Society*. Weber used his vast historic knowledge to provide examples from a wide range of societies to illustrate the dynamics of each of these forms of domination. He was less interested in how people resisted or overthrew the power structures and focussed more on how they were maintained. He assumed that domination was natural and drew from the philosophy of Friedrich Nietzsche a belief that the 'will to power' pervaded all human relationships.

We shall start this chapter by looking at the influence of Nietzsche on Weber's writings and then outline the main differences between the three categories of domination. We shall seek to draw out the assumptions which underlie his analysis before critically discussing, in more detail, traditional, charismatic and rational legal forms of domination. Our aim in each case is to provide a critical overview.

NIETZSCHE AND THE WILL TO POWER

Friedrich Nietzsche died in 1900 and the following year the first edition of his book *The Will to Power* appeared from a collection of his notes. Its central idea can be summed up in the aphorism 'The world is the will to power and nothing else besides! And you yourselves are also this will to power and nothing else besides.'[1] Nietzsche railed against the levelling tendencies of modernity that had produced a mass society. He despised the 'slave morality' and 'herd instinct' of Christianity and celebrated the values of aristocratic societies. These societies had produced 'pathos of distance'[2] from the mass and so allowed key individuals ' – the highest exemplars'[3] of humanity – to rise above the herd. Human creativity was all about imposing one's will on others.

Weber had little time for Nietzsche's celebration of aristocratic societies, as he believed the spread of capitalism was inevitable. However, alongside Marx he counted Nietzsche as one of the key philosophers of his age. From Nietzsche, he took the view that the world was comprised of shifting power struggles. There could be no objective truths but rather multiple perspectives on the world. These perspectives were in turn shaped according to values, which had no other foundation than, as Mommsen put it, 'the spontaneous decision of the personality'.[4] This viewpoint, as we have seen, played a major role in Weber's writings on methodology. More generally, the belief that power and domination were at the heart of all human relations was an intrinsic part of Weber's vision.

As the struggle for domination was eternal, Weber believed that there would always be a ruling class and a ruled. 'Any thought ... of removing the rule of men over men through the most sophisticated forms of "democracy" is utopian',[5] he told his friend Robert Michels. His focus on power and domination put him at odds with other theories that held society together. He did not believe, like Jeremy Bentham and the utilitarians, that society was held together simply by self-interested contracts. Nor did he fully accept the opposing view of the French sociologist Durkheim that it was glued together by a moral consensus on values. For Weber, force and violence played a much more central role. 'Violent social action', he claimed, 'is obviously something absolutely primordial.'[6] All political structures used force and domination pervaded every aspect of human life from erotic relationships to scholarly discussions.

This rather gloomy outlook meant that Weber had little time for pretence. He did not see the state simply as an expression of the common good or as an institution which rose above the conflicting interests of civil society. His definition of the state was that it was a political institution which 'upholds the claim to the *monopoly* of the *legitimate* use of physical force in the enforcement of its order'.[7] In other words, it was built on legal violence. In modern parlance all other groupings in society had to be disarmed, persuaded to de-commission or labelled as 'terrorists'. State violence or the threat of violence was the key element in bringing this about. His definition of the state is strikingly similar to Lenin's much quoted observation that all states are based on 'special bodies of armed men'.[8]

Weber's definition of power has also become a classic in sociology. Power, he argued '*is the probability that one actor within a social relationship will be in a position to carry out his own will despite resistance, regardless of the basis on which this probability exists*'. [9] This definition focuses on the individual actor and their will – on this inner mental capacity to enforce their desires. There is no reference to resources – either economic or military – which the particular actor might need. As Brennan has pointed out, it is a subjective definition of power and one more likely to flatter existing power holders. Those at the bottom are more likely to experience power as an objective constraint – they obey the capitalist or the slave owner because these hold the machinery or the whip, not necessarily because they respect his or her will.[10]

TYPES OF DOMINATION

Weber acknowledged that his definition of power was amorphous because it could refer to all conceivable circumstances. His principal writings focus instead on domination, which he saw as a special case of power. Domination is defined as '*the probability that a command with a given specific content will be obeyed by a given group of persons*'.[11] This is again a broad opening statement but Weber soon moves to distinguish between two main forms of domination. There is, first, domination by monopoly control of economic resources. So a central bank or a multinational like Standard Oil can enforce their command over debtors or on garage retailers because they hold the economic monopoly. Second, there is domination by the authority of office. Thus state officials or army generals use non-economic sources of power to dominate. The distinction between them can be fluid and one form of domination can develop into another. Weber, however, concentrates on the latter, narrower form of domination. This authoritarian power of command, as he calls it, occurs in situations where

the manifested will (command) of the *ruler* or rulers is meant to influence the conduct of one or more others (*the ruled*) and actually does influence it in such a way that their conduct to a socially relevant degree occurs as if the ruled had made the content of the command the maxim of their conduct for its own sake.[12]

What is noticeable here is that orders from on high appear to be met by a positive commitment to obey. Power, it appears, elicits a desire for obedience. This obedience is willingly given and, in a dominant relationship, this is not simply a matter of external appearance: 'The merely external fact of the order being obeyed is not sufficient to signify domination in our sense; we cannot overlook the meaning of the fact that the commandment is accepted as a "valid" norm.'[13] This definition of domination provides the cornerstone for his celebrated sociology of legitimate authority. Weber argues that there are three ideal types of legitimate authority in history. These ideal types are not necessarily found in pure forms in the real world but they are useful yardsticks to measure reality against.

- *Traditional authority* rests on beliefs in the sanctity of immemorial tradition and custom. This type of domination is exercised by tribal chiefs, patriarchs, feudal aristocrats.
- *Charismatic authority* rests on devotion to the exceptional sanctity, heroism or personal magnetism of a heroic figure. Revolutionary leaders, prophets and warriors, for instance, exercise this type of authority.
- *Legal Rational authority* is based on properly enacted rules and is given to office holders rather than specific persons. Bureaucrats and government ministers have authority of this type.

Weber's three ideal types distinguish between the grounds on which obedience is based. Parkin provides an excellent, succinct summary (see table).[14]

Type of domination	Grounds for claiming obedience
Traditional	Obey me because that is what our people have always done.
Charismatic	Obey me because I can transform your life.
Legal Rational	Obey me because I am your lawfully appointed superior.

WEBER'S ASSUMPTIONS

There are two central assumptions in Weber's sociology of domination that need to be made explicit. The first is that forms of domination that arise from market mechanisms can be dismissed. As we have seen, he only made a brief reference to monopoly power in the market and then concentrated solely on the authority that arose from political offices. However, in the market place itself, of course, domination is not confined to monopolies. Big companies that compete against each other can sack workers, cut their wages or ban unions. Competition between companies does not diffuse power or protect the workers – if anything it can strengthen management's desire to enforce obedience. Weber did not wish, however, to examine the actual workings of the market. His separation of political and economic power – which is a feature of most conventional thinking – led him effectively to discard a major reason why people obey their 'leaders'. The 'dull compulsion of economic necessity' means that obedience is given grudgingly and without inner conviction because people need money and a roof over their head.[15] It is not a question of legitimacy but the necessity for survival.

Weber also assumes that domination eventually evokes its own legitimacy. Political elites certainly need force but they cannot rule by that alone and they need 'self-justification through appealing to the principles of its legitimation'.[16] If they have survived for any appreciable length of time, this implies they have won this legitimacy. A ruler eventually gets into the happy situation where, as Luhmann summarising Weber puts it, he 'has the opportunity to make his ends the ends of others'.[17] However, rulers can rule for long periods without being legitimately accepted by the majority of their population. The apartheid regime in South Africa, the Chilean dictatorship of Pinochet, the Burmese military, and the present Saudi royal family have all had a considerable period in office through sheer bloody force.

Even where regimes acquire some legitimacy, it may still be interesting to ask: to what degree? There can be various combinations of force and fraud, of the carrot and stick, and people can accept rulers for all sorts of reasons – they may be politically kept in ignorance; the regime may temporarily bring material rewards; the opposition may be demoralised or co-opted. Weber, however, ignores the varied reasons for why people obey and instead implies that they give their rulers a blank cheque. The 'masses' appear to accept the general legitimacy of the status quo and then inscribe their rulers' commands in their own consciousness and will. Weber's failure to examine the contradictory motives for why people obey means that he could not allow much scope for fundamental change or revolution. What is entirely lacking from his work is any analysis of how masses of people overthrow rulers they previously thought of as legitimate.

Weber's sociology of domination is therefore a top-down sociology that reflects the vantage point of an elite bourgeois man in imperial Germany. There is a degree of realism about the level of force in political life but it is a realism that has its limits. The masses are objects not the subject of history and appear only as instruments of their rulers' wills. As Brennan put it, Weber's 'ruler-centric approach accords little or no significance to the role of underdogs like workers or citizens'.[18] The real actors for Weber are elites, charismatic heroes and the leaders of great states who enforce their domination.

TRADITIONAL AUTHORITY

Traditional authority is based on respect for the sanctity of age-old rules and customs and involves loyalty to a personal master. Obedience is not given simply to an office but to a lord or a prince. All traditional authority involves a double sphere. On the one hand, the master has personal discretion in a wide area. They are entitled to make arbitrary and unilateral demands when it suits and expect obedience precisely because they are seen as a personal master. On the other hand, obedience is delivered within the bounds of a tradition that places limits on the arbitrary power of the ruler. Custom dictates that the church provide alms for the poor, for example, and so bishops cannot simply collect tithes and not give something back. There are no formal principles in all of this but rulers have to walk a line between arbitrary power and a tradition that limits the content of their commands.

Throughout his sociology of domination, Weber's primary focus was on the relationship between the ruler and their administrative staff. The administrative staff make up the apparatus that carries out and enforces the ruler's wishes among the masses. Any relationship of domination has three elements – the ruler, the administrative staff, and the ruled. Weber, though, focused only on the first two. He paid particular attention to the material interests of the staff, the organisational principles through which they operate and their wider relationship to the ruler. He simply assumed that they conquer 'the masses'.

Under traditional authority, the staff have no well-defined areas of jurisdiction but there is a series of overlapping tasks and powers that are assigned at the masters' discretion. There is no evidence of rationally organised functions in the titles of officials who work for traditional rulers. Instead of a clear hierarchy or system of promotion, the structure revolves around the whims of the master. Ideally, the staff are normally recruited from direct family dependents of the ruler, conscripted subjects, mercenaries or from slaves. The role of slaves is particularly interesting here. The famous story of Joseph in the Bible indicates how a 'special' slave can be picked out by the master and elevated to a major role in the court. Weber pointed out that it was not uncommon for grand viziers – high officials in the Ottoman Empire – to have been former slaves.[19] They are 'favourites' of the ruler and so, not only their status, but their whole life was dependent on pleasing the ruler's will. Traditional staff are recruited from such groupings precisely because relations of personal dependence are so necessary. They do not receive a regular, fixed salary as of right. Instead they are supported directly from the ruler's own household or by grants once they move away from that household.

Strains and conflicts can develop in these societies but abrupt overall system change is ruled out. Where a ruler overstretches the mark, they encounter resistance in the name of the same tradition that was supposed to grant them legitimacy. The result is a 'traditionalist revolution'[20] whereby another member of the household or the elite displaces the lord or the prince. Instead of bad King John, there is a call for good King Richard.

Weber was at pains to suggest there is no pattern of historical evolution. Nevertheless, he produced a set of subcategories that imply an evolutionary process within the overall sphere of traditional authority. The original cell from which traditional authority is formed is the *patriarchal household*. Here the members of the household stand in an entirely personal relationship to a father figure. The basis for solidarity is the permanent sharing of lodging and food. There is no administrative staff but the system works purely on 'piety toward tradition and toward the master'.[21]

Strong patriarchal households eventually come to control a wide territory and this leads to *patrimonial domination*. Key offices are separated off from the original household and a military force and an administrative staff are formed. The officers and the key members of this staff are no longer fed at the household table but receive a benefice that is given to the individual and is not hereditary. These benefices are granted in return for services rendered. Those who receive them try to 'stereotype' them into rights but for a period they remain privileges that can be withdrawn at the discretion of the master. Crucially, the military force remains the ruler's personal instrument and its equipment and maintenance are supplied from the ruler's household. The ruler is still caught in the double sphere of tradition and arbitrariness but where it leans to an extreme version of the latter, Weber calls it *sultanism*.

The most developed version of traditional authority occurs under *feudalism*. This arises when administrative staff extract concessions from the patrimonial rulers and start to de-centre authority. They turn the benefices into fiefs that are a personal and inalienable possession. Feudalism is based on a contract between free people – the knight enters into service of his lord but, ironically, this service is linked with high social honour and prestige.

> The feudal system produces men who can equip themselves and handle weapons professionally, who in war identify their own honour with that of the lord, who see in the expansion of his power the chance to secure fiefs for their heirs and, above all, find the only *basis for the legitimacy of their own fief* in the preservation of *his* personal authority.[22]

Feudalism creates the basis for a separation of traditional authority. As Bendix puts it, 'feudalism is domination by the few who are skilled in war; patrimonialism is domination by one who requires officials for the exercise of his authority'.[23]

Late feudalism as it developed in Europe created openings for modern capitalism but Weber's central argument is that traditional domination tends to block the market. Economic relationships are tradition bound and arbitrary taxes are imposed which militate against a culture of calculation. The rulers and their administrative staff monopolise the main source of wealth in trade. Tax farming and the sale of offices divert energy away from accumulating wealth from production. The disorganisation that results from the absence of clear rules leads to bribery and corruption. Finally, economic activity is geared to immediate use, to the welfare of elites or to absolute values.

A RULER-CENTRIC VISION

Weber provides many important insights into the dynamics of traditional authority and the features of feudal society. But his account is marred in two key areas. First, the original patriarchal household is seen as the cornerstone of the whole system. This household is a natural unit of authority and becomes the primordial centre from which other forms of authority radiate out. Second, the main population in traditional societies – the peasantry – play no role in the shaping of authority structures. In Weber's ruler-centric vision, they are simply a pliable mass that is shaped by traditional leaders. Let us look at each of these problems in turn.

Bryan Turner has acknowledged that Weber has 'a theoretical blind spot concerning the social functions of the family in relation to the economy and the social role of women'.[24] The blind spot extends, however, well back in time because Weber regarded the patriarchal family as primordial and natural. His dismissed socialist theories about the evolution of the so-called normal family.[25] There was never any form of mother right. There was never a time when spontaneous sexual relations with more than one person were normal. Rather, prostitution existed from time immemorial.[26] Marriage did not arise from the desire of male property owners to pass on their possessions to legitimate offspring.[27] Rather, the family and domination by the father were effectively natural institutions. Weber provided no adequate explanation for why rule by tribal elders was replaced by rule by one dominant patriarchal household who broke away from the tribe. He simply assumes it was a natural progression. Within that household, obedience to the father arose because 'the woman is dependent because of the normal superiority of the physical and intellectual energies of the male, and the child because of his objective helplessness'.[28]

Many of these sexist assumptions had been questioned by the appearance of Engels' book *The Origin of the Family, Private Property and State* in 1884. Weber's positive fury about its arguments was evident when he berated historians for not 'telling us about the war-like deeds of our ancestors (but instead) they dilate at length about "mother-right", that monstrous notion'.[29] He saw the model for all traditional authority as the father–son relationship and so there was little need to look at anything as complex as different modes of production. The different forms of traditional authority were analysed primarily in terms of their increasing distance from the original patriarchal household. It is almost as if the patriarchal household was the original nucleus of an authority cell that later split, differentiated and spread. Thus, the formation of social classes and the conflict between them are replaced by an analysis of how patrimonialism and feudalism differed from the original household. One important consequence of this method of analysis is that an undue emphasis is put on personal loyalty, which is seen as the basis of all traditional authority. The possibility that there are other reasons for obeying traditional rulers apart from loyalty is effectively discarded.

Another major problem stems from Weber's elitism. The peasantry quite simply disappear from the analysis and the focus is kept firmly on the apex of the feudal pyramid. There is no discussion on why the mass of the population obeys the knights and kings. It is assumed that they accept feudal society as legitimate because their landlords do. However, why assume that the downtrodden peasantry had the same motive for obedience as those who battened on their labour? Even if the courtiers obeyed a king from loyalty to his person, why assume that the peasants who carried terrible burdens did so for the same reason? Moreover, because Weber saw the development of feudalism arising from a separation from the original patriarchal household, there is no room in his account for how the class struggles of the peasantry might affect that society. Robert Brenner wrote a celebrated article on how the class struggles of the peasantry played an important role in the divergent patterns of agrarian capitalism in France and England.[30] Others have put a greater emphasis on the role of technology or population growth in explaining the spread of agrarian capitalism.[31] However, whatever the merits of each side in the debate, it could not occur within Weber's framework. The fate of the peasantry was unconditional obedience to their lords and masters.

CHARISMATIC AUTHORITY

The term charisma in Christian theology means 'the gift of grace'.[32] Weber took over the term and added 'charismatic leader' to modern political vocabularies. No account of modern elections is now complete without some reference to the semi-magical, mysterious quality of charisma. However, the coinage has been debased. Charisma can apparently be won by a hairdo, an engaging smile, a vague sex appeal or whatever the PR agents dream up.

For Weber, charisma had an altogether more important meaning. Charismatic leaders were seen by their followers to have some extraordinary power or quality that commanded obedience. In more primitive societies, these powers were magical and the leaders were either superhuman or supernatural. In modern society, charismatic leaders arise in periods of great turbulence or crisis and answer a need. The leader is literally blessed with a sign of grace or, in secular terms, is a genius. As Bendix puts it, 'it is associated with a collective excitement through which masses of people respond to some extraordinary experience and by virtue of which they surrender themselves to a heroic leader'.[33] The use of the word 'surrender' is key – charismatic leaders are spellbinders who command fanatical support.

Weber's methodology of ideal types allows him to cull different examples from history to fill the rubric. So, the founder of the Mormons, Joseph Smith, is grouped with the Bavarian Marxist revolutionary Kurt Eisner as a charismatic leader.[34] Both are joined by magicians, bounty hunters, heroic warriors and Chinese monarchs as exemplars of charismatic leaders. All, apparently, share a number of common characteristics for how they legitimate their authority.

Their personal charisma overrides economic considerations. People follow these leaders because they feel a 'call' or believe they are part of a 'mission'.[35] They obey because of a force that is akin to spiritual duty. The charismatic leader does not gain his authority from any established authority or tradition but solely by proving his powers in practice. He must bring well-being to his followers and 'if they do not fare well, he obviously is not the god-sent master'.[36] If this success is eluded for a long time, then the charismatic authority disappears. Floods or droughts often forced the abdication of Chinese monarchs because they were no longer seen as the 'Son of Heaven'.[37]

The administrative staff of charismatic leaders are not chosen because of qualifications, social status, or family loyalty. They are recruited simply as followers. There is no set hierarchy, no prospect of promotion or career. There is not even a regular salary because pure charisma is foreign to economic considerations. The staff can be looked after by the seizure of booty or by gifts but any provision for a regular career structure is despised. In order to live up to their mission the leader and his followers 'must be free of the ordinary worldly attachments and duties of occupational and family life'.[38] A form of communism exists between the charismatic leader and his followers so that the authentic revolutionary heroism is preserved by sharing property and sacrifice.

THE ROUTINISATION OF CHARISMA

For Weber there are two major revolutionary forces in history. One is the wider tendency towards bureaucracy, which spreads inextricably throughout modern society. However, the other is the eruption at periodic intervals of charismatic movements, which break the institutions, traditions and forms of rational management. Bureaucracy revolutionises society from the outside because it sets up material conditions which people are forced to adapt to. Charisma, however, brings a revolution from within because it changes people's psychology and beliefs. Only after it changes outlooks does it shape 'material and social conditions according to its revolutionary will'.[39] History for Weber is, as Runciman put it, an eternal struggle between charismatic innovation and bureaucratic rationalisation.[40]

It is important to stress, however, that the former, more genuinely revolutionary force arises solely from exceptional personalities. There can be no real explanation or analysis of why it emerged at a particular time. Charismatic movements are also inherently unstable:

> Every charisma is on the road from a turbulently emotional life that knows no economic rationality to a slow death by suffocation under the weight of material interests: every hour of its existence brings it nearer to this end.[41]

One can clearly sense Weber's yearning for charismatic figures, particularly in his native Germany. However, the dark side to his writings came primarily from the depiction of charismatic movements as romantic souls that are doomed to extinction as soon as they are born.

The 'routinisation of charisma' occurs when people try to transform a unique gift of grace into a permanent possession of everyday life. Two main factors are involved. There is, first, the problem of succession. If the charismatic leader's qualities are exceptional, then what happens when they die? Traditionally the problem of succession has been dealt with through mechanisms such as *revelation*, whereby an oracle or wise men select the new leader; *designation*, whereby the charismatic leader chooses the new leader before his death; or a *search* for a new figure with particular qualities as occurs in the case of a new Dalai Lama. These mechanisms, however, suffer from one major defect – there is a time gap between the discovery of the new charismatic leader and the confirmation that they are indeed charismatic. In other words, there can be a major period of instability before the new leader is found or proves their exceptional qualities.

This brings us to the second problem. The 'ideal and also the material interests'[42] of the administrative staff create a pressure to regularise the situation and deal with the problem of succession.

Sometimes they do this by depersonalising the gift of charisma. Instead of an individual possessing it, charisma is deemed transferable to the blood relations of the leader or to a particular institution. A particular household, for example, is deemed to be magically blessed and they alone are the bearers of charisma. The 'divine right of kings' whereby the Saxe-Coburgs, or the Bourbons were seen to be appointed directly from God may have originated here. Where this has occurred, charismatic powers have slowly evolved into a form of traditional authority. The Christian churches, by contrast, provide an example of charisma being transformed into bureaucratic authority. For what is a priest but someone who lays claim to charisma by virtue of occupying the office?

Weber understood the dynamics of this shift in a most perceptive way:

> The bureaucratisation of the church was possible only if the priest could be absolutely depraved without endangering thereby his charismatic qualification; only then could the institutional charisma of the church be protected against all personnel contingencies.[43]

After all the child abuse scandals that have swept the Catholic Church in the US, Australia and Ireland, this sounds highly prophetic. The Catholic Church has brought the 'routinisation of charisma' to the full scope of its development. It claims for the *office* of the priesthood the gift of charisma – even if the actual holders fall well short of the mark.

Weber begins his analysis from the pure, ideal type of charisma but he uses this as a tool to consider all sorts of possibilities. In doing so, he produces many genuine insights. He notes, for example, how elites often seek to 'sanctify' their position by protecting their claims to charisma quite carefully. So a monarch may be insulated by 'the specialists in tradition and ceremony'[44] from the day-to-day running of their state. The grand vizier or the chief minister will then take responsibility for the acts of government, especially for the failures and unpopular measures. In brief, there will be a fall guy for the wider system of privilege.

WHY DO PEOPLE FOLLOW CHARISMATIC LEADERS?

Nevertheless, despite these insights there are serious problems with Weber's argument. First, there is no discussion on the reasons why people follow charismatic movements. Instead Weber sees them as being swept away, surrendering all powers of rational thought to their leader. Charisma appears as the ultimate expression of a leader entirely shaping a movement or state by the sheer dint of his personality and will. This brings us very close to the Great Man Theory of History. Or as Gerth and Mills put it, 'the monumentalised individual becomes the sovereign of history'.[45] In reality, of course, no leader creates a movement purely from their will. There is nothing about charisma which transcends particular situations and contexts. In the 1930s, the Irish leader Eamonn de Valera had a spellbinding effect on his followers but when young Irish people today listen to his speeches they find them incredibly boring and dull.[46] In Argentina, Perón inspired an extraordinary adulation from his followers in the 1950s and 1960s but when he returned from exile in the 1970s 'the charisma' was gone. Alternatively, to take a particularly nasty example, Hitler spent most of his early years in Vienna as an eccentric anti-Semite whose influence did not extend far beyond his dosshouse but by the late 1920s, he was leading a mass movement.[47]

It is not necessary to deny the role of individuals in history or the particular talents or insights they bring to a movement. The Russian revolutionary Trotsky dismissed the mechanical approach of Plekanov who effectively wrote the individual out of history and instead produced an account of Lenin's role in the Russian Revolution which deemed it quite decisive. However, he also showed there was dialectic involved. Lenin's ideas were crucial to overcoming his own party's conservatism and so reached out to the aspirations of masses of people for change.[48] In Weber there is no dialectic – the leader is the subject and the followers his object. There is no space for a discussion of the social and economic conditions or the complex interplay of political conflicts which raise dull orators or fanatical eccentrics into the role of national heroes. The process is literally mystified.

Second, Weber's elitism in assigning the leader the only active role is also married with a strong formalism. Charismatic leaders are found in groups as diverse as 'robber capitalists'[49] who are engaged in piracy, slave hunting and colonisation *and* Marxist revolutionaries. But what possible connection is there between a slave hunter and an opponent of capitalism? Both may exhibit, we can concede, certain psychological characteristics of bravery or daring but is this not entirely marginal to a discussion about the content of what they are fighting for? Weber, however, shows little interest in the actual programme of charismatic leaders because he is not developing a historically specific analysis of actual change. His ideal types are not categories of reality so it is pointless asking about the actual political context of the different 'charismatic' movements of the left or right. Instead, they are lumped together and contrasted with the normal forms of traditional or bureaucratic rule.

Finally, if charisma is the only genuinely revolutionary force in history, then fundamental change only occurs through the accidental qualities of individual geniuses. However, history is shot through with revolutions or attempted revolutions. Weber can produce no understanding of why these revolts occur because he fails to see the source of change in deep contradictions in existing society. For him societies are always controlled by the leaders who more or less effortlessly wrap themselves in the mantle of legitimacy. He has therefore to resort to the wild card of charisma – an outside spirit that visits society and reshapes it in its image. This is not a theory of change – it is a *deus ex machina* that is bolted on to cover a missing gap in his sociology.

LEGAL RATIONAL AUTHORITY

The normal means of domination in modern societies is legal rational authority and bureaucracy. Weber's main concern was with the culture of rationality that led to bureaucracy and the consequences this held for the world. We shall deal with these issues in the next chapter but here we will look at third ideal type in terms of its more static, more formal characteristics.

Legal authority rests on a number of interdependent factors. There has to be a legal code which covers everyone in a particular territory. It has to be based on consistent, abstract rules – so that people know in advance the penalties for infringements. Crucially, the rulers themselves must also be subject to these rules. The arbitrary discretion that was granted to charismatic or traditional rulers is removed. People obey authority in their capacity as citizens or members of particular associations. There is often a 'personal sphere' where the rules do not apply. So, aside from Enver Hoxha's Albania, there normally are not rules about the length of hair or men's beards. Crucially, obedience is given to an office holder and not the person.

The administrative staff in this form of authority are more highly developed and in their purest form become a bureaucracy. The staff operate continuously according to rules that govern the conduct of their official business. They each have a definite specified area of competence that is laid down by their job descriptions. These areas of jurisdiction give them powers to fulfil their duties only in these specific areas. The jurisdictions do not overlap but are based on a rational division of labour. The whole system forms a hierarchical pyramid so that the higher offices supervise the lower offices. Rules are laid down for each office and the official is given specialised training so that he or she can meet them.

A crucial development is the separation of the office from the incumbent. In an imaginative adaptation of Marx, Weber compared the official to the worker. 'The bureaucratic structure', he claimed, 'goes hand in hand with the concentration of the material means of management in the hands of the master.'[50] Officials do not own their office and cannot pass it onto their offspring. The property which the officials work with – the pens, staplers, files – are not their own. They have no right to use their office for their own purpose. In the past, officials in patrimonial regimes might have been tax farmers who could take a cut from what they gathered but not so in a modern bureaucracy – office holding is no longer considered a source of income. There is a radical separation of 'the organisation's property (respectively, capital) and the personal property (household) of the official'.[51] When big research laboratories are established, for example, the material means of operation are controlled by the heads: 'The mass of researchers and instructors are separated from their "means of production", in the same way that workers are separated from theirs by capitalist enterprises.'[52]

Unlike the worker, however, the official is compensated for this separation. They receive a pension and a monthly fixed salary as distinct from a wage, which in Weber's time was often measured by work done. There is a career structure through which they can aspire through promotion. Normally they have a job for life in public bureaucracies but Weber predicted this would increasingly become the case in private sector bureaucracies. Crucially, the modern official 'always strives for and usually attains a distinctly elevated *social esteem* vis a vis the governed'.[53] The educational qualifications they need to attain office are used to raise their status. All sorts of catch-all rules are invented to protect their social status. The Prussian state, for example, had a special prohibition against 'insults to office'. The rules of modern trade unions usually include a clause against 'bringing the union into disrepute', which can be used against those who criticise union officials.

All these features help to give the individual bureaucrat a material incentive to function as 'a small cog in a ceaselessly moving mechanism, which prescribes for him an essentially fixed route of march'.[54] He or she is dependent on their superiors and so becomes a malleable instrument in their hands. The precondition for all this is that the official has to be appointed rather than elected. Elections cut across a bureaucratic apparatus because candidates can be pressurised by their electorate rather than their superiors. They have to articulate the grievances of their constituents and, as Gramsci put it, give expression to 'the fickle eddy of moods and currents of the great tumultuous masses'.[55] By contrast, an appointee can be more easily trained into the existing bureaucratic culture and will identify their own aspirations with those of their superiors.

The axial principal of bureaucracy is 'domination through knowledge'.[56] It is popular today to disparage bureaucracy as 'red tape' and to caricature the way that officials fill in forms and memos in triplicate. This misses the point, however. The modern office is indeed based on the management of files but this is to ensure that those at the top have 'a special knowledge of facts and have available to them a store of documentary material peculiar to themselves'.[57] They know more about the ruled than any previous authorities in history. They also know exactly how their commands will be implemented since the room for personal discretion among their staff is virtually nil. Bureaucracy has invented the concept of the 'official secret' which means that information can be gathered and exact commands transmitted in a secretive way. Individual officials can be penalised for divulging these official secrets to the public. Normally, however, it does not come to this because 'bureaucratic administration always tends to exclude the public, to hide its knowledge and action from criticism as well as it can'.[58]

A bureaucracy, therefore, is a permanent machine and different rulers can use it. After the country is defeated, for example, the bureaucratic apparatus survives and is usually taken over by the new rulers. This suggests that 'at the top of a bureaucratic organisation, there is necessarily an element which is at least not purely bureaucratic'.[59] At the apex of the system, there is a will, a personality whose wishes have to be enforced. Weber's central argument, though, is that bureaucracy is the most efficient way of conducting this rule. He writes,

The decisive reason for the advance of bureaucratic organisation has always been its purely technical superiority over any other form of organisation. The fully developed bureaucratic apparatus compares with other organisations exactly as does the machine with non-mechanical modes of production. Precision, speed, unambiguity, knowledge of the files, continuity, discretion, unity, strict subordination, reduction of friction and of material and personal costs – these are raised to the optimum point in strictly bureaucratic administration.[60]

Weber had little time for the modern right-wing catch cry that the bureaucracy is linked to the state and public ownership. This line of argument is often used to justify privatisation as this is supposed to be more dynamic and less hidebound by 'red tape'. Weber argued instead that 'the very large modern capitalist enterprises are themselves unequalled models of strict bureaucratic organisation'.[61] The reason being simply that bureaucracy is the most efficient form of rule.

THE WEAKNESS OF BUREAUCRATIC RULE

However, Weber got it wrong on a number of points. First, he generalised from the high status of the Prussian official to argue that officials would normally attain a higher status than the rest of the population. Implicitly, Weber equated, 'officials' with what we might today call white-collar employees. Yet, as we have seen, the high status of these officials was not maintained in the late twentieth century. In many countries, civil servants receive low wages and increasingly find themselves in contract employment. They join unions and, even more bizarrely from Weber's viewpoint, they strike. In other words, the cogs occasionally rebel and their superiors are sometimes forced to make concessions.

Second, Weber took the formal character of bureaucracies at face value. However, the notion that all levels are bound by rules is an ideological device used by elites. Gouldner has pointed out that in factories rules are 'fully developed for the lower strata' but 'conversely relaxation of certain rules increases as one goes up the hierarchy'.[62] Think of the difference, for example, in timekeeping between the manager's 'business lunch' and the worker's 'tea-break'. All business operates by a double code. There is the formal rule-bound culture and an informal culture based on connections and personal networking. Formally, arms contractors do not bribe government officials; informally, all manner of 'sweeteners' are offered to win contracts. The higher up the hierarchy you go, the more it operates by implicit understandings between the 'right people'. In Hill's study of a board of directors, for example, informal networks are far more important than rigid rules.[63]

Third, Weber's elitism led him to believe that the issuing of top-down commands is the way to maximum efficiency. As Carl Friedrich put it, his writings on bureaucracy 'vibrate with something of the Prussian enthusiasm for the military type of organisation'.[64] However, this ignores how 'adherence to the rules, originally conceived as a means, becomes transformed into an end-in-itself'.[65] In other words bureaucracies breed a culture of conformism and become rigid as individual officials mechanically comply with rules and forget the original goals. The culture of a bureaucracy can have dysfunctional effects such as 'timidity, conservatism and technicism'.[66] It is precisely for this reason that modern corporation seeks to loosen up the bureaucratic structures with 'flat hierarchies' and 'teamworking' which encourage more autonomy. The aim of companies is often to intensify the rate of exploitation but they find that their own bureaucratic hierarchies have become an obstacle.

Finally, Weber did not fully appreciate how bureaucratic organisations can fragment into competing subgroups. The line of command from the top may have to go through a number of competing factions. H. Kaufman has written about US federal bureaucracy, for example:

> The federal bureaucracy is such a collection of diverse, often competing and contradictory, antagonistic interests that many of its components check and neutralise each other. As a result of such divisions, rivalries and opposing missions and interests, one of the principal barriers to an assumption of dominant power by bureaucrats is other bureaucrats.[67]

The same might have been written about the administration of large multinationals. Bureaucracies in both the public and private sectors tend to develop fast growing sub-bureaucracies who develop interests in, for example, protecting their budgets. Instead of keeping cost down, they have an interest in 'spending all they can' to keep up their allocation for the following year. This often leads to the employment of further controllers and consultants to counteract the tendency to self-expansion.

Many of these inefficiencies occur precisely because bureaucracies seek to rule over people and cut back on the space for self-administration. Weber's dismissal of the very notion of genuine democracy meant that he failed to see the inherent weaknesses in structures built on control freakery.

CONCLUSION

Weber's sociology provides interesting insights into how forms of power are exercised. His discussion on how the Catholic Church manages to 'routinise' charisma through the office of the priesthood is fascinating. So too is his discussion on how revolts against traditional rulers take a personalised form. But the insights are limited by the fact that Weber has no sense of how the mass of people can resist, mock and undermine the most powerful spellbinder or bureaucrat. Weber has a top-down vision that sees rulers as the sole agents capable of moulding society. There is no history of revolts – only of different forms of obedience. Instead, leaders induce a desire to obey in the compliant mass. There is no sense that, sometimes, the mass of people may have well-thought-out aspirations and desires that they charge the leader with meeting. The concept of charisma, in particular, loads everything onto the exceptional qualities of individual rulers. The overall effect is to deny the possibility that any subordinate class is ever capable of liberating itself. That is useful for Weber because his overall sociology suggested that there must be a tragic acceptance of capitalism.

8
The Fall and Rise of the West

Weber assumed the superiority of Western society. It was not a matter for debate, discussion or argument. It simply was. This superiority was identified with a more rational framework for organising social action.

The 'specific and peculiar rationalism of Western culture'[1] was the foundation stone for modern capitalism and bureaucracy, according to Weber. An important element in its creation was the Protestant ethic. However, he insisted that this was just one factor among many. There was a wider causal chain with religion being just one link. Weber's sociology focussed on where this unique culture of rationality came from. This involved a wide historical exploration that ranged from classical civilisation to modern times.

Weber's writings on the history of Western civilisation began in his early years with a series of essays on the ancient world. However, these became a preface to a wider interpretation of Western rationality that underlay much of his other writings. In this chapter, we will begin by looking at how he applied a neo-Marxist interpretation to ancient civilisation. We shall then try to reconstruct the wider conjuncture of factors that he claimed gave rise to a peculiar Western rationality. Finally, we shall offer a critical assessment of his theory of history, stressing how it masks many fundamental conflicts.

THE SOCIOLOGY OF ANCIENT CIVILISATION

Like many educated Germans of the nineteenth century, Weber had a classical education. He had been influenced by the famous German classicist Theodor Mommsen who drew parallels between the problems of antiquity and modern society.[2] Mommsen had attended Weber's doctoral dissertation on 'The History of Trading Companies in the Middle Ages' and was fulsome in his praise of the budding genius. He proclaimed that 'when I have to go to my grave someday, there is no one to whom I would rather say "Son, here is my spear; it is getting too heavy for my arm" than the highly esteemed Max Weber'.[3] After his dissertation, Weber's next study, completed in

1891, was on *The Agricultural History of Rome and its Relation to Public and Private Law*. The method of investigation in this publication is explicitly attributed to Mommsen.

What is remarkable about this study is Weber's emphasis on social class. The book looks in detail at the struggles over land and how political developments are closely connected to class conflict. One of the central issues in Roman society was the control of the *ager publicus* – land that was in theory owned by the Roman state after it was acquired in conquest. Contrary to the formal legal status, this land came to be exploited by private interests after an intense struggle between the independent peasant proprietors and the larger patrician landowners. Weber noted that 'never before in a large scale political system was political power so directly connected with money'.[4]

Weber's use of a class analysis, in a manner reminiscent of Marx, is all the more interesting because subsequent classical scholars such as Moses Finley have claimed that his concept of status had more explanatory power than Marx's approach. Finley had originally worked with the Marxist influenced Institute for Social Research in the 1930s but by the time he came to Britain in the 1950s he 'preferred to give primacy to Weber's concepts of "order" and "status"'. [5] Finley has been extremely influential in claiming, for example, that the slaves of antiquity could not be regarded as a distinct social class but should be viewed as a collection of status groups with few common interests. The irony is that classicists such as Finley and later Keith Bradley drew on Weber's writings on modern society to make their case about status while Weber's own writings on antiquity had a distinct Marxist ring to them.

This is most evident in his essay on 'The Social Causes of the Decay of Ancient Civilization' that was published in 1896. It makes a distinction between the end of ancient civilisation and the actual decline of the Roman Empire. Ancient civilisation had declined centuries before the political structures of the Empire fell apart and an internal barbarism had conquered the Empire from within.[6] 'The civilisation of Ancient Europe', Weber claimed, was 'a coastal civilisation and its history was above all a history of the coastal cities'.[7] This civilisation co-existed with a different type of society based on a 'natural economy' of primitive peasants in the interior who lived in tribal communities or under the domination of patriarchs. The existence of the two different socio-economic systems eventually caused major problems. The cities, which were based on trade, could only expand if there was an increased differentiation of wealth in the countryside. In other words, city traders needed to increase their supply of goods beyond the range of a small stratum of the wealthy. They needed to sell goods to the masses if they were to grow and prosper but this was blocked by slavery. The widespread use of slavery meant that the market could not expand intensively as only a few people could buy goods. The cities therefore grew extensively on an international scale, based on large establishments of unfree labour supplying the consumption needs of the upper class. As a result, trade became 'a thin net spread over a large natural economy'.[8]

The thin net eventually snapped when the contradictions in the slave economy came to the surface. In a later book-length essay, *The Agrarian Sociology of Ancient Civilisations*, Weber spelled out the problems that faced a slave economy by drawing a contrast with wage labour. He showed in some detail how slave labour is less productive and ultimately more costly to a slaveholder than free labour is to a modern employer. His argument represented a fruitful challenge to common sense, as it might at first sight seem that far greater profits could be made from slavery. However, Weber showed otherwise.

CONTRADICTIONS IN THE SLAVE ECONOMY

The employment of slaves involved a greater capital outlay than wage labour as a full living human being had to be purchased rather than simply their labour. Once the slave was bought, the slaveholder had little flexibility in the deployment of their labour. Slaves could not be laid off if the harvest was poor – they still had to be maintained and fed. The slaveholder also faced considerable risks of losing their capital. Slave mortality was high and the shifting fortunes of war meant that the price of slaves could drop if more slaves were taken. There was also no firm basis for efficient cost accounting with slavery, especially if the slaves were part of the master's household. Finally, slaves had no interest in any technical advance or in any increase in the quantity or quality of production. No major improvement was made in the standard instrument of slavery, the plough. All of this meant that: 'Large-scale use of slave labour was in general really profitable only when the land was fertile and the market price of slaves was low. Hence, slave labour was normally used for extensive agriculture.'[9]

The low productivity of slaves could be overcome only if more and more slaves were captured. Historically every slaveholder from the Roman latifundia owner to the plantation lords of the southern states of America had a natural tendency to expand the slave population. Writing of the former Weber noted that, 'the ancient plantation consumed slaves the way a modern blast furnace consumes coal'.[10] This was not a problem as long as the Roman Empire was expanding. However, the decision of the Emperor Tiberius in the first century AD to abandon the conquests on the Rhine and Hadrian's subsequent evacuation from Dacia in the second century signalled the end of this phase of expansion. The ending of a steady supply of new slaves had a dramatic effect on the Roman economy. Four major consequences followed.

First, the slave owners were forced to move away from a system of slave barracks to allowing slaves to form families in order to replace the shortage of labour. More female slaves were needed for reproduction but this increased the overall costs on the system. Ultimately the shift to slave families living outside of barracks paved the way for a new system of serfdom.

Second, to compensate for these new costs the conditions of the free *coloni* – Roman settlers on conquered land – worsened. Henceforth they were tied to the land and increasingly labour services were demanded of them. This was the other route into the creation of unfree serfs.

Third, the large estates broke away from cities to save taxes. The Empire moved inland and the state came to depend more and more on local landowners to supply recruits to the army.

Finally, the decline of the cities was hastened by the measures taken to alleviate the situation. The state took more direct control over taxes and created new state monopolies. However, the effects were to 'arrest private capital formation and check every tendency towards the emergence of a class corresponding to the bourgeoisie in modern times'.[11]

Overall, the essay on 'The Social Causes of the Decay of Ancient Civilization' had a decidedly Marxist tone. Ancient society was seen to rest on slavery and the contradictions in its mode of production ultimately determined its fate. Weber explicitly argued that economic developments shaped the 'superstructure' of the ancient world:

> the disintegration of the Roman Empire was the inevitable consequence of a basic economic development: the gradual disappearance of commerce and the expansion of a barter economy. Essentially this disintegration simply meant that the monetarized administrative system and political superstructure of the Empire

disappeared for they were no longer adapted to the infrastructure of a natural economy.[12]

No wonder that the main Weberian writer in this area, John Love, noted that the essay had a 'materialist thesis', which was 'remarkably close to Marxism'[13] while Antoni has even argued that Weber's 'historical materialism had freed him from any tendency to moralize'[14] about the decline of Rome.

Nevertheless, there was one aspect of Weber's analysis of the ancient world which was closer to Mommsen than Marx. Marx had derided Mommsen for claiming that capitalism existed in the ancient world[15] but Weber's subsequent book on *The Agrarian Sociology of Ancient Civilisations* took up and amplified Mommsen's theme that capitalism existed in these societies. This was all the more odd because Weber's introduction challenged the arguments of the modernist Eduard Meyer that concepts such as 'factory' and 'factory worker' could be applied to Athens of the time of Pericles.[16] Yet a few pages later Weber himself was happily applying the concept of 'capitalist' to the ancient world. Capitalism was defined here as 'wealth used to gain profit in commerce'.[17] This equation of capitalism with commerce, however, meant that virtually all societies had elements of capitalism within them. The Middle Ages, ancient Greece, the civilisations of Babylon were all 'capitalist' because individuals traded for 'profit'. By divorcing the concept of capitalism from any connection with class relations and free labour, Weber had effectively rendered it so broad as to be meaningless.

However, his intention was clearly ideological. Weber wanted to assert that capitalism was natural. Just as Adam Smith had said there was a natural propensity to truck and barter, so Weber also contended that capitalism had existed almost from the dawn of time. He disputed Marx's contention that it was a specific system that had come into existence at a certain point in time and might equally go out of existence at a different historical moment. Moreover, he also wanted to associate the achievements of ancient civilisation with capitalism. Thus he claimed that 'capitalism shaped whole periods of Antiquity, and indeed precisely those periods we call "golden ages"'.[18] This is an extraordinary claim and so it is hardly surprising that Weber concluded *The Agrarian Sociology of Ancient Civilisations* with a strong moral tale:

Bureaucracy stifled private enterprise in Antiquity. There is nothing unusual in this, nothing peculiar to Antiquity. Every bureaucracy tends to intervene in economic matters with the same result. This applies to the bureaucracy of modern Germany too ... Thus in all probability some day the bureaucratisation of German society will encompass capitalism too, just as it did in Antiquity.[19]

The story of ancient Greece and Rome was often used to illustrate lessons for contemporary society. Edward Gibbon saw the decline rooted in the growth of Christianity. Among the ancient writers, Annimanus Marcellinus, for example, began the now familiar story that moral degeneration was to blame for the demise. So it was not entirely unusual for Weber to add his unique story – that the glories of antiquity rested on ancient capitalism and that its decline arose from a stifling bureaucracy.

Yet, if we leave aside the ideological claims and the moral lessons, Weber's writings on antiquity were unusual. He embraced a materialist analysis and acknowledged that class conflict and the contradictions in a particular mode of production acted as fetters on the development of that society. The reason for this openness was that he was looking at a society that had decayed. From the vantage point of modern capitalism, he could see the contradictions inherent in the exploitation of slaves. However, when writing about modern capitalism, Weber's approach was entirely different. Marxists start from an assumption that capitalism can be transcended by a new social order. However, as Giddens points out, the possibility of a transcendence of capitalism is completely eliminated for Weber.[20] He therefore never examined the contractions in his own society but assumed it would last until the end of time.

WEBER'S THEORY OF HISTORY

The study of classical civilisation was only the start of a wider analysis of how the unique culture of Western society developed. Weber was keen to suggest that his theory of history was not deterministic but open-ended. He didn't over-emphasise the material or the cultural but sought to grasp the complex interplay between them. Any one factor could have a multitude of effects depending on other factors it was combined with. The historical process was a product of infinite complexity and openness. There were no fixed evolutionary stages of development set by the mode of production. Nonetheless, Weber claimed to have detected at least one pattern, claiming that 'there is a long run cultural tendency towards increasing rationalization'.[21]

This leads to a particular difficulty in Weber's sociology. The rationality of the West appears as the end point of history. However, this unique point only emerged because of a combination of necessary elements. No one element in this combination is deemed to have a causal primacy – it is the combination as a whole that counts. It is like entering into a casino and putting your bet on red and then waiting not just for one spinning wheel but several to click onto a combination of colours which mixed together form red. As Collins concedes, 'this makes world history look like the result of configurations of events so rare as to appear accidental'.[22]

Weber, of course, was trying to develop a powerful intellectual alternative to Marx's historical materialism. His desire to claim the mantle of sophistication led him to acknowledge the importance of economic factors but these were then subsumed into a more complex whole. To explain his historical method he used the metaphor of the signal box on an old railway system: 'Not ideas, but material and ideal interests, directly govern men's conduct. Yet, very frequently, the "world images" created by "ideas" have, like switchmen, determined the tracks along which action has been pushed by the dynamic of interest.'[23] Different cultures will apparently send the trains in different directions. Different economies could experience population growth and a price revolution that were preconditions for advance but the Protestant Ethic sent European society down a different direction than China, for example. The analogy of the signal box and the railway track sought to combine the material and cultural but there was a subtle bias towards the cultural. This became evident when Weber came to his argument about how the process of rationalisation emerged. His peculiar insight was that all the great rational ways of living had to have 'irrational presuppositions'. Rationality could only have been created on irrational foundations. In addition, the primary source of these foundations was religion. In a key passage, that soon follows the signal box metaphor, Weber writes that:

> wherever the direction of the whole way of life has been methodically rationalized, it has been profoundly determined by the ultimate values toward which this rationalization has been directed. These values and positions were thus *religiously* determined. Certainly they have not always, or exclusively, been decisive; however, they have been decisive in so far as an *ethical* rationalization held sway,

at least so far as its influence reached. As a rule, these religious values have been also, and frequently absolutely decisive.[24]

Weber assumed that religion arose from an innate 'metaphysical need for a meaningful cosmos'.[25] People needed explanations of suffering and religion offered an account of this by seeing it as a sign of the anger of the Gods. The fortunes of humanity also differed widely and people demanded to know why their fate differed from the fate of their fellows. Even those who had good fortune needed to be convinced that they deserved it. Religions therefore arose naturally – almost from the human condition itself. The particular belief systems, however, had very different impacts as we have seen. In addition to the actual beliefs, Weber placed a particular emphasis on the organisations that promoted religious ideas. The 'charisma' which religious figures claimed was embedded in different types of church organisation. So Weber often shifted from cultural analysis to what Michael Mann later called 'organisational materialism'[26] to explain why the process of rationalisation developed in the West. Overall, however, religion played a primary role in a complex of factors that shaped the culture of particular societies. Let us look at some of the key factors which produced the culture of instrumental rationality.

THE SOURCES OF WESTERN RATIONALITY

One of the early sources of Western rationality was ancient Judaism. As an ardent German nationalist, Weber wished to dispute Sombart's contention that the origins of capitalism lay in Jewish culture. Nevertheless, his focus on the Protestant Ethic necessitated some acknowledgement of Jewish influence on the Old Testament. Judaism's main contribution was disenchantment with the world. According to Weber, Judaism was unique in waging a determined conflict with all forms of magic. It was built around prophets who spoke freely and were not beholden to any civic authority. They were demagogues who were answerable only to God and insisted that their fellow Jews honour a contract with him. Like Puritanism, the Jewish religion stressed that the Holy Scripture was a binding law which the individual must know and interpret correctly. Judaism provided 'a highly rational religious ethic of social conduct; it was free of magic and all forms of irrational quest for salvation; it was inwardly worlds apart from the paths of salvation offered by Asiatic religions'.[27] Its 'prophecies have released the world from magic and in doing so created the basis for our modern science and technology and for capitalism'.[28]

Another source of the West's rationality was its legal system. Legal systems often started from charismatic prophets who made revelations through an oracle or by staging ordeals. After a certain period, higher authorities emerged to interpret these revelations and so 'enact' laws. With the decline in magic, they had to give reasons for their judgements and so a certain standardisation emerged. Wars, however, disrupted these older legal traditions and so new laws had to be systematised and made more explicit. Roman law, for example, developed as a highly codified and logically consistent system. The tradition of rational law-making reached its apex in the West because of two central factors. First, the Catholic Church developed its own system of canon law and a trial procedure – the inquisition – in order to 'obtain evidence in a rational manner'.[29] This in turn influenced the secular system of justice. Second, universities in medieval cities revived Roman law and produced trained jurists and notaries who formed an important part of the urban bourgeoisie. All of this led to a practice of continuous law-making and rational jurisprudence that was unique to the West.

Additionally, Schluchter has argued that Weber's theory about the uniqueness of Western rationality can be best understood as the intertwining of three main revolutions.[30] The first might be termed the papal revolution and the growth of monasticism. The period between 1046 and 1122 is known in church history as the Age of Gregorian Reform after Pope Gregory VII. It was characterised by the struggle of the investiture after the papacy wrested from secular powers the right to appoint priests and bishops.[31] The change helped to produce a unified Christian culture, which in turn had a number of key consequences. A professional priesthood arose which was removed from the 'world'. Through the pope, it made a claim for universal domination and so sought to overcome all claims of primary loyalty to household or tribe. The dogma and rites of this church were also rationalised and based on set commentaries from the scriptures. No longer was religious organisation reliant on either the patronage of aristocrats or on the deeds of charismatic individuals. Instead there was 'the separation of charisma from the *person* and its linkage with an institution and, particularly, with the *office*'.[32] In other words, instead of religion being based on individual holy men or charismatic prophets, the church became the trustee of a '"trust fund" of eternal blessings, that are offered to everyone'[33] and dispensed by priests.

The church's claim to the charisma of office led to a new relationship with the medieval state. In return for using its charisma to bestow a legitimacy of kings and rulers, the church secured immunity from secular jurisdiction and exemption from taxation. All of this created the space for the growth of monasticism.

The original monks belonged to charismatic communities which disdained normal economic concerns. They lived alone in freely formed 'herds'; they were unmarried and free of family responsibilities. They followed an ascetic life based on methodical practices. The goal of every monk was the achievement of complete control over his natural drives as these were seen to impede his unity with God. In the past, this type of ascetic Holy Man often fled into deserts or wilderness and developed an implicit critique of their bishops and the established state.[34] However, after the Gregorian reforms the monks were fully integrated into the church. Their withdrawal from the world and the rational organisation of their work led to huge advances in science and knowledge.

For Weber, these monastic communities were 'the first rationally administered manors and later the first rational work communities in agriculture and crafts'.[35] The great irony was that the energy and passion of religious faith led to the creation of enormous wealth. The monasteries exemplified how irrational religious feelings led to rationalised economic conduct:

The ascetic monk has fled from the world by denying himself individual property; his existence has rested entirely upon his own work; and, above all, his needs have been correspondingly restricted to what was absolutely indispensable. The paradox of all rational asceticism, which in an identical manner has made monks in all ages stumble, is that rational asceticism itself created the very wealth it rejected. Temples and monasteries have everywhere become the very *loci* of rational economies.[36]

The second great revolution which paved the way for Western rationality was feudalism. Western feudalism arose when vassals succeeded in undermining a system of pure domination and established fixed contractual relations with their lords. As a system, it developed when they equipped themselves with the instruments of war and developed skills to handle weapons professionally. This made possible forms of knighthood, which held to a unified code of conduct based on honour. Feudalism contributed to Western rationality by creating a constellation of rights and by laying the basis for a separation of powers.

The original tribal leaders were typically warriors who demanded loyalty almost like patriarchs who ran an extended household. These rulers resisted any codification of rights as it restricted their powers. However, as society expanded and these rulers came to rule over larger areas, they needed to cede rights to their barons and knights. As Bendix put it, 'feudalism replaces the paternal relationship by a contractually fixed fealty on the basis of knightly militarism'[37] The knights won bilateral contracts with their lords whereby they guaranteed to provide men and weapons in return for tax exemptions and privileges. They set out to limit through fixed norms the maximum annual tribute they had to grant the lord. They also succeeded in establishing feudal courts, composed of fellow vassals to adjudicate on rights. Weber is at pains to stress that what was won was 'congeries of acquired rights'[38] rather than any abstract system of rules that characterises modern capitalism. Hence, even though feudalism restricted access to moneymaking and tried to channel it into land, it was a step on the road to rationalisation because arbitrary rule was diminished in favour of codes of acquired rights.

Ultimately feudalism helped create a separation of powers which Montesquieu would later claim was characteristic of modern society. It produced a 'quantitative division of authority'[39] because there was a social contract between the ruler and his representatives. This separation of powers ultimately created cracks and crevices in the wider society that were not completely controlled by the rulers. Instead of the bureaucratisation that developed in ancient Egypt where the Pharaohs imposed heavy liturgies – duties – on a subject population, a space was created for new forms of economic energy to emerge. Specifically, the separation of powers was a key precondition for the emergence of the Western city.

Weber's writings on the medieval city describe the third revolution in Schluchter's interpretation. Cities, of course, were not peculiar to Western Europe. However, the character of the Western medieval city was unique and held for Weber 'a special developmental position'.[40] Cities were normally established by feudal lords primarily for economic reasons rather than military purposes. The same lords often lacked a trained apparatus of officials and were divided among themselves and so the cities were not easy to control. As a result,

The urban citizenry therefore usurped the right to dissolve the bonds of seigniorial domination; this was the great – in fact, *revolutionary* – innovation that differentiated the medieval Occidental cities from all others. In the central and Northern European cities appeared the well-known principle that *Stadtluft macht frei* (City air gives freedom) which meant that after a varying but always relatively short time the master of a slave or a serf lost the right reclaim him.[41]

What developed was the city commune. Typically, it had a market, which acted as a seat of trade and commerce. It was surrounded by a fortress that offered some protection against looting. It had its own court of law and, crucially, the administration was in the hands of the city burghers. The burghers grew out of medieval guilds and were often the master craftsmen. Alternatively, in Italy, they arose through the *coniurationes* – sworn confraternities that regulated the right to engage in economic activities. In other words, the Western cities were linked to a distinct bourgeois class that did not exist elsewhere.

The medieval urban communes gained a degree of political independence from the surrounding feudal society. In some cases, such as Vienna and Genoa, the cities pursued their own foreign policy and established trading outposts. Inside the city there was a system of autonomous law creation, which was dominated by the guilds and, later, the crafts. There were also separate judicial and administrative agencies – what Weber calls autocephaly – which had developed to high degree in Italy and to a lesser extent elsewhere. City courts increasingly dispensed with irrational forms of evidence based on duels and ordeals in favour of rational procedures. They developed their own procedures for tax raising. They often had to make a collective lump sum payment to feudal lords but could then take the collection of taxes under their own management. Finally, the cities were able to regulate their own markets and the craft associations determined who could and who could not trade and produce.

All of this meant that the Western city produced the concept of citizenship, which was unique. The idea of citizenship grew out of institutionalised associations of burghers who were subject to special laws and so formed a distinct status group. Originally the term citizenship meant a man of property and culture. It stood in contrast with both the nobility on one hand and the proletariat on the other. It entitled someone to pursue certain occupations in the medieval city. For these citizens formal legal restrictions – such as

feudal obligations and membership of certain religious groupings
– were waived. Citizenship, Weber therefore argued, is 'a specifically
modern and Western concept like that of bourgeoisie'.[42]

COMPLEXITY OF FACTORS

This then was the complex of reasons which led to Western rationality
and Western capitalism. There was not one single determining cause
but a collection which worked together to lay the foundation for the
modern 'sober bourgeois capitalism' that Weber described in *The
Protestant Ethic and the Spirit of Capitalism*. Protestantism provided
the psychological trigger which enabled the modern entrepreneurial
spirit to be released but Weber's later writings point out that Western
rationality had deep roots that stretched back to ancient Judaism and
developed in complex fragile ways that were not repeatable elsewhere.
Capitalism had existed since the dawn of time but early capitalism
was non-rational. It needed Western culture to transform it into its
modern form. In this sense, there is a mutually reinforcing dynamic
between capitalism and the Western culture of rationality.

In his last work, *General Economic History*, Weber summarised the
complex matrix that made up his overall theory. By itself, capitalism
had led to a 'rational organisation of labour, which nowhere
previously existed'.[43] Unlike slavery or serfdom, it was based on
free labour, which was bought and sold in the market place. This
allowed a strict calculation to be made about what was profitable
and productive. Capitalism helped to dissolve clan and caste ties; it
cut open all 'primitive economic fixity'[44] and replaced all forms of
ethics which distinguished between in-groups and out-groups with
a commercial spirit. These developments could only flourish in the
West because of 'the special features of its general cultural evolution
which are peculiar to it'.[45] Only the West produced a rational science
and rational technology. Only the West had 'a religious basis for
ordering life which consistently followed out must lead to explicit
rationalism.'[46] Only the West knew a rational legal state based on a
professional administration, specialised officialdom and law based
on citizenship. Only the West produced a rational nation state
that allowed capitalism to develop. This latter point represented a
significant shift from Weber's earlier work as he was now claiming
that the modern bourgeoisie arose from the alliance of the state with
capital: 'It is the closed national state which afforded capitalism its

chance for development – and as long as the national state does not give place to a world empire, capitalism will also endure.'[47]

ASSESSMENT

Weber's general theory of history is difficult to assess without going into a long excursus on the key turning points of Western Europe. However, there are a few general points that can be made.

There is a pronounced teleological character to the argument. The story of the West is one of progressive movement to the end point of rationality. There is little differentiation between societies within the West and instead it is defined as a united whole in opposition the Orient. In fact, England had a more centralised system of feudalism than, say, France. However, while this is briefly acknowledged by Weber it does not detract from his overall argument that feudalism produced a separation of powers and, thus, represented a new stage on the road to rationality. There is also little discussion of the crisis in feudal society in the fourteenth century, which brought considerable disruption in Europe. Instead, the process of rationalisation is discussed at a high level of generality. History seems to build upon its previous achievements to deliver the final, unique culture of the West.

Underlying this teleology is an intertwining of capitalism and rationality. As long as there is profit from trade, capitalism exists. Western culture, however, facilitates the transition from earlier commercial activity to full-blown capitalism while Oriental culture impedes it. As Wood put it, Weber,

> always tended to talk about factors that impeded the development of capitalism in other places – their kinship forms, their forms of domination, their religious traditions and so on – as if the natural, unimpeded growth of towns and trade and the liberation of the towns and burgher class would by definition mean capitalism.[48]

Weber's general account assigns an unduly important role to religion. He assumes that there is a metaphysical need for religion and can barely countenance the idea of society living without a religion. It might equally, however, be argued that religion arose from alienation, when people could not control their lives.[49] More than that, Weber assumes that religious ideas and institutions are crucial for social change. The active elements in history are the religious 'virtuosos' such as the Protestant sects. Sometimes they struggle against the inert bureaucratisation of their church while at other times they come to an accommodation with it. However, their particular theologies are the most active ingredient in shaping the 'economic ethic' of their societies. As Weber puts it 'the peculiar nature of the concrete religiosity of the virtuosos has been of decisive importance for the development of the way of life of the masses'.[50]

Weber never considered how 'the life of the masses' might be a major factor in shaping 'the concrete religiosity' of the virtuosos. Yet, history is full of examples where the social concerns of the masses helped shape religious outlooks. Heretical movements such as the Albigensians in France or Hussites in Bohemia often reflected the aspiration of the peasantry for an end to corruption within the church. The Waldensian movement of the twelfth century, for example, emphasised the virtues of the poor, equality between men and women, and a direct relationship between God and human beings.[51] In England in the seventeenth century, the aspirations of the lower orders found expression in all sorts of millenarian sects such as the Muggeltonians and groups such as the Fifth Monarchists.[52] Weber neglects this aspect because he sees the mass of people as pliable putty in the hands of the theological virtuosos.

Weber's account is fundamentally elitist, as it gives no explanatory space to the role of the mass of people in shaping the history. This occurs because Weber virtually ignores the contradictions in the feudal economy. The principal surplus that sustained the feudal aristocracy came from the peasantry. The peasantry faced considerable difficulties in organising but the conflict between these classes must have played some role in shaping society. Hilton has argued, for example, that by the fourteenth century falling agricultural prices, growing expenditure by the aristocracy and the heavier burdens of war led the upper class to place greater pressure on the peasantry for increased rent.[53] One result was a series of medieval peasant rebellions such as the revolt in maritime Flanders in 1323–27; the Jacqueries in the Paris region in 1358; the Tuchin movement in central France from the 1360s to the end of the fourteenth century; the peasant revolt in England in 1381; and the wars of the *remensas* in Catalonia during the 1460s and 1480s.[54] The peasant revolt in England led at one stage to a general charter of manumission from Richard II relieving all villeins in particular counties from the obligations of servile status.[55] This was later revoked but in the following centuries there was a withering away of these feudal obligations, mainly due to continuing peasant resistance.

Robert Brenner has argued that differing levels of peasant resistance to the claims of the aristocracy had important repercussions for the future of European countries.[56] East of the river Elbe in Germany, peasant resistance was weak and so an intensified class structure of serfdom re-emerged. This consolidated the power of the landed aristocracy and created barriers to future industrialisation. By contrast, peasant resistance in Western Europe was stronger and peasants were able to establish fixed rents, ensure rights of inheritance and eventually dissolve serfdom. However, even when serfdom was removed, there were still differences between countries in terms of land consolidation and capitalist methods of agriculture. England, for example, moved to capitalist agriculture far quicker than France, which maintained a stronger tradition of peasant proprietorship. Again, Brenner argues that the key factor was the level of peasant resistance. There is certainly a huge debate about the Brenner thesis and in particular Brenner's location of the origins of early capitalism in agriculture. However, this debate is impossible within the framework established by Weber because he sees the peasantry simply as the raw material of history – shaped and manipulated by others.

Finally, Weber's concept of citizenship masks the conflicts and violence associated with the rise of the urban burghers. Weber is strongest when he shows how the Western cities grew from the fragmentation of feudal authority, which stood in marked contrast with the more centralised authority of countries such as China. He also correctly points to the role of the organised trading interests in developing their own laws and system of justice. However, he plays down the degree of class conflict that occurred in favour of a focus on law-making. The rising 'burgher plutocracy' often usurped the older guild associations to take control of town governments. Dobb, for example, shows that in Coventry, the Gild Merchant excluded all craftsmen and became the governing body of the town. In Florence, bankers and export merchants took control from the middle thirteenth century and forged alliances with the surrounding landed nobles, sometimes against their own population. In Paris, the richer weavers formed themselves into the Drapers and subordinated other craftsmen to them.[57] Citizenship was riven with conflict as former rights that were bestowed on city communes were hallowed out and usurped by richer sections.

In his *General Economic History*, Weber argues 'that the accumulation of wealth through colonial trade has been of little significance for the development of modern capitalism'.[58] However, it is difficult to see how cities such as Liverpool, Genoa or Barcelona developed without the colonial trade. Italian cities such as Genoa and Venice participated in the Crusades for the express purpose of gaining plunder. Later the wealth of Italian cities was based on a monopoly of trade they established in Egypt, which functioned as an entrepôt for Eastern spices. Weber did not fully acknowledge the reliance of many Western cities on the colonial trade because ultimately he wished to assert that Western rationality was the key to history. However, without taking into account the fabulous wealth that was accumulated through colonial trade it is hard to explain how the burghers emerged as a stratum between the nobility and the proletariat.

CONCLUSION

Benedetto Croce said that all history is contemporary history and we see this clearly in Weber. He produced a brilliant materialist analysis to explain the fall of antiquity. His analysis of slavery and the contradiction in the mode of production had a decidedly Marxist ring. Yet, this appreciation of the historic limits to any one economic form deserted him when he reached more modern times. Instead, his key explanatory variable became a set of conjunctural factors which created the unique constellation of Western culture.

The strangeness of his original question – what made Western rationality possible? – meant that his genuine insights were covered in a whitewash. The stories of exploitation, violence and irrationality were played down to paint capitalism in more glowing colours. Concepts like citizenship were used to present a benign image of shared values and privileges. Religion was assigned an unduly positive role in developing a methodical approach to life. Missing entirely was any possibility that revolts from below effected major changes – or even forced the ruling elite to adopt new forms of rule. Once again, Weber revealed a top view vision of society that ultimately implied a satisfaction with the achievements of his own culture.

9
Capitalism, Socialism and Bureaucracy

Karl Lowith made a celebrated comparison between Marx and Weber, claiming that they differed mainly on their master concept for discussing modern capitalism. For Marx it was 'alienation', for Weber it was 'rationality'.[1] By alienation, Marx meant that humans create a power, capital, which comes to dominate and demean their lives. What Weber meant exactly by rationality is, as we shall see, much more controversial.

Nevertheless, Lowith's comparison has conveyed an impression that Weber was somewhat of a left liberal. He too, apparently, wanted to critique capitalism – but through a more humanist approach which warned against bureaucratisation. His focus on bureaucratisation is deemed more relevant in an age that has seen the failure of Soviet communism.

This chapter disputes this emphasis. It seeks to show that Weber was deeply influenced by the forerunner of neo-liberal economics – the Austrian school. From this influence, he developed a robust defence of the free market – equating it with the highest peak of economic rationality. Finally this chapter examines his particular explanation of bureaucracy and questions the argument that the 'iron cage of bureaucracy' is inevitable.

WHAT IS RATIONALITY?

Collins has argued that there are three meanings of rationality in Weber's work.[2] One is to be found in Weber's theory of action. Here instrumental rationality means that actors make choices and calculations about the most efficient means to achieve their ends. It involves 'the rational consideration of alternative means to the end, of the relations of the end to secondary consequences and finally of the relative importance of different possible ends'.[3] People calculate how much it costs to reach goals and examine the importance of each goal according to its costs. This form of thinking had become dominant in modern society. In brief, modern humanity was calculating, predictable and cold.

A second meaning is to be found in Weber's theory of the economic ethic of world religions. Rationality here refers to an active force that seeks to master the world rather than succumbing to it through mysticism. So Puritan asceticism is rational whereas many Eastern contemplative religions are not.

A third meaning of rationality is to be found in Weber's discussion of institutions in the West. Bureaucracy is a rational form of administration as opposed to the irrational elements found in patrimony. The free market is also rational when compared with attempts to regulate production. The criteria here are that both bureaucracy and the market operate through calculation and predictability.

Rationality also involves the secularisation or 'disenchantment' of the modern world. Modern humanity has dispensed with spiritual forces as explanations of nature or society. The world has become 'intellectualised' because we seek explanations in the form of scientific laws. Even if one has not got such an explanation at the moment, there is an assumption that one could eventually discover one:

> Hence, it means principally there are no mysterious incalculable forces that come into play, but rather that one can, in principle, master all things by calculation. This means that the world is disenchanted. One need no longer have recourse to magical means in order to master or implore the spirits, as did the savage, for whom mysterious powers existed. Technical means and calculation perform the service. This is above all what intellectualisation means.[4]

The growth of science has been the key element in this. Science contributes to the technology of controlling life but it also leads to methods of thinking that emphasise clarity about the means to achieve goals. Like Nietzsche, Weber did not believe science was about pursuing 'progress' or the pursuit of human happiness. It was a value-free practice that did not subject human aims to critical scrutiny but instead provided an objective assessment of the means that people might use to achieve them.

WEBER AND THE AUSTRIAN SCHOOL OF ECONOMICS

In addition to this broad cultural analysis, Weber advanced the much more controversial claim that modern capitalism was the highest expression of rationality. His argument was strongly influenced by

Eugen Bohm-Bawerk, one of the key writers in the Austrian marginalist school of economics. Bohm-Bawerk wrote his two-volume piece *Capital and Interest* between 1884 and 1889 as an explicit challenge to Marx's theories. Later he became Minister for Finance in Austria on three occasions in the 1890s before returning again to full-time academic work. He laid the theoretical basis for the neo-liberal economic policies which dominate the modern world.

Bohm-Bawerk's economic analysis coincided with Weber's on a number of key areas. Bohm-Bawerk rejected Marx's labour theory of value, which claimed that the value of commodities was determined by the amount of socially useful labour contained in them. He denied that commodities had any objective value, arguing that value depended on the 'desires' of particular individuals. As individuals had different desires the value of a commodity derived from their subjective estimation of the utility they got from each extra amount (marginal utility) of this commodity. In *Economy and Society*, Weber explicitly supported Bohm-Bawerk and made the concept of 'utility' the cornerstone of his theory of economic action. He defined utilities as, 'the specific and concrete, real or imagined, advantages of opportunities for present or future use as they are estimated or made an object of specific provision by one or more economically acting individuals'.[5]

Behind this rather abstract theorising, there was a notion that society was a collection of individual interests who were connected through the market. Marx had denounced the notion that society was built on many individual Robinson Crusoes and argued that people only achieved individuality in and through society. Bohn-Bawerk and Weber, however, took the ideological image of man in a market society as an isolated, selfish soul and generalised it throughout all history. Yet, there are good grounds for questioning this approach, as Bukharin has pointed out in his critique of the marginalist school:

> Society ... is not an arithmetical aggregate of isolated individuals; on the contrary, the economic activity of each specific individual pre-supposes a definite social environment in which the social relation of individual economies finds its expression. The motives of the individual living in isolation are entirely different from those of the 'social animal' ... The economic subject, in its actions, adapts itself to the given condition of the social phenomena; the latter imposes barriers upon his individual motives. Thus, for example, the individual estimate of price always starts with prices

that have already been fixed; the desire to invest capital in a bank depends on the interest rate at the time; the investment of capital in this industry or that is determined by the profit yielded by that industry ...[6]

Weber's use of marginal utility theory ruled out questions about the social usefulness of production and consumption. His assumption that 'desire' was the basis for value 'creates the space for anything to become a utility irrespective of its social usefulness'.[7] It can mean for example that a millionaire's 'desire' for an extra yacht is to be taken as an unquestioned economic given – as much as an African peasant's 'desire' for water purification tablets to save their children from water-borne diseases.

Another implication of Bohm-Bawerk's theory was to deny that profit was based on exploitation. Marx had argued that workers did not receive payment for the full value of their labour, which they transmitted into commodities. As labour was the basis for the value of commodities, this meant that workers were exploited. Bohn-Bawerk, however, saw profit arising from the difference between the price of future goods and the price of commodities used in the production process. Capitalists, in effect, granted an advance to workers to allow them to receive a wage. There was no exploitation and workers owed a debt of gratitude to their employer for their entrepreneurship and foresight. When asked how the capitalist got his original stock of capital, Bohm-Bawerk simply associated capital with possession of tools in general. In other words, there was nothing unique about capital. Marx, by contrast, ridiculed those who saw 'the stone of the savage as the origin of capital'[8] and argued that capital was a unique economic power, which arose from dispossession, slavery and exploitation. Weber, however, endorsed Bohm-Bawerk's theory that profit had nothing to do with exploitation. He claimed that 'profitability depends on the prices which the "consumers", according to the marginal utility of money in relation to their income, can and will pay'.[9]

The founders of modern sociology and neo-liberal economics agreed, therefore, on breaking the link between profits and human labour. Both assigned an active and almost heroic role to the entrepreneur. Both prized the competitive struggle between individuals as a supreme value to be cherished. Both attempted to place the capitalist system beyond any effective criticism by defining it as the most rational possible imaginable. Critiques could still be made from an ethical, utopian or traditionalist perspective but they could offer no rational alternative. Hegel's revolutionary dialectic may have farcically collapsed in his assertion that the 'rational' was finally embodied in the 'real' world of the Prussian monarchy. Although Weber despised Hegel's grand dialectic, his own sociology of modern rationalisation is equally teleological as capitalism represents the end point of rationality.

FORMAL AND SUBSTANTIVE RATIONALITY

Weber makes an important distinction between 'formal rationality' and 'substantive rationality'. Economic activity is 'called "formally" rational according to the degree in which the provision of needs, which is essential to every rational economy, is capable of being expressed in numerical, calculable terms and is so expressed'.[10] Accounting and calculation are, therefore, the defining terms of formal rationality. Weber's definition of 'substantive rationality' is less clear-cut. Substantive rationality applies to 'certain criteria of ultimate ends, whether they be ethical, political, utilitarian, hedonistic, feudal, egalitarian or whatever, and measure the results of economic action ... against these scales of "value rationality" or "*substantive* goal rationality"'.[11] This second category of 'substantive rationality' is, therefore, very much a catch-all space for anything that is not formally rational. Weber acknowledges that the concept of 'substantive rationality' is 'full of ambiguities'[12] precisely because it is defined in opposition to the category of formal rationality. The important point is that it is only used to 'measure the results of economic action'.[13] In other words, it essentially involves a form of political moral commentary after the event. As Weber's sociology purports to abstain from value judgements, it is not surprising that he rarely uses the concept of substantive rationality. It is, he claims, an 'abstract, generic concept'[14] that helps to delimit what he means by formal rationality. Rationality for Weber, therefore, virtually always means action based on calculation and accountancy.

This ignores the most obvious question: what is the calculation and technical control of figures being used for? A number of modern examples illustrate the difficulty. A nuclear power plant operates on the highest level of formal rationality. There are sophisticated schemes to monitor all inputs, to control energy usage, to calculate the relative cost of labour. There are dials, balance sheets, monitors of all kinds. However, producing the deadly waste product of plutonium is the height of irrationality because it does not disintegrate for tens of thousands of years and remains a danger to human health. It is only 'rational' to those who regard nuclear weaponry as a plausible method of defence.

Or let's apply Weber's concept to the infamous example of the Ford Pinto. This small car was rushed into production because of competition from Japanese rivals. Pre-production tests indicated that its fuel system would rupture easily in a rear-end collision but, because expensive assembly equipment was already in place and Ford was under pressure, the car went into production. The decision to go ahead was based on the most sophisticated forms of calculation. Ford compared the litigation costs from lost lives with the costs of scrapping production and decided to go ahead with production. Ford's calculations were most precise and 'formally rational'. They estimated that the defects in the Ford Pinto would lead to 180 deaths and about the same number of injuries. Placing a cost of $200,000 per person, Ford decided that the total cost of these deaths and injuries would be less than the $11 per car it would cost to repair the defect.[15] All of this may fit into a narrow definition of rationality but it is absurd in terms of any concept of rationality that starts from human needs.

As Marcuse has pointed out, the main basis for Weber's concept of rationality is an abstraction that reduces quality to quantity. The concept fits well with a society which reduces all of human life to 'exchange values' which are traded on the market place.[16] It mystifies accountancy by transforming it into an activity that transcends human interests. After recent scandals involving the giant firm Arthur Anderson, we now know that accountancy firms do not produce 'objective' figures that are divorced from the class interests of those who employ them. The Enron scandal revealed all too nakedly that 'balancing the books' is influenced by such venal concerns as share prices, dividend payments and consultancy fees.[17] Weber's defence of capitalism rests, therefore, on an avoidance of questions about the goals of economic activity and their social usefulness. Instead capitalism is simply deemed to be formally rational because 'of the unprecedented extent to which the actions of economic agents are calculated'.[18]

ECONOMIC RATIONALITY

The sources for economic rationality are to be found in the market, capital accountancy and wage labour. Weber's arguments about the market belong firmly in the realm of conventional economics. Economic activity is supposed to be characterised by conflicting individual desires. There has to be a way of establishing 'effective demand' and this occurs through price competition. Capital accounting, which Weber regards as the high point of economic rationality, 'presupposes the battle of man with man'[19] with money being 'primarily a weapon in this struggle and prices are expressions in this struggle'.[20] The market also sets clear, rational limits on people's desires. Weber argued that socialism had no way of determining effective prices because it abolished the market. He insisted that once the population reached a certain density an economy could only be maintained on the basis of accurate price calculation. As Mommsen has pointed out, economic rationality for Weber therefore depended on the 'essentially unrestricted struggle between autonomous economic groups in the market'.[21]

A second condition for economic rationality, according to Weber, is the wide-scale use of capital accountancy. Money makes for precise rational economic provision but it obtains its 'highest level of rationality' when it reaches the level of capital accounting. Capital accountancy means putting a value on the total assets of goods and money at the beginning of the profit-making cycle and then comparing this value with that attained at the end of the cycle. In brief, it is a measure of the rate of return on capital. The search for a rate of return forces each capitalist to impose 'shop discipline' on employees and maintain a close check on capital costs. Weber's defence of the free market is total at this point. He claims that capital accountancy must rest on ' unrestricted market freedom'.[22]

A third condition for economic rationality is wage labour based on the expropriation of workers from the means of production.[23] Weber's language follows Marx at certain points but his standpoint is entirely different. He is willing to describe very bluntly the actual process of capitalism but he wants to justify it as a technical necessity for achieving the highest level of rationality. Weber claims that in all societies human economic activity has to be divided into either 'managerial' activity or labour which is 'orientated to the instructions of a managerial agency'.[24] In other words, the distinction between mental labour and manual labour that took on an extremely pronounced character under capitalism is projected back into history and given a permanent character. As this distinction is absolute, there is no prospect of self-management in any society. The issue then becomes: how do you get people to work? Weber's answer is that:

It is generally possible to achieve a higher level of economic rationality if management has extensive control over the selection and the modes of use of workers, as compared with the situation created by the appropriation of jobs or the existence of rights to participate in management. These latter conditions produce technically irrational obstacles as well as economic irrationalities.[25]

Weber's bluntness has at least the advantage of clarity. Attempts by workers to gain a say over management prerogatives lead to irrationality. Free labour and the complete appropriation of the means of production, claims Weber, create 'the most favourable conditions for discipline'.[26] Sometimes Weber's bluntness is unpalatable to modern defenders of the status quo. He argues that there has to be a strong compulsion to work, based on either physical force or the probability of a drop in earning if effort is not increased. This in turn 'presupposes the expropriation of the workers from the means of production by owners is protected by force'.[27]

Weber has sometimes been presented as being close to Marx in wanting a more humane version of capitalism to protect workers' interests. Writers in this vein often point to his odd complimentary remark about Marx or to his defence of the socialist Robert Michels who was denied a PhD by reactionary university authorities. However, the image of Weber as a forerunner of a more humane society is gravely mistaken. His second chapter of *Economy and Society* was as robust a defence of deregulated free markets as one can get. With great gusto he expressed the outlook of modern bourgeois who see balance sheets, competition, and shop discipline as the high point of rationality. Weber assumed that individualistic self-interest is the motive force for all progress, claiming that 'one of the most important aspects of the process of rationalization is the substitution for unthinking acceptance of ancient custom, of deliberate adaptation to situations in terms of self-interest'.[28] The possibility that ancient custom and tradition might be replaced by planning for collective interests is not even countenanced. His defence of capitalism has since become the standard one – it may lead to huge inequality but it is the only technically efficient system possible.

If the standard used is that of a certain minimum of subsistence for the maximum size of population, the experience of the last few decades would seem to show that formal and substantive rationality co-incide to a relatively high degree. The reasons lie in the nature of the incentives, which are set in motion by the type of economically orientated social action, which alone is adequate to money calculations.[29]

THE IRON CAGE OF BUREAUCRACY

Weber's defence of capitalism was, however, by no means a joyful celebration but was rather bleak and gloom ridden. Mommsen has argued that Weber's thought is often 'antinomical' in that he adopts starkly counterposed positions, which are held together in tense combinations.[30] So there is a fulsome defence of the market but a recognition that bureaucracy and capitalism go hand in hand. The balance shifts depending on the age of the system. In *The Protestant Ethic and the Spirit of Capitalism*, Weber celebrated the arrival of a dynamic enterprising system, which was born with a sense of a mission. However, in *Parliament and Government in Germany*, which was written in 1917, there is a fatalistic acknowledgement that the system has been ossified. It is like an old person whose energies are sapped by bureaucratisation. The only hope lies in a charismatic leader who will revive its energies.

One of the first warnings Weber issued on this score was to the Russian liberals during the 1905 revolution. He was acutely aware of their weaknesses and wished to shock them out of any sentiment that their political philosophy would inevitably win out in the rapids of revolution. His writings on Russia were a clarion call to liberalism to break from any smug optimism and 'to see its vocation as fighting against both bureaucratic and Jacobin centralism and working at the permeation of the masses with the old individualistic ideas of the "inalienable rights of man"'.[31] Against the naïve optimists, he warned that,

'Democracy' and individualism would stand little chance today if we were to rely for their 'development' on the 'automatic' effect of *material* interests. For these point as clearly as they can in the opposite direction. Whether in the shape of American 'benevolent feudalism', the German 'welfare institutions' or the Russian factory constitution – everywhere the empty shell for the new serfdom stands ready.[32]

Russian liberalism originally had quite a close relationship to the 'legal Marxist' movement which stressed a need to follow the objective laws of history. Peter Struve, who became one of leaders of the liberal movement, once wrote as a legal Marxist and followed Plekanov's position that change in Russia would occur in two distinct stages.[33] Before socialism could be achieved, it was both necessary and inevitable that a 'bourgeois liberal revolution' take place. This dogmatic position of historical stages permeated both the Marxist and liberal movements. Weber wanted to polemicise passionately against its fatalism but he went further and struck an even more pessimistic note:

> Any sober observer would have to say that all economic indicators point in the direction of growing 'unfreedom'. It is absolutely ridiculous to attribute to high capitalism ... any elective affinity with democracy let alone liberty (in *any* sense of the word). The question should be: how can these things exist at all for any length of time under the domination of capitalism? In fact they are only possible where they are backed up by the determined *will* of a nation not to be ruled like a flock of sheep. We 'individualists' and supporters of 'democratic' institutions must swim 'against the tide' of material constellations.[34]

Some see this passage as evidence of Weber's critique of capitalism itself, arguing that he condemned the inhumanities of modern society. There is certainly a grain of truth in this – but only a grain. Weber's central argument was that 'liberty' arose from a unique and never to be repeated combination of factors. Among these factors were the socio-economic structure of Western Europe, the values of particular religions, the conquest of science and, importantly, overseas expansion. With the ending of this unique constellation, modern conditions had undermined the individualism of early capitalism and produced a more passive population. However, it was not capitalism itself which was to blame for the new serfdom but rather the exhaustion of its colonies and 'free markets'. Serfdom was growing, Weber argued, due to a combination of slowing technical and economic progress, the domination of rentier income over profit and the 'exhaustion of what remains of "free" lands and the "free markets"'.[35]

Weber did, however, acknowledge that there were features of capitalism that helped to create bureaucracy. It needed an efficient administration that responded continuously and speedily to its needs. This was true at the level of 'very large modern capitalist enterprises (which) are themselves unequalled models of bureaucratic organisation'.[36] It was also true at the level of public administration. Capitalism needed a nation state that had a rational legal system and provided it with an efficient infrastructure. In addition, the market had a levelling effect on society – militating against status differences and reducing everything to naked economic interest. In this way an elective affinity emerged between late capitalism and bureaucracy. Bureaucracy meant,

> Objective discharge of business (which) primarily means a discharge of business, according to *calculable rules* and 'without regard for persons'. 'Without regard to person' however is also the watchword of the market and, in general all pursuits of naked economic interest ... Bureaucracy develops the more perfectly, the more it is 'dehumanised', the more completely it succeeds in eliminating from official business love, hatred, and all purely personal, irrational and emotional elements which escape calculation. This is appraised as its special virtue by capitalism.[37]

Weber's liberal opposition to bureaucracy was mixed with a strong element of Nietzsche's philosophy.[38] In the wider liberal tradition, freedom is also associated with differences in wealth. It arises when men of property gain the ability to stand against the herd instincts of the masses. Liberty is thus invariably opposed to equality because it arises in the realm of 'freedom of the mind'.

PARLIAMENT AND DEMOCRACY

Weber's debt to Nietzsche came out most clearly in 'Parliament and Government in Germany' where he found new sources of bureaucratisation in the growth of mass democratic politics. Weber did not believe that parliaments represented the will of the people and held quite a jaundiced view of their role:

> Modern parliaments are assemblies representing the people who are *ruled* by the means of bureaucracy. It is, after all, a condition of the duration of any rule, even the best organised that it should enjoy a certain measure of inner assent from at least those sections of the

ruled who carry weight in society. Today parliaments are merely the means whereby this minimum of assent is made manifest.[39]

His scepticism about parliament did not spring from any concern about the influence of the corporate elite. The focus of his disdain lay in the growth of state officials whose influence increased in parliamentary democracies. These paid officials decided on the daily needs and complaints of the population and so they often became the real decision-makers rather than the politicians. The power of the officials arose from the technical need for mass administration in modern society. If this administration broke down or was temporarily suspended chaos would result. The fate of the masses literally depended on the efficient functioning of officialdom.

Alongside state officialdom, parliamentary democracy also created mass parties. Inside these parties, there was a general tendency to dispense with rule by hereditary or honoury 'notables' and replace it with rule of the paid official. Weber agreed with his friend Robert Michels that in all mass associations there was an 'Iron Law of Oligarchy' whereby effective domination rested with a small number of full-time officials.[40] People might believe their organisation to be democratic but they had little chance against a full-time apparatus that controlled knowledge and was able to dominate their moods: 'in the administration of *mass* associations the permanently appointed officials with *specialist training* always form the core of the apparatus, and its "discipline" is an absolute prerequisite of success'.[41]

Professional politicians were also a necessity in parliamentary democracy and they came in two forms – they might either be living *from* politics or living *for* politics.[42] The politician who lived *from* politics derived an income from the party and blended in more easily with the needs of the full-time officials. Those who lived *for* politics had independent means and were be able to devote themselves to pursuing their political beliefs without deriving an income from the party. The main social group that was able to assume this latter role were solicitors and barristers because they had enough money but they were not tied to running a business as entrepreneurs were. Their legal training also gave them the necessary fighting skills. Weber's elitism was undisguised as he asserted that only a person who lived for politics,

can become a politician of great stature. Naturally, this is easier for him, the more he has a fortune which gives him independence and makes him 'available', not tied to a business (as entrepreneurs are) but a person with an unearned income.[43]

In other words, only members of the upper middle class had the ability to achieve a great stature because they were not dependent on the full-time apparatus.

Only a tiny number of groups could therefore challenge the bureaucratisation of modern society. Weber singled out three particular leading roles that differed from the bureaucratic spirit pervading society – the entrepreneur, the 'real' politician and the army commander.[44] Even here, it very much depended on whether these assumed a leadership spirit or simply occupied their office. Weber certainly believed they should live up to their role because, 'the struggle for personal power and acceptance of full *personal responsibility for one's cause* which is the consequence of such power – this is the very element in which the politicians and the entrepreneur live and breathe'.[45]

On one point, however, Weber was clear: there was simply no conceivable way that the masses could resist bureaucratisation. Their fate was to be governed either by a bland cold officialdom or great leaders. Even their parliamentary representatives were effectively voting fodder for this small elite:

> It is not the many-headed assembly of parliament as such that can 'govern' and 'make' policy … The entire broad mass of deputies functions *only* as a following for the 'leader' or small group of leaders who form the cabinet and they obey them blindly as *long* as the leaders are successful. *That is how things should be.* The 'principle of the small number' (that is the superior political manoeuvrability of *small* leading groups) always rules political action. This element of 'Caesarism' is always ineradicable (in *mass states*).[46]

Weber's elitism therefore led him to the one central question that is at the core of his sociology: under what conditions can 'real leaders' emerge? His answer, which we will examine in the next chapter, showed a profound antipathy to any form of democratic values. However, before examining his proposals, let's look at his view of the tragic fate that awaited us without these leaders.

Weber was deeply pessimistic and believed that 'the future belongs to bureaucratisation'.[47] Bureaucratic administration had progressed further in Germany than elsewhere but for Weber there was no 'escape clause' left in any society that modernised.[48] The previous bureaucratic regimes of China, Egypt and the late Roman Empire were much more amateurish than their modern counterparts but, nonetheless, history knew of no instances where bureaucracy disappeared once it achieved domination. Weber noted that 'wherever the trained, specialist, modern official has once begun to rule, his power is absolutely unbreakable, because the entire organization of providing even the most basic needs in life then depends on his performance'.[49] Private capitalists might be removed but if that happened the situation would be even worse because 'private and public bureaucracies would then be merged into a single hierarchy, whereas they now operate alongside and, at least potentially, against one another, thus keeping one another in check'.[50] In brief, there was little hope because the 'congealed spirit' of modern bureaucracy was already manufacturing the housing of 'that future serfdom to which, perhaps, men may have to submit powerlessly, just like the slaves of ancient Egypt'.[51] Humanity was being dragged towards an iron cage of conformity. In this nightmarish world

> The performance of each individual worker is mathematically measured, each man becomes a little cog in the machine and aware of this, his one preoccupation is whether he becomes a bigger cog. It is horrible to think that the world would one day be filled with these little cogs, little men clinging to little jobs, and striving towards bigger ones ... this passion for bureaucracy is enough to drive one to despair.[52]

MARX ON BUREAUCRACY

This is certainly a vision of unremitting gloom yet Weber's writings on bureaucracy have been hailed for filling an important gap that Marx left out. After the collapse of the Berlin Wall in 1989, they were taken as almost prophetic. Thus Weber is credited with recognising the consequences of a culture of instrumental rationality:

> this abstraction has gone beyond capitalism itself and we will not get rid of it by changing the title deeds of property (or still less capturing state power). This is the enduring importance of Weber's analysis of rationalisation and bureaucratisation which is its ubiquitous concomitant.[53]

More generally, he offers intellectual sustenance to those who warn that every attempt to make a change from capitalism can only end up in a worse bureaucratic nightmare. The reality, however, is that Marx was more than aware of the danger of bureaucracy and there still are viable non-bureaucratic alternatives to capitalism.

One of Marx's earliest writings, 'The Critique of Hegel's Doctrine of the State', attacked Hegel's view that the state bureaucracy represented a universal class that stood over and against the conflicting interests of civil society. Marx argued that the bureaucracy advanced its own private interests and did so through the control of knowledge:

> The bureaucracy is a magic circle from which no one can escape. Its hierarchy is the hierarchy of knowledge ... The bureaucracy holds the state, the spiritual essence of society, in thrall, as its private property. The universal spirit of bureaucracy is secrecy.[54]

In his 'Civil War in France', Marx extolled the Paris Commune for doing away with bureaucracy. He noted that 'The Commune made the catchword of bourgeois revolution, cheap government, a reality by destroying the two great sources of expenditure – the standing army and state functionarism.'[55] Lenin's classic work, 'State and Revolution', returned to these writings to argue that a workers' state could barely be a state in the conventional meaning of the word. It was necessary to suppress the power of the old elite but the more successful the state was, the more this power would wither away – 'instead of the special institutions of a privileged minority (privileged officialdom, the chiefs of a standing army) the majority itself can directly fulfil these functions'.[56]

These brief points are necessary simply to indicate that Weber did not fill a gap in bureaucracy left behind by Marxists. Rather, he developed a different theory of why no *modern* society could do without bureaucracy. As Gouldner put it, his theory helped to create the 'metaphysical pathos'[57] that modern human beings were doomed to live with bureaucracy. This meant that Weber could both passionately condemn the dead weight of bureaucracy and also, in effect, offer an apology for its existence because he saw it as the only possible way of organising. His pessimism led to an injunction that no change should be attempted because no real change was possible.

In fact, he went a little further claiming the bureaucratic era removed even the possibility of revolution. He wrote that the power apparatus

> makes 'revolution', in the sense of a forceful creation of entirely new forms of authority, more and more impossible – technically, because of its control over the modern means of communication (telegraph etc) and also because of its increasingly rationalised inner structure. The place of 'revolutions' is under this process taken by coups d'etat.[58]

The notion that the powerful are just too powerful to be overthrown is a familiar argument. But Weber's timing was woeful. The First World War was, in fact, ended by the outbreak of revolution in Russia in 1917 and in Germany in 1918. When the revolution occurred in Russia, Weber claimed that it was due to 'the purely personal conduct of the Tsar' and argued that there had been no revolution 'but merely the removal of an incompetent monarch'.[59] He predicted that it would last only a few months. On this point, at least, his analysis proved to be sorely wrong.

THE WEAKNESS OF WEBER'S THEORY OF BUREAUCRACY

This particular failure might alert us to the danger of relying on highly general assertions that bureaucracy was unbeatable to explain the failure of the Russian revolution. Instead of assuming that bureaucracy was inevitable, an alternative method might be to analyse the specific historical circumstances of Russia to see why its revolution failed. Thus one might look, for example, at how bureaucratic tendencies grew from Russia's international isolation, the destruction wrought on the country by the civil war and the conflicts that arose between the peasantry and the urban workers.[60] It is not necessary to accept an 'original sin' theory of modern history.

Weber's theory of bureaucracy has another fundamental blind spot: there is no attempt to analyse bureaucracy in terms of its links to a specific class. There was simply an all-pervasive bureaucracy – rather than different bureaucracies. However, the need for bureaucracy varies according to different class interests. The ruling class needs a bureaucracy because it has to supervise the labour of others and ensure that their work effort is maintained at a regular level of intensity. Even though capitalists have to compete with each other, they also have to ensure that the state caters for the general interests of their economy – even if these conflict with the private interests of individual capitalists. The only way this can be done is through 'a rigid system of formal, hierarchically organised rules, regardless of the immediate effects these might have upon the personnel who adhere to them'.[61]

The bureaucracy in workers' organisations arises for different reasons and has altogether different effects. Trade unions are contradictory organisations because they represent both an opposition to capitalism and also an acceptance of it. In order for workers to survive, a separate bureaucratic layer emerges to negotiate with the employers and form relations of trust. These negotiations bring gains for workers but they also enforce a particular framework on workers' organisations. The union officials develop certain privileges of their own and cut back on workers' democracy to ensure that negotiated deals are not subject to the fickle moods of the masses. They come to prize the organisational apparatus from which they derive their livelihoods over all else and seek not to put it at risk. As Gramsci put it,

> The union bureaucrat conceives of industrial legality as a permanent state of affairs. He too defends it from the same viewpoint as the proprietor. He sees only chaos and wilfulness in everything that emerges from the working class. He does not understand the workers' act of rebellion against the capitalist discipline as a rebellion; he perceives only the physical act, which may in itself and for itself be trivial.[62]

In other words, whereas bureaucracy is an absolute necessity for the employers, for workers it arises from their conditional acceptance of the system and becomes a block once they move into opposition to it. However, Weber completely avoids these issues because he sees bureaucracy as a necessity for society as a whole.

IS BUREAUCRACY INEVITABLE?

This raises the question: is modern society doomed to accept bureaucracy? An alternative account to Weber's sees bureaucracies developing in societies where there is both a social division of labour *and* high levels of scarcity and restriction on human labour. A social division of labour means there is a requirement for co-ordination and administration between different sectors. However, this co-ordination will be carried out differently in class societies and non-class societies. Under capitalism, the ruling class needs a specialised bureaucratic apparatus that stands above and monitors society. In a non-class society, such a specialised apparatus is no longer *necessary*. Self-administration becomes a real possibility.

Bureaucracy, however, could persist if people do not have enough free time or cultural resources to take part in the general affairs of society. A radical shortening of the working day could create opening for new methods of organisation where the majority of people could combine work with self-administration. It would also require a challenge to the division of labour established in capitalist society between mental and manual labour. The whole structure of work under capitalism is based on separating the functions of conception and planning from execution. The former becomes the preserve of management who centralise knowledge about how work is to be organised and pass it out as orders to their staff. [63] This division between mental and manual labour pervades the whole of society, with education for the majority often consisting of rote learning and passive acceptance of the 'facts' while education for the elite stresses confidence, leadership skill and analysis. The majority in society are trained to believe that administration is for others – they are 'not paid to think'. A conscious struggle against these patterns is a requirement for eliminating bureaucracy.

Of course, time constraints and limited cultural resources are not the only obstacles to self-administration. The persistence of scarcity in the basic goods required by society always gives rise to privileged minorities who undertake to distribute those goods according to specific rules – and award themselves in the process. Trotsky put this well in his analysis of the Russian bureaucracy:

> The basis of the bureaucratic rule is the poverty of society in objects of consumption, with the resulting struggle of each against all. When there are enough goods in a store, the purchasers can come when they want to. When there are few goods, the purchasers are compelled to stand in line. When the lines are very long, it is necessary to appoint a policeman to keep order.[64]

The development of the productive forces so that this level of scarcity is removed is also a requirement for eliminating bureaucracy.

Weber's gloomy belief that there will always be bureaucracy reflects the outlook of liberal capitalists who need a specialised administrative apparatus for their system but who also dislike the restrictions it places on their 'market freedom'. A less ideological view might hold that while bureaucracy cannot be abolished overnight, there is a host of measures which can be taken to reduce, curb and eventually eliminate its dominance.

Weber's dismissal of self-administration springs from his elitism and market fundamentalism. The economic man of liberal theory is taken as an absolute so people have only self-interests and are naturally apathetic about public states of affairs. Their withdrawal from public life means they have to either submit to great leaders or passively accept bureaucracies. However, the separation of private interests from public interests is linked to lack of control over the resources of society. As Mandel has pointed out, if the majority of people had really the power to decide on issues which shaped their lives, they would have an interest in collective forms of self-administration:

> If a quarterly residents' meeting decides on the provision of adequate heating for the block or neighbourhood, will the relevant household really not be motivated to attend? Is it not also their concern at what frequency buses run in a given area, or where the stops are located? Do they not have vital interest in the workloads and rhythms of their workplace? Are they indifferent to the choice of canteen food at their office or factory, or their children's school? Are they passive on such general questions as pollution in their town and the relationship between their money income and the price of accommodation, food, holidays or public transport (insofar as these are not yet distributed free of charge)? And will they not feel moved to act to defend the guarantee of full employment?[65]

The real issue is not the ability of humans to administer themselves – it is how much of society do they collectively control. In other words, whether there is both economic and political democracy.

CONCLUSION

Weber has little in common with any form of left-wing thought. He uses the theory of marginal utility to rule out questions about the usefulness of production for the majority of society. Instead, he sees society as an aggregate of individual interests and desires. This leads to a robust defence of private ownership of the means of production. Like a true ideologist, Weber in his justification for private ownership barely touches on the question of whose interest it really serves. Rather he defends capitalist control as a more rational form of production. Despite making a distinction between formal and substantive rationality, Weber, in practice, identifies formal rationality as his master concept. This involves an excessive emphasis on quantitative measurement as the criterion for rationality – rather than asking the most basic question: why is anything produced and does it serve the interests of society as a whole?

Weber's theory of bureaucracy is much more sophisticated than the normal arguments raised by small businesspeople about 'red tape'. His argument has the merit of not assuming that bureaucracy is the exclusive preserve of state-owned firms. He acknowledges quite forcefully that large private enterprises need an extensive bureaucracy. However, his pessimism about the spread of bureaucracy leads back into an elitist approach. Parliamentary democracy is scorned and deemed to be only of use when it produced great leaders. There is no critique that parliamentary structures are not democratic enough.

His abiding legacy is to promote a view that bureaucracy is inevitable. This fits neatly with the later 'Animal Farm' notion of revolution – the more things changes, the more they become a bureaucratic nightmare. However, Weber makes no distinction between the different types of bureaucracies that emerge in workers' movements and in wider society. He does not seek the roots of bureaucracy in any material factors – or in cultures that deny the capacity of the majority to administer themselves. He assumes apathy is a permanent state of affairs and can simply not explain how the process of revolt is possible.

10
War and Revolution

On 4 August 1914, the German Kaiser appeared at his Berlin palace to announce that his country was at war and that henceforth, he 'recognised no parties only Germans'.[1] Soon war fever was everywhere as the population were subjected to a steady diet of propaganda warning that hordes of Russians were massing for an attack. The frenzied enthusiasm spilled onto the streets as rumours abounded among mobs who hunted for 'Russian spies' and French 'bomb makers'. Young men rushed to enlist for the front in large numbers.

Just over a week before the declaration of war, the Social Democratic Party had denounced war. Socialist mass meetings had adopted strongly worded resolutions stating that 'The warmongers must realise that if a war breaks out with all its sufferings and atrocities, the political and economic crisis caused by it will inevitably ... powerfully accelerate the development of the capitalist order towards socialism.'[2] Leading party officials such as Friedrich Ebert transferred large sums of money to Switzerland in preparation for a crackdown. However, within days, the opposition of the SPD dissipated. The party had become an electoral machine and feared annihilation at the polls. Its huge bureaucratic apparatus, which employed 11,000 people, stood on the point of destruction. The old fears of Russia and the desire to stand by 'the fatherland' in its hour of danger won out.

This chapter examines how the founding father of sociology responded to these momentous events. War tests the responses of all intellectual systems like nothing else. It is not possible to bracket out Weber's support for the First World War as something which belonged to his time and was divorced from his more general sociological analysis. As we have tried to illustrate, Weber's elitism and his imperialist attitude pervaded his sociology.

A WONDERFUL WAR

August 1914 was a defining moment for Max Weber as he embraced the cause of war. In fact, according to his wife, Marianne, he positively celebrated, thanking his lucky stars for having let him live to see the war. He wrote, 'for no matter what the outcome – *this war is great and wonderful'*.[3] His only regret was that he could not go to the front but instead had to serve as a disciplinary officer with the Military Hospitals Commission of the Reserve Corps. The war eventually touched Weber personally when his younger brother Karl was killed in 1915 but even this did not dim his enthusiasm. He wrote that 'he had a beautiful death in the only place where it is worthy to be a human being at the moment'.[4]

Weber's support for the war should come as no surprise because all his life he had advocated a form of liberal imperialism. He had argued that Germany needed to become a truly great world power and this would entail military strength and prowess. As early as the Freiburg address in 1896 he had chastised those who did not face the reality that military strength had to supplement economic greatness. Germany had certainly expanded dramatically in the decades before 1914. Between 1870 and 1913 its coal production grew by seven times, its steel expanded five fold, and its overall GNP by six times.[5] This expansion brought it into direct conflict with the dominant empire of the day, Britain. The First World War arose from the deep-seated conflicts that had been brewing between the rival powers in Europe since the end of the nineteenth century. Weber regretted that an accommodation could not have been reached with Britain but he still thought it was the destiny of great powers to fight for their honour. Drawing a sharp contrast with 'lesser nations' such as the Swiss or the Danes, he proclaimed,

Because we are a people of seventy and not seven million, because by contrast with those small nations we therefore tip the scales of history with our weight, it is our bounden duty ... to history ... to pit ourselves against the swamping of the entire world by those two powers (England and Russia). The *honour* of our people bade us not to shrink this duty in a cowardly and slothful manner; this war is being fought for *honour*, not for changes in the map and economic gains.[6]

When the war started, few of the politicians and military commanders believed that it would last long. Schliefen, the first German chief of staff, thought a long war inconceivable. His successor, Moltke, thought the conflict would last two years. The government's economic calculations assumed a nine-month war.[7] Weber also was firmly convinced that a short war was necessary for German stability because he had little confidence in the leadership qualities of the Kaiser. He also feared that the sacrifices of war would breed the spirit of revolution if it lasted too long and when the war continued against expectations, Weber's pessimism grew. He intervened ever more sharply to seek more modest war aims but his attacks on the bombast and rhetoric of the ultra conservatives were entirely tactical. He never flinched in his support for war and sometimes even reversed his position if he thought his tactical criticisms lent comfort to the enemy.

Weber's fear of a long war proved quite realistic. Germany's central weakness was that it was dependent on imported raw materials and it soon experienced a shortage of labour. Few provisions had been made to sustain the enormous waste of manpower or the problems caused by the Allied blockade. At the start of the war, 5 million men were enlisted but this gradually rose to 11 million or 16.5 per cent of the population.[8] In the famous 'turnip winter' of 1916, food distribution in cities virtually broke down and many who had supported the war originally began to turn against its horrors. In May 1916, for example, revolutionary socialists led by Rosa Luxemburg and Karl Liebknect called a demonstration of several thousand in Berlin. When Liebknect was arrested in its aftermath, 55,000 workers struck in solidarity.[9] Weber resolutely opposed the strikes while arguing within elite circles for a curtailment of war aims. His fear was that the new accommodation which had been forged between the SPD and the political establishment would be lost in the flames of revolution. In his view Germany had at last a 'mature' working-class movement that was integrated in the framework of great power politics.

WEBER'S MODERATION

From early in 1915 a debate broke out in Germany about the conduct of the war. The German army had smashed through Belgium but had come to a standstill at the battle of the Marne. The Western front barely moved more than ten miles either way for the rest of the war. One group around the pan-Germans called for the annexation of Belgium and its transformation into a vassal state of Germany, which supplied it with raw materials. Leading industrialists such as Hugo Stinnes supported this policy of permanent conquest and argued that the ore deposits of Normandy should be plundered for German interests.[10] This group also called for a policy of unrestricted submarine warfare to enforce a blockade on Britain by attacking merchant ships but this threatened to involve the US on Britain's side. It was therefore opposed by the Chancellor, Bethmann-Hollweg, who claimed that 'if Germany resorts to such methods, the whole world will kill it like a mad dog'.[11] The debate over the issue of submarine warfare eventually led to the resignation of the naval minister Admiral Tirpitz who believed that his prime minister was too soft.

Weber intervened actively in these debates to encourage a policy of moderation. He rejected the annexation of Belgium and signed a letter opposing the agitation of the pan-Germans. But while resisting annexation and permanent occupation, Weber still believed that Belgium should be used as a 'pawn'[12] in future negotiations. He opposed the unrestricted use of submarine warfare but his concern had little to do with moral considerations – he believed that American intervention would be disastrous for Germany. He thought advocates of unrestricted use of submarine warfare were succumbing to moods of desperation rather than engaging in clear-sighted thinking about how victory could be won. He wrote, for example, that 'people with courage and strong nerves are not the ones that scurried behind the submarine warfare demagoguery, but hysterically weak people who were no longer able to bear the burden of war'.[13] Thus his opposition to particular tactics never signified any lessening of his enthusiasm to pursue the war to victory.

Weber was in practice a supporter of Bethmann-Hollweg. He wrote in July 1916, that 'next to the military leadership, the *current chancellor deserves* credit in every trench'[14] and he regarded his policies as the best tactical options. By limiting the aims and avoiding a conflict with America, Weber thought that a German victory could be secured. His objection to dragging out the war was expressed in a letter to Naumann:

> Today, the most important question is how it will be ever *possible* to agree to a 'peace'; since the dragging on of the war means: (1) the multiplication of those on pension: 40–50 million more in fixed pensions applied against German means; 2) a lack of capital for the use of areas that may be annexed; (3) the weaning of the nation from the adjustment to work; (4) the passage of economic supremacy to America.[15]

Here Weber's support for war is mixed in with the traditional concern of the modern bourgeoisie about paying its costs. He wanted war to further the great power ambitions of Germany but he dreaded the cost that German capitalism might have to pay for a long war.

Weber's desire to achieve German hegemony on the cheap was evident in his discussion on desirable conquests. Like most other advocates of empire, he took it as an unquestioned assumption that Germany had a right to 'the delineation of colonial spheres of influence in the uncivilised regions of Africa'.[16] However, he also thought that the major gains for Germany were not to be found in this continent. His main ambition was to reach a future understanding with Britain and to concentrate on spreading German domination into Central and Eastern Europe.[17] He considered a strategy of expansion into Western Europe to be highly unrealistic as it would unite Britain and France against Germany. The primary enemy was Russia and he, therefore, advocated a reorganisation of Central and Eastern Europe under German hegemony.

Weber was quite specific about what this strategy entailed. He wanted first to 'liberate' a number of smaller nations such as Lithuania, Latvia and the Ukraine from the Russian yoke. Instead of full independence, they were to be granted a wide-ranging form of autonomy, which kept in them in an association with the German Reich. Weber demanded, for example, the right to maintain German garrisons in Latvia and Lithuania and a tariff union which tied these countries to the German economy. Whereas in the past Weber had urged the closing of the eastern German frontiers to Polish migrants he now advocated a peculiar form of Polish 'independence'. The new 'free' Poland was to grant Germany the right to maintain fortifications on its eastern border, stretching northward from Warsaw. It was also to be enmeshed in 'an indissoluble, permanent [Central European] union of states with a common army, trade policy [and] tariffs'[18] under German domination. Weber's enthusiasm for this course led him to join Naumann's Arbeitsausschuss fur Mitteleuropa, a grouping that promoted this particular imperialist project.

Weber's pro-war activities are clearly an embarrassment to those who wish to portray him as an ardent liberal who championed a value-free sociology. The traditional defence is to assume that there are two Webers – a professional sociologist who could work away on research on the world religions while the guns of war blared and another who had a personal standpoint which was influenced by the society he lived in. This separation of the professional and the personal will not do, because Weber's sociology is not divorced from arguments that led him to support the war. His academic work also reflects an obsession with great power relations, an imperialist outlook and a virulent opposition to Marxism.

Moreover, Weber was not just a passive receptacle of the pro-war mood in German society – he was an active creator and advocate of it. Millions of working people were certainly caught up in war hysteria in August 1914 but the privations of war and the terrible suffering shook many out of it. Weber, however, continued to support the war to the very end. Even when the German Reich appeared on the point of collapse, Weber argued for a national guerrilla war to continue the conflict. He urged young nationalist students to risk imprisonment and summary trials to ensure that 'the first Polish official who dares enter Danzig will be met by a bullet'.[19] When Germany was forced to sign the humiliating Versailles Treaty, Weber still did not give up. He told a trusted student that he had no further political plans 'except to concentrate all my intellectual strength on the one problem, how to get once more for Germany a great general staff'.[20] He had many tactical disagreements about the conduct of war, but his sole concern was with the strategies that might guarantee victory for Germany and stability for its society afterwards. Far from merely reflecting the war hysteria, he was an advisor to the German elite who created that sentiment. He virulently opposed the only force that brought the terrible carnage of the First World War to a halt – the revolutions in both Russia and Germany.

THE RUSSIAN REVOLUTIONS

Few people had expected a revolution to break out in Russia. In January 1917, Lenin told a meeting of young Germans 'We of the older generation may not live to see the decisive battles of the coming revolution.'[21] Six weeks later on International Women's Day – which was celebrated in Russia on 23 February – a protest of working women over bread prices in Petrograd turned into a massive 400,000-strong strike. Soldiers sent in to break the revolt fraternised with the workers and eventually came over to their side. On the morning of 2 March, the all-powerful Tsar of Russia abdicated and two competing sources of power emerged. On the one hand, there were workers' delegates, drawn together in workers' councils or soviets, which were modelled on the revolution of 1905. On the other hand, there were the official liberal politicians from the Duma, a truncated parliament elected under a system of suffrage, which radically discriminated against the working class. The latter eventually formed the government and nominated Kerensky, one of their number with the most radical of credentials, to head it up. However, as Kerensky's regime failed to solve the decisive issues which produced the revolution – those of land, peace and bread – support ebbed away to his left. By November 1917, the Bolsheviks had won a majority in the soviets and under the battle cry 'All Power to the Soviets' staged a successful insurrection.

Weber's attitude to the February Revolution was dismissive. Formally, he wrote an article entitled 'Russia's Transition to Pseudo Democracy', which purported to provide an objective analysis of the events. In reality, he was motivated by a deep fear that German workers might emulate the example of their Russian counterparts. To counter this possibility, he produced a highly torturous, tendentious piece that got it wrong on many points. Bizarrely, he claimed that no revolution could survive without the involvement of the bourgeoisie because they alone could guarantee it creditworthiness. He claimed that what had occurred in Russia was that the bourgeois intelligentsia had joined the revolt because they opposed the behaviour of the Tsar. Their intervention was, apparently, far more decisive than the actions of the thousands of workers who struck and risked their lives to fraternise with the troops. The socialist element in the revolution, Weber argued, was doomed to play the role of 'second fiddle and are happily tolerated in that role because they provide the illusion of the revolutionary character for the government'.[22]

The February Revolution had, therefore, only produced a pseudo democracy and Russian society was still dominated by imperialist interests who wanted to dominate other foreign nations. Their only hope was that German socialists might be fooled into thinking that more genuine peace moves were afoot:

> With an army of negroes, ghurkas and all the barbarian rabble in the world standing at our borders, half crazed with rage, lust for vengeance and the craving to devastate our country, they [Russia] assume that German Social Democracy will still be a party to the fraudulence of the present Russian Duma plutocracy and, morally speaking, stab the army which is protecting our country from savage nations in the back.[23]

Weber had a point about the incomplete nature of the February Revolution but he was attacking it from the right not the left – in the name of his own imperialism. The aim of his article was to discourage a rapprochement between German socialists and Russian revolutionaries. To reach this conclusion he had to play down the self-activity of Russia workers and to see them as pawns in the hands of bourgeois intellectuals.

The subsequent revolution in October – or November in the Russian calendar – proved just how wrong Weber's analysis was. And the mistake did not just occur because Weber was producing an immediate journalistic account. Weber's whole sociology rested on the notion that power elites were the real subjects of history and the masses were inevitably passive. The very notion that workers who were organised through soviets and through a mass party such as the Bolsheviks could seize power was anathema to him. He therefore claimed that the new revolution was 'a pure military dictatorship, only one of corporals rather than generals'[24] and predicted that it could only last a few months.

Weber's concerns about links between German socialists and Russian revolutionaries grew as peace negotiations opened between the Russian government and the German General Staff at Brest-Litovsk in December 1917. The Russian revolutionaries were determined to spread the message of peace to rank-and-file soldiers and workers in the warring nations. This desire was symbolised by Karl Radek, who distributed anti-war pamphlets among German soldiers right in front of the diplomats and officials sent to conduct negotiations at Bresk-Litovsk. By contrast, Weber claimed that the only thing which had changed in Russia was that 'Bolshevik soldier imperialism' had replaced 'Russian popular imperialism'.[25] He defended the German delegation who demanded vast swathes of lands of the old Russian empire in return for peace, claiming that 'it is impossible to conclude a peace with ideological fanaticism. It is only possible to neutralize it and that was the intention of the ultimatum and the dictated Brest-Litovsk peace settlement'.[26]

THE GERMAN REVOLUTION

However, anti-war pressure was growing in Germany itself. In Austria, a quarter of a million workers struck after the negotiations at Brest-Litovsk appeared to break down. Workers' councils were elected which demanded an end to censorship, martial law and the release of the imprisoned socialist Friedrich Adler. Hundreds of thousands of German workers also struck in solidarity. Weber's answer was to urge immediate changes in the nature of the regime. He called for an end to the three-class suffrage system in Prussia and the development of a full parliamentary system in Germany. However, his respect for democratic values was limited. He believed that the war had exposed the weakness of a political structure that rested on aristocratic domination and wanted a change to full-scale bourgeois rule. The 'parliamentarization' of Germany was the only way to preserve stability and to ward off the danger of revolution. Three days after the outbreak of strikes in Vienna, he claimed that 'parliamentarization is also the only way to save the dynasty and the monarch, for the current regime is heading for catastrophe both at home and abroad'.[27]

Weber was a least correct on the latter point. By November 1918, the German High Command was desperate and tried suddenly to conclude an immediate armistice with its enemies but was repulsed. Its Austrian ally had collapsed as huge crowds tore down the emblems of its monarchy, the heirs to the 1,200-year-old Holy Roman Empire. In one last desperate move, the German High Command ordered their naval fleet to sail against Britain but the sailors were not prepared to risk death for a discredited elite. In Kiel, sailors armed themselves, marched through the town alongside striking dockers and established a soldiers' council. The fuse for the German revolution had been lit. By 6 November, the north-west of Germany had been conquered by the revolution. In Munich, revolutionaries took over the royal palace and nominated Kurt Eisner as Prime Minister of the Bavarian Free State. On 9 November it was Berlin's turn. Here, as vast crowds began to assemble, the SPD finally moved sharply left.

With the tacit agreement of the pro-war authorities, the SPD placed itself at the head of the movement, declaring a general strike – four hours after it had already begun. While the veteran anti-war activists were calling for a socialist republic and world revolution, SPD ministers from the former government proclaimed a republic. A joint revolutionary government was established composed of the pro-war majority SPD and the anti-war Independent Socialists. The Kaiser fled to Holland but within 24 hours of the establishment of the new regime, its Prime Minister, Ebert, was on the phone to General Groner of the military High Command to agree a strategy to restore order.

Weber was outraged by these events. He had hoped that Wilhelm II might abdicate to save the monarchy and blamed his failure to do so for the onset of revolution. However, he was also adamant about defending the old order. Even in the midst of the November Revolution, he stood by generals Ludendorf and Hindenburg from the Imperial High Command, claiming that 'he who insults our commanders in chief in the hour of defeat is a cur'.[28] A day after the Kiel rebellion began, Weber gave a speech in Munich, where he appealed to 'instincts of manly self preservation in the face of the enemy and to the will for the preservation of the Reich'.[29] He denounced the growing revolt as 'a bloody carnival that does not deserve the honourable name of a revolution'.[30] Later he argued that the revolution had knocked weapons out of Germany's hands and was responsible for selling the country out to alien rule.[31] He denounced the workers' councils that had sprung up all over Germany and disliked how the new government in Berlin related to these councils. He claimed that the government was 'carrying out a policy of hatred, or has to do so since it must defer to the demagogues and has no troops that it can depend upon. You can work with people as individuals, but as a mass they are stupid, as always.'[32]

Despite his abhorrence of the revolutionary process, Weber soon recognised that the SPD had become a force for order. As soon as they had ensconced themselves in power through the use of left rhetoric, the SPD leaders worked assiduously to construct a new army that could break the revolt. Leaders such as Noske co-operated with the General Staff in the formation the Frei Korps, a highly paid privileged layer of right-wing officers and troops. As masses of people moved further left, the SPD prepared for a crackdown on the 'extremists' to break the revolution. Weber quickly understood the tactical manoeuvres and for a brief period began to adopt a left rhetoric. He claimed that 'he was very close to the views of many Social Democratic leaders who had received some training in economics'[33] and even made vague references to the socialisation of the economy.

ATTACKING THE REVOLUTIONARY LEFT

This flirtation with the workers' council movement did not last long. Weber's main aim was to attack the forces of the revolutionary left. He claimed that

What is decisive now is whether the crazy Liebknecht gang will be kept down. They are going to make their putsch; that cannot be changed. But what matters is that it be put down quickly and that it be followed by level headed policies rather than wildly reactionary ones.[34]

From December 1918, Weber came out more openly against the government giving support to the workers' councils. He charged that they encouraged 'a shameless lack of discipline and looting and made it impossible ... to oppose the Poles even in regions inhabited only by Germans'.[35] They had indulged 'pathological personalities such as Liebknecht' and instead of forming a coalition with liberal bourgeois parties, they had tolerated in their midst 'unclean elements' such as the anti-war independent socialist Hugo Haase and Emil Barth, one the leaders of the left-wing shop stewards movement. Above all 'they do not recognise ... the *currently* inevitable need for bourgeois help, or at least they only lay claim to it in a form that makes it *impossible* for an honest man to put himself in their service'.[36]

In January 1919, as the crisis matured, Weber embarked on a speaking tour to rally the more conservative forces. He launched tirades against the revolutionary socialists, claiming for example that 'Liebknecht belongs in the madhouse and Rosa Luxemburg in the zoo.'[37] This type of hysterical propaganda was quite typical of right-wing forces that were planning to put down the far left forcibly. He denounced the 'stupid hatred of the domestic entrepreneurs, the only result of which will be that *foreign* capital will control the German economy'.[38] In brief, Weber placed himself firmly on the side of bourgeois order.

Once the Spartacist revolution had been crushed in January 1919, Weber was able to return to the more conventional calmer waters of elite politics. At the suggestion of Prince Max of Baden, he joined with other intellectuals in preparing a detailed German reply to an Allied memorandum on German war guilt. He accompanied the German peace delegation to the Versailles Treaty and agonised about his country signing the Treaty. By October 1919, he was, once again, worrying about 'the preservation *of the traditions of our military science instruction in spite of* the ban of the *peace treaty*'.[39] When a parliamentary commission was established to look into the origins of war, Weber objected when that there too many Jewish people represented on it. His wife claimed that he remained opposed to anti-Semitism to the end of his life, but he regretted that 'in those days there were so many Jews among the revolutionary leaders'[40] and so claimed it would be better if they stepped aside from such a commission.

It is sometimes assumed that towards the end of his life Weber dropped his passionate nationalism and embraced a more liberal pluralism. Such a belief, of course, rests on the assumption that there is a dichotomy between nationalism and liberalism. This dichotomy seems more apparent when the term nationalism is applied to the activities of smaller countries that resist colonial oppression rather than to the activities of great powers. In Weber's case, there is no evidence of a transition from nationalism to liberalism. He remained to the very end a passionate defender of the war effort of Germany, even though 2 million of his compatriots lost their lives and 4 million were wounded in its senseless slaughter. He denounced those Germans who acknowledged any form of war guilt or criticised the generals who were responsible for the slaughter. After Germany's defeat, his prime interest lay in restoring the army and its traditions of 'military science'. He saw not the slightest irony in attacking the 'violence' of the revolutionary left while advocating policies to restore the power of the German High Command.

Weber's liberalism was summarised in one bizarre incident in 1920 when he was attacked by right-wing students for criticising the pardoning of Count Arco, the assassin of the Bavarian revolutionary leader Kurt Eisner. Weber made it clear that he thought Arco's conduct was 'chivalrous and manly' in court.[41] He also agreed with Arco's argument that Eisner's actions brought disgrace to Germany. However, he was against the assassination because Eisner had been turned into a martyr in people's hearts and the pardoning of Arco would mean that 'political murders will become the fashion'.[42] In brief, Weber's liberalism amounted to saying that it was the task of the legitimate authorities to suppress the left. Weber's own work was designed to create the intellectual conditions for such suppression – the proper authorities would do the rest.

ON SOCIALISM

Weber's ideological attacks on the left during the war and the revolutionary crisis should not be divorced from his sociology – rather, the pressure of events forced him to bring out the bitter political logic of that sociology. Instead of the implicit, relatively oblique attacks on Marxism, which characterised monographs like *The Protestant Ethic*, there was now a full frontal assault. But this assault continued to draw on his wider sociological theories, which had been developed in the previous decades. This is illustrated by his article 'On Socialism'.

This article was an address to army officers in Vienna in 1918 on the ideological arguments against socialism. The invitation to speak came from a military intelligence section known as the 'Section for the Defence against Enemy Propaganda'.[43] Vienna at the time was rapidly entering the throes of revolution and even though the strikes in January 1918 had been defeated, they clearly worried the officer corps. 'Enemy propaganda' in this instance did not, therefore, refer to the 'Russian hordes' but to the enemy within Vienna itself.

Weber was clearly aware of the propaganda work being undertaken by the army officers. His lecture started off by referring to the 'work of enlightenment'[44] – a euphemism for political propaganda – being conducted by the officers. He mentioned that he often travelled in third-class carriages of trains and listened to the talk of men returning from the front. On the basis of these conversations, he warned the officers that 'enlightenment practised in the wrong way could perhaps damage the authority of the officer'.[45] Specifically, he warned them to ensure that their propaganda did not appear as party propaganda and he advised them to move away from the cruder right-wing attacks on SPD officials. They should recognise that 'we now stand on a good footing with the trade unions'[46] as a result of the formal recognition bestowed on them by the German government during the war years. Weber's aim was to provide the officers with a better understanding of socialism so that they could be more effective in their attacks.

Weber argued that socialism arose in opposition to the discipline imposed on the proletariat by modern industry. Socialists had claimed that the suffering of workers resulted from their separation from the means of production. In fact, according to Weber, the same style of discipline was imposed in armies, universities and offices. It existed, therefore, due,

> Partly to purely technical considerations, to the nature of modern means of operation – machines, artillery and so on – but partly simply to the greater efficiency of this kind of human co-operation …. In any event, it is a serious mistake to think that this separation of the worker from the means of production is something peculiar to industry, and moreover, to *private* industry.[47]

Ruling elites often claim that their rule has nothing to do with personal greed or aggrandisement – but is simply a technical necessity. The mere fact that Weber drew on a body of sociology to make the same case does not alter this fact. However, he never explained what possible reasons of 'technical efficiency' required the mass of people to be permanently bossed around so that a small elite could maintain their life of privilege.

Weber's next argument was that the *Communist Manifesto* represented a set of prophecies which had been disproved. It had predicted the 'immiseration of the working class' – but this had not occurred. It had predicted the growing concentration of capital so that a few entrepreneurs dominated each sector making it easier to expropriate them – but again Weber claimed that the prophecy had not happened. Finally, it had predicted that capitalism would enter a series of economic crises which would lay the basis for revolutionary upheavals. Weber, however, claimed that the growth of cartels had changed this because they undermined the tendency towards overproduction.

Weber's refutation of each of the three arguments was shoddy at best. He acknowledged that the prediction about the 'immiseration' of the working class was not central to Marx and Engels' argument but never addressed the more central claim that capitalism had a tendency to reduce the share of the overall economy going to workers in favour of capitalists. In other words, that it tended to increase the rate of exploitation.

His denial of the tendency for a concentration of capital is palpably wrong. In Weber's own period, there was an enormous growth in monopolies in the US and in cartels in Germany. Since then, the process has accelerated. Expropriating the tiny number of large capitalists has in fact technically become much simpler than in Marx's day.

Weber's argument that business cycles would disappear with the growth of cartels was also proved wrong. Less than a decade after his death, the Wall Street Crash reaped devastation on much of the advanced industrial world. And a full 80 years after his prediction about the disappearance of the business cycle no less a figure than Edward Mortimer of the *Financial Times* could gloomily pronounce that 'Marx and Engels described a world economy more like that of 1998 than 1848.'[48]

Alongside these arguments, Weber claimed that the growth of large-scale industry would not lead to a united working class which could confront capitalism. The spread of shareholding capitalism and state enterprises was, instead, creating a vast army of 'officials' who had different interests from the working class. By officials, Weber meant white-collar employees. It was in this context that he advanced his own prognosis that 'it is the dictatorship of the official, not that of the worker, which, for the present time at any rate, is on the advance'.[49]

However, as we have seen, the link between white-collar employees and a privileged bureaucratic stratum is tenuous. The nature of capitalism has been precisely to undermine the privileges and conditions of office workers and to subject them to ever-growing pressure to raise productivity and to suffer growing insecurity.

Finally, Weber informed the army officers about the different varieties of socialism and urged them to pinpoint the main enemy, which he referred to as 'syndicalism'. He claimed, with some justification, that orthodox Marxism in Germany had based itself on the dogma of evolution. By this was understood a theory that socialism could not come into existence until capitalist society had fully matured. The Russian revolutionaries and the 'syndicalists' who advocated a general strike had broken from this dogma. The Russian Revolution was attempting to hop over the bourgeois stage of development and therefore Weber urged the army officers to ask what was such a revolution designed to achieve, as according to orthodox Marxism, socialism was impossible in a backward country.[50]

This was a relatively clever attempt to exploit the conflicts within Western labour movements about the Russian Revolution. Nevertheless, Weber was ill-equipped even to understand its ethos. Whereas mechanistic Marxists such as Karl Kautsky had argued that socialism could only be achieved in each individual country after capitalism was fully developed, the Bolsheviks changed the paradigm by focussing on a global economy which imperialism had created. The theoretical justification for the Bolshevik Revolution was that capitalism *internationally* had more than matured – as the war demonstrated – and that the Russian Revolution was the springboard for an international challenge to capitalism. Weber's nationalism made it exceedingly difficult even to comprehend this fundamentally internationalist spirit. He was therefore forced to rely on torturous caricatures to distort the actual project of the socialist revolutionaries.

POLITICS AS A VOCATION

These distortions are most evident in Weber's celebrated work, 'Politics as a Vocation'. In this article, which originated in a series of lectures to the Union of Free Students in 1919, he claimed revolutionary socialists, 'espoused a principle which one might characterise thus:

"If the choice lies between a few more years of war, followed by a revolution and peace now but no revolution, we choose a few more years of war"'.[51]

This cynical piece of propaganda is disproved by the mere fact that Rosa Luxemburg and Karl Liebknecht opposed the war from the start when there was little chance of revolution. Luxemburg's *Junius Pamphlet* positively resonates with outrage at the horror of war – while Weber was celebrating its virtues. Luxemburg received a harsh period of imprisonment for her efforts – while Weber, enjoyed a more elevated status in official German society for his support for the carnage. The briefest reading of Luxemburg will demonstrate that she opposed war for its own sake – with the same passion with which Weber defended it.

In an attempt to disparage the efforts of revolutionaries, Weber introduced a bizarre distinction between two sorts of ethics – the 'ethic of principled conviction' and the 'ethic of responsibility':

> There is a profound opposition between acting by the maxim of the ethic of conviction (putting it in religious terms: 'The Christian does what is right and places the outcome in God's hands') and acting by the maxim of the ethic of responsibility, which means one must answer for the (foreseeable) *consequences* of one's action.[52]

The 'ethic of principled conviction' was associated with the morality espoused in the sermon of Jesus Christ known as the Sermon on the Mount. According to Weber, this morality had to be accepted in its entirety, which specifically meant not going on strike since strikes are a form of coercion; not using weapons; not talking about 'revolution' since it means violence. Rather oddly, 'the ethic of principled conviction' was also supposed to include 'the syndicalists' who refused to accept the framework of contemporary politics and who, according to Weber, professed to follow absolute ends. As these 'syndicalists' did not abstain from strikes or attempted revolutions, they were, apparently, inconsistent! The alternative for Weber was to accept 'the ethic of responsibility' which meant making choices within the framework of the existing status quo. However, as we have seen, this particular ethic for Weber himself amounted to offering tactical advice on the conduct of war – rather than opposing war itself.

Although sometimes hailed as a major work 'Politics as a Vocation' clearly contains an odd argument because it seeks to make a piece of Christian theology into a universal article of faith. The aim of the verbal tricks and dichotomies is to claim that if one is not willing to abide by an absolute form of pacifism and love, then one must accept the existing order. Like his hero Dostoyevsky, Weber implies that those who follow 'absolute ends' take no account of the consequences of their actions: 'if evil consequences flow from an action done out of pure conviction, this type of person holds the world, not the doer, responsible'.[53] However, all of this merely reflects the conflicts in Weber's own mind between his religious background and his acceptance of a disenchanted world. It has precious little to do with the mind frame of revolutionaries. Far from claiming to follow an absolutist morality, they simply believed a better world was possible.

THE DEATH OF A LIBERAL

As social tension grew in the war years, Weber advocated a parliamentary system in Germany as a way of stabilising the existing order. He stated that 'we demand the "democratisation" (as it is called) of German political institutions as an indispensable means for securing unity of the nation ... and Parliamentary government as a guarantee of uniformity in the direction of policy'.[54] Mommsen has stressed the limited nature of Weber's support for parliamentary democracy, stating that 'Lukács' pointed judgement that for Weber democratisation was only a "technical means to achieve a better functioning imperialism", is very difficult to quarrel with.'[55]

However, even this technical support for parliamentary democracy was blown apart in the post-war years when Weber came to argue for a form of plebiscitary democracy. Under this system, the people would be granted a formal choice of electing a leader who then reigned supreme over parliament and selected his government at will. Weber hoped that this constitutional structure would produce great charismatic leaders who could rally the nation. He had become profoundly disillusioned with the actual functioning of parliament claiming that it was composed of people 'who operate under an imperative mandate from economic interests'.[56] It had become in 1919 'a "banausic" assembly, incapable in any sense of providing a selection ground for political leaders'.[57] Weber had hoped that parliament could function like a gladiatorial contest to produce great political warriors who could lead the nation but when German society was riven by class conflict the space for gladiatorial games was limited. A strong man was now required to impose his will:

the only choice lies between leadership democracy with a
'machine' and democracy without a leader, which means rule by
the 'professional politician' who has no vocation, the type of man
who lacks precisely those inner, charismatic qualities, which make
a leader.[58]

Leadership democracy meant the rule of a great man who did not
live *from* politics but *for* politics. Because he had independent means,
he could face up to the bureaucracy and subjugate it to his will.
Leaderless democracy by contrast was rule by politicians who lived
off politics and so were dependent on the political machine and its
bureaucracy. Once again, Weber's framework was entirely conservative
and elitist as the key problem was how could great leaders be found.
Weber claimed that with mass suffrage 'a Caesarist plebiscitarian
element in politics – the dictator of the battlefield of elections – had
appeared on the plain'.[59]

Weber's cult of leadership – which runs right through his whole
sociology – was now given a free rein. He claimed that 'True democracy
means, not a helpless surrender to (parliamentary) cliques, but
submission to a leader whom the people have elected themselves.'[60]
Just what that submission might entail was outlined in a dialogue
between Weber and Ludendorff on the nature of democracy, which
Weber's wife, Marianne, recounts.

> *Ludendorff*: What is your idea of democracy, then?
> *Weber*: In a democracy the people choose a leader whom they trust.
> Then the chosen man says, 'Now shut your mouths and obey me.'
> The people and the parties are no longer free to interfere in the
> leader's business.
> *Ludendorff*: I could like such a 'democracy'!
> *Weber*: Later the people can sit in judgement. If the leader has made
> mistake – to the gallows with him! ...[61]

Not only were the mass of people to be treated as pliant putty in the
hands of great leaders, but even the political activists who surrounded
such leaders were to be reduced to yes-men and yes-women. Weber
explained the new role of the party apparatus as follows:

> The leadership of parties by plebiscitary rulers means the
> 'depersonalisation' of the followers, their spiritual proletarization,
> one could say. In order to be useful as an apparatus for the

leader they must be blindly obedient machines in the American sense and not beholden to the vanities and pretensions of party functionaries ...That is the price that must be paid for the leadership of leaders.[62]

CONCLUSION

Weber's embrace of authoritarianism illustrates the classic dilemma of all liberals. There is room for democracy, tolerance, debate and dissension – as long as there is a fundamental consensus about the maintenance of the existing order. As soon as a real challenge emerges to that order, as occurred in post-war Germany, the room for dissent vanishes. Capitalism required a 'strong man' who could demand unquestioned obedience. And Weber understood this more than most – hence the death of his liberalism.

Herbert Marcuse has aptly summarised the irony and contradictions inherent in Weber's final arguments. Weber, he argued, had set out to solve social contradiction with a 'plebiscitary democracy.'

In which trained (and terrorised) masses install their own leaders, periodically ratify their position and even determine their policy – under prescribed conditions carefully controlled by the leaders. Thus, for Weber, universal franchise is not only a result of domination, but also an *instrument* of domination in the period of technical perfection. Plebiscitary democracy is the political expression of irrationality turned to reason.[63]

11
Conclusion

'The present age and its presentation of itself is dominantly Weberian', Alasdair MacIntyre once wrote.[1]

Max Weber is certainly not short of devoted admirers. He is often seen as a value-free sociologist who rose above petty party conflicts. Divorced from a specific political and social context, his work can appear sufficiently ambiguous to attract support from both the left and the right.

Weber's concept of rationality, for example, was taken up by Georg Lukács in his celebrated discussion on 'Reification and the Consciousness of the Proletariat'. The young Lukács was part of the Max Weber Circle in Heidelberg but whereas Weber supported the war and attacked the Russian Revolution, Lukács drew opposite conclusions and became a fully-fledged Marxist.[2] In his essay on Reification, he attacked a system whereby social relations appeared to have a 'thing like' quality that was beyond human control. He referred to Weber's view that modern capitalism needed an administration whose workings could be rationally calculated 'just as the probable performance of the machine can be calculated'.[3] Later Lukács became one of the most trenchant critics of Weber but for some, his earlier sympathetic references appeared to show that Weber's sociology might be integrated into a wider critique of the present order. Thus, Keller has suggested that Weber played an important role in the development of critical theory, particularly in the hands of Adorno, Horkeimer and Habermas.[4]

However, the aim of this book has been to challenge this ambiguity and to see Weber as a sophisticated ideologue for capitalism. He drew a fundamental link between the market and rationality and saw any interference with the private ownership of capital as irrational. He was concerned about the bureaucracy of late capitalism and was disappointed by the political immaturity of the capitalist class in his native Germany. Yet, these concerns did not lead to a wider critique of a system based on exploitation. Quite the opposite. Weber sought to awaken the German bourgeoisie to a sense of its heroic mission by romanticising the origins of capitalism and creating an image of the moral entrepreneur. He naturalised the imperialist outlook of his day by blaming the religious cultures of colonised countries for why they had to be colonised. More fundamentally, his peculiar view of rationality conveyed an impression that capitalism and bureaucracy were inevitable.

Weber's most famous book, *The Protestant Ethic and the Spirit of Capitalism*, located the origins of the present economic order in the ethos of the early Protestant sects. The story of slavery, the theft of common lands, the ruthless economic terrorism used to turn peasants into workers virtually disappeared. Instead, the activities of religious virtuosos who sought to honour God in the daily world of work moved centre stage. Early capitalists, Weber stoutly asserted, were above all moral and honest. In a revealing argument about why it was the Protestant sects rather than the Jews who were responsible, he claimed that 'their superior, religiously-determined ethics gave them superiority over the competition of the godless according to the principle "honesty is best policy"'.[5] The Puritan never placed himself at the disposition of

> colonial capitalism, of the state purveyor, ancient tax- and custom farmer, or monopolist. These specific forms of ancient, non-European and pre-bourgeois capitalism to him were ethically objectionable and God disapproved forms of brutal accumulation of money.[6]

Ideologues often try to create myths about the origins of their favoured nation or social groups. In Weber's case, the myth arose from a method of 'reading off' social behaviour from religious texts. Little consideration was given to the contradictory ways in which people interpreted these texts and instead a thought experiment was conducted so that the 'logic' of Reformation texts was illuminated. The entrepreneur arose because Protestants took the higher morality reserved for clergy in monasteries and brought it into the daily world of work. The capitalist was the embodiment of the rationalisation of religious ethics. Throughout Weber's writings, there is nostalgia for this lost world. He worried that the mission of the early entrepreneurs was being lost under a tide of bureaucracy and hoped for charismatic leaders who could break through the 'iron cage'.

In his sociology, Weber was a methodological individualist. He was deeply influenced by the marginalist school of economics, which stressed that the value of commodities was derived from subjective estimations. Weber generalised this outlook into a meta-theory of society. Individuals and their cultural universe were the starting point for any analysis and could be accessed through the *Verstehen* method. Instead of a focus on social structures, sociology had to start from how the acting individual attached meanings to his or her behaviour. The result was often a highly formal method, which showed many affinities with conventional economics. Weber's sociology was full of careful, formal definitions and of typologies but the content to fill these categories was often drawn at random from very diverse phases of history. Thus, the meaning of the term charismatic leadership was stretched to cover such diverse groups as bounty hunters, monarchs and revolutionary socialists – from the dawn of time to the early twentieth century.

Although values held by individuals were central to Weber's sociology, these could not be subject to critical scrutiny. Values were fundamental, irreducible and beyond any objective analysis. Weber did not accept that there might be a rationality which arose from wider social needs and which could be used to judge the value choices of the individual. Yet, society does face a choice about whether the subjective needs of a millionaire for an extra yacht should be equivalent to the demand for food from thousands of impoverished people. Under the name of value-free research, Weber tried to grant the atomised individual of the free market immunity from criticism. In reality, he only smuggled in the dominant political values of the present order.

Weber's defence of individualism sat uneasily with his enthusiastic advocacy of 'great power politics'. From his inaugural address as Professor in Freiburg to his political writings during and after the First World War, he was an ardent supporter of German imperialism. He wanted his country to be 'a nation of masters' rather than becoming the equivalent of Switzerland. His nationalism, his advocacy of war, his support for Germany gaining more 'elbow room' are often deemed irrelevant to his wider more 'academic' sociology. Worse, there are plain distortions such as the extraordinary claim that Weber helped sociology to 'break from Eurocentric ideas'.[7] However, Weber's imperialism deeply affected his sociology, distorting how he viewed non-European countries such as China and India.

Weber toyed with – but ultimately rejected – explanations of national differences based on biological heredity.[8] However, if he rejected socio-biological explanations of 'race' differences, he still held that there were superior and inferior national cultures. In the case of the Poles, he thought that their 'inferior'culture might allow them to survive harsher economic conditions to the disadvantage of German agricultural labourers. He used the most specious of arguments to suggest that the Chinese were incapable of logical thinking because of the nature of their language. He assumed that the people of India were incapable of nationhood unlike European peoples. These claims did not appear simply as throwaway comments – they went right to the heart of Weber's analysis of colonised societies because he naturalised their conquest. Throughout his analysis of why India and China failed to develop, there is no discussion on the role of colonialism. It is as if it belonged to the natural order of things. So his discussion on Indian society ranges from the earliest origins of civilisation right up to the contemporary period, yet there is not one single reference to the East India Company.

This failure even to acknowledge the impact of colonialism meant that Weber uncritically accepted the views of missionaries and colonial adventurers as objective. China and India were presented as unchanging societies, imprisoned in a cultural time warp until colonialism arrived. The technological and commercial developments of these two countries were played down. There was no real appreciation of how economic developments in China far surpassed those of Europe before the mid seventeenth century. A rigid caste structure was assumed to be primordial in India, stretching back to the early religious texts. There was no attempt to analyse the caste structure as the outcome of a complex interaction between colonial intervention and indigenous tradition. The religions of China and India were, thus, abstracted from their social and economic foundations and held up as implicitly less rational than the superior ethics of Protestantism. Weber's legacy has lived on in the sociology of development in the writings of Cold War ideologues such as Walter Rostow who blamed the cultures of underdeveloped countries for their failure to modernise. Unfortunately, it still reaches students of today in the packaged form of sociology textbooks which construct the spurious debate between 'modernisation theory' and 'dependency theory'.

Mommsen has suggested that Weber 'comes close to the modern concept of "social imperialism" as a manipulative strategy of ruling elites designed to defend their own privileged positions in the existing social system and to forestall the imminent rise of the working class'.[9] Weber's political ambition was to see a mature working class in Germany, which co-operated with a re-energised bourgeoisie in building a great nation. The major obstacle to this was the Marxist politics of the SPD and he therefore sought to challenge this influence. Instead of a direct attack, there were often attempts to develop a more 'sophisticated' alternative while making oblique reference to Marxist arguments. Thus, Weber's celebrated distinction between 'the ethic of principled conviction' and the 'ethic of responsibility' appears at first sight to be rooted in Christian theology and to contain a sophisticated discussion on how religious ethics deal with the evilness of the world. However, Weber's actual target in 1919 was revolutionary socialists, who were referred to obscurely as 'syndicalists'. The point of the distinction was to lay the now familiar charge that these revolutionary 'extremists' cared little about human suffering compared with those who worked inside the existing order. Weber's argument, however, would have been stronger if his own 'ethic of responsibility' had not led to support for the carnage that was the first World War!

Weber's sophisticated attack on Marxism has become the staple diet of modern sociology. His discussion on 'Class, Status and Party – compiled from fragmentary notes in two different volumes on *Economy and Society* – forms the central core of most modules on stratification. Typically, a dry formal account of Marx's 'two-class model' versus Weber's 'multi-class model' is presented. As Weber introduces a more sophisticated discussion of 'status' distinctions, he is deemed the implicit winner. What is often neglected is that Marx's theory was based on the concept of exploitation whereas Weber saw social class as only a collection of individual life chances formed in the market place. Important implications follow from this crucial conceptual distinction. Weber's focus on market transactions meant that, rather oddly, he claimed that slaves were not a class purely because they did not live in a market economy. Similarly, because he dismissed the idea of exploitation he treated 'work effort as primarily a problem of economic rationality (and) directs class analysis towards a set of normative concerns centred on the interest of capitalists: efficiency and rationalization'.[10] The issue is not that Marx had a political agenda whereas Weber had a more objective and sophisticated account. Rather that by dismissing the issue of exploitation, Weber wrote from the vantage point of a supporter of capitalism.

Weber's discussion on status has achieved even more prominence in sociology. Yet the confusion that stemmed from Weber's original conceptual framework has barely been untangled. He tended to use the concept of status in relation to both feudal estates in pre-market societies and 'the educated' strata or white-collar employees of modern capitalism. The legacy of this confusion is that sociologists have often seen much a greater separation between white-collar and blue-collar employees than actually exists. This might have been understandable in Weber's day but today the majority of routine white-collar employees face higher levels of exploitation and control at work. Stress, insecurity and low wages form the core experience of many white-collar employees and not surprisingly many have joined unions. Imprisoned within a Weberian framework, however, many conventional sociologists tend to see this grouping as 'middle class' and as having different interests to the older manual working-class movement. Yet, a sociology that started from the central conception of exploitation might have a greater appreciation of the growing cynicism and resistance of white-collar employees to 'flexibility' and 'performance enhancement'.

In the years after the fall of the USSR and the East European regimes, Weber's standing grew amongst sociologists. Yet, ironically, the elitist bent in his sociology led to a poor appreciation of the possibility of revolt. His 'ruler-centric' focus played down the role of masses of people in bringing change. The dialectic of history, for Weber, was torn between bureaucratisation and charismatic leaders who acted as spellbinders for a passive population. Revolts of whatever kind – particularly those in highly-bureaucratised societies – simply did not figure in his vision.

Despite all this, Weber's warning on bureaucracy was taken as prophetic. His implicit claim that the capitalist, the army general and the charismatic leader offered the main safeguarded against bureaucracy was barely examined. His writings fitted neatly with the dominant view that a change from capitalism would only lead to bureaucratic nightmares. This, however, was always an ideological assumption because Weber was convinced that genuine rule by the people was an impossibility. He gave limited support to parliamentary democracy, seeing it more as a gladiatorial chamber that might produce great leaders. He saw any participation by workers in their own enterprise as a recipe for inefficiency and irrationality. His implicit contempt for the self-activity of masses of 'ordinary people' led to an overarching pessimism that ultimately justified an acceptance of capitalism and bureaucracy.

Up until recently, market fundamentalism and the argument about 'the end of history' reigned supreme. Only small numbers held onto the hope that 'another world was possible' – a world based on greater democracy and equality. Since 1999, with the great Seattle protest, though, much has changed. Outside academia, there is a ferment of discussion and debate about how there might be an alternative to capitalism and what it might look like. Across the globe millions have marched against war, debt, environmental decay and for workers' rights. The ivory towers of academia have only just begun to awaken to the clamour. Inside the discipline of sociology, the hegemony of Weberian sociology has provided a shutter against this new storm. It has justified an intellectual pessimism that tries to put down the new radicalism. But the time has come to lift the shutter and let the light – and the wind – in.

Notes

1 INTRODUCTION

1. I. Horowitz, *The Decomposition of Sociology* (Oxford: Oxford University Press, 1994), p. 13.
2. Ibid.
3. P. Bourdieu, *Acts of Resistance: Against the New Myths of Our Time* (Cambridge: Polity, 1998), p. 34.
4. A. Giddens, *The Third Way: The Renewal of Social Democracy* (Cambridge: Polity, 1998), pp. 43–44.
5. T. Bilton, K. Bonnet, P. Jones, T. Lawson, D. Skinner, M. Stanworth and A. Webster, *Introducing Sociology* (London: Palgrave, 2002), p. 185.
6. Max Weber, *Economy and Society Vol. 2* (Berkeley: University of California Press, 1978), p. 919.
7. G. Schroeter, 'Max Weber as Outsider: His Nominal Influence on German Sociology in the Twenties' *Journal of the History of the Behavioural Sciences* Vol. 16, 1980, pp. 317–32.
8. D. Kaesler, 'From Academic Outsider to Sociological Mastermind: The Fashioning of the Sociological "Classic" Max Weber', paper delivered to UCD Department of Sociology, 2002, p. 3.
9. W. Mommsen, *The Political and Social Theory of Max Weber* (Cambridge: Polity, 1989), p. 171.
10. Kaesler, 'From Academic Outsider to Sociological Mastermind', p. 2.
11. Mommsen, *The Political and Social Theory of Max Weber*, p. 170.
12. Mommsen, *Max Weber and German Politics 1890–1920* (Chicago: University of Chicago Press, 1984), p. xix–xx.
13. Ibid. p. 263.
14. B.S. Turner, *The Talcott Parsons Reader* (Oxford: Blackwell, 1999), p. 2.
15. A. Gouldner, *The Coming Crisis of Western Sociology* (London: Heinemann, 1971), p. 149.
16. Ibid. p. 149.
17. Ibid. p. 146.
18. T. Parsons, 'The Circumstances of My Encounter with Max Weber' in R. Merton and M.W. Riley (eds), *Sociological Traditions from Generation to Generation: Glimpses of the American Experience* (Norwood: Ablex Publishing, 1980), p. 38.
19. T. Parsons, *The Structure of Social Action* (Glencoe: Free Press, 1949), p. 721.
20. Gouldner, *The Coming Crisis of Western Sociology* p. 177.
21. Parsons, 'The Circumstances of My Encounter with Max Weber', p. 42.
22. J. Cohen, L. Hazelbrigg and W. Pope, 'DeParsonizing Weber: A Critique of Parsons' Interpretation of Weber's Sociology' *American Sociological Review* Vol. 40, No. 2, 1975, pp. 229–41.

23. K. Tribe, 'Translator's Introduction' in W. Hennis, *Max Weber, Essays in Reconstruction* (London: Allen and Unwin, 1988), p. 8.
24. E. Shils, 'Max Weber and the World since 1920', in W. Mommsen and J. Oesterhammel (eds), *Max Weber and His Contemporaries* (London: Allen and Unwin, 1987), p. 547.
25. Ibid. p. 552.
26. Ibid. p. 554.
27. S. M. Lipset, 'The End of Ideology', in C. Waxman (ed.), *The End of Ideology Debate* (New York: Simon and Schuster, 1969), p. 69.
28. D. Bell, *The End of Ideology: On the Exhaustion of Political Ideas in the Fifties* (New York: Free Press, 1960), p. 279.
29. Ibid. p. 280.
30. H.H. Gerth and C.W. Mills, 'Introduction: The Man and His Work' in *From Max Weber: Essays in Sociology* (London: Routledge and Kegan Paul, 1948), p. 41.
31. Ibid p. 41.
32. Ibid p. 41.
33. Ibid p. 41.
34. Ibid p. 73.
35. Ibid p. 49.
36. Ibid p. 73.
37. E.V. Schneider, 'The Sociology of C. Wright Mills' in J. Alexander, R. Boudon and M. Cherkaoui (eds), *The Classical Tradition in Sociology: The American Tradition* (London: Sage, 1997), p. 279.
38. Kaesler, 'From Academic Outsider to Sociological Mastermind', p. 15.
39. G. Roth, 'Political Critiques of Max Weber: Some Implications for Political Sociology' *American Sociological Review* Vol. 30, No. 2, 1965, pp. 213–23.
40. D. MacRae, *Weber* (Glasgow: Fontana/Collins, 1974), p. 14.
41. P. Hirst, *Social Evolution and Sociological Categories* (London: Allen and Unwin, 1976), Chapter 7.
42. T. Bottomore, *Sociology and Socialism* (Brighton: Harvester, 1984), p. 132.
43. See A. Seligman, *The Idea of Civil Society* (New York: Free Press, 1992) and J. Femia, 'Civil Society and the Marxist Tradition' in S. Kaviraj and S. Khilnani (eds), *Civil Society: History and Possibilities* (Cambridge: Cambridge University Press, 2001), pp. 131–46.
44. W. Hennis, *Max Weber, Essay in Reconstruction* (London: Allen and Unwin, 1988), p. 21.
45. A. Gouldner, *For Sociology* (London: Allen Lane, 1973), p. 14.

2 THE SOCIOLOGIST OF EMPIRE

1. Quoted in W. Mommsen 'Max Weber as a Critic of Marx' *Canadian Journal of Sociology* Vol. 2, 1977, p. 373–98. Reprinted in P. Hamilton, *Max Weber, Critical Assessments* (London: Routledge, 1991), p. 115.
2. Max Weber 'The National State and Economic Policy' (Freiburg Address) in K. Tribe, *Reading Weber* (London: Routledge, 1989), p. 204.

3. Marianne Weber, *Max Weber: A Biography* (New York: John Wiley, 1975), Chapter 2.
4. Ibid. p. 132.
5. Ibid. p. 133.
6. M. Sturmer, *The German Empire 1871–1919* (London: Weidenfeld and Nicolson, 2000), p. 53.
7. Weber, *Max Weber*, p. 135.
8. W. Mommsen, *Max Weber and German Politics 1890–1920* (Chicago: University of Chicago Press, 1984), p. 55.
9. Weber, 'The National State and Economic Policy', p. 203.
10. D. Blackbourn, *Fontana History of Germany 1780–1918:The Long Nineteenth Century* (London: HarperCollins, 1997), p. 332.
11. Sturmer, *The German Empire*, p. 69.
12. Blackbourn, *Fontana History of Germany*, p. 333.
13. J. Sheehan, *German Liberalism in the Nineteenth Century* (London: Methuen, 1982), p. 275.
14. D. Beetham, *Max Weber and the Theory of Modern Politics* (London: Allen and Unwin, 1974), p. 128.
15. Mommsen, *Max Weber and German Politics*, p. 137.
16. Ibid, p. 139.
17. Quoted in G. Mann, *The History of Germany Since 1789*, (Harmondsworth: Penguin, 1974), p. 434.
18. See P. Theiner, 'Friedrich Naumann and Max Weber: Aspects of a Political Partnership' in W. Mommsen and J. Osterhammel (eds), *Max Weber and His Contemporaries* (London: Allen and Unwin, 1987), pp. 299–310.
19. Beetham, *Max Weber and the Theory of Modern Politics*, p. 134.
20. Max Weber, 'Germany as an Industrial State' in Tribe, *Reading Weber*, p. 214.
21. Ibid. p. 214.
22. Ibid. p. 218.
23. Ibid. p. 213.
24. Max Weber, 'Developmental Tendencies in the Situation of East Elbian Rural Labourers' in Tribe, *Reading Weber*, p. 159.
25. Quoted in K. Tribe, 'Prussian Agriculture – German Politics: Max Weber 1892–7 in *Reading Weber*, p. 112.
26. Ibid. p. 114.
27. Weber, 'Developmental Tendencies' p. 182.
28. Tribe, 'Prussian Agriculture', p. 115.
29. W. Falk, 'Democracy and Capitalism in Max Weber's Sociology' *Sociological Review* Vol. 27, 1935, pp. 373–93.
30. Max Weber, 'Parliament and Government in Germany' in *Political Writings* (Cambridge: Cambridge University Press, 1994), p. 269.
31. K. Marx and F. Engels, *Collected Works Vol. 8* (London: Lawrence and Wishart, 1975), p. 162.
32. G. Eley, 'The British Model and the German Road: Re-Thinking the Concept of German History before 1914' in D. Blackbourn and G. Eley (eds), *The Peculiarities of German History* (Oxford: Oxford University Press, 1984), p. 84–5.
33. Weber, 'Germany as an Industrial State', p. 215.

34. Beetham, *Max Weber and the Theory of Modern Politics*, p. 160.

35. W. Hennis, '"A Science of Man". Max Weber and the Political Economy of the German Historical School' in *Max Weber, Essays in Re-Construction* (London: Allen and Unwin, 1988), pp. 107–45.

36. See M. Schon, 'Gustav Schmoller and Max Weber' in Mommsen and Osterhammel, *Max Weber and His Contemporaries*, pp. 59–70.

37. Weber 'The National State and Economic Policy', p. 196–7.

38. Ibid. p. 198.

39. Ibid. p. 194.

40. Ibid. p. 194.

41. Ibid. p. 203.

42. Ibid. p. 202.

43. Ibid. p. 204.

44. Ibid. p. 202.

45. Ibid. p. 197.

46. Ibid. p. 198.

47. Ibid. p. 207.

48. V. Berghahn, *Imperial Germany 1871–1914*, (Oxford: Berghahn Books, 1994) p. 336.

49. See 'Erfurt Programme' in S. Miller and H. Potthoff, *A History of German Social Democracy* (New York: St Martin's Press, 1986), p. 240–2.

50. W. Mommsen, 'Robert Michels and Max Weber: Moral Conviction versus the Politics of Responsibility' in Mommsen and Osterhammel, *Max Weber and His Contemporaries*, p. 129.

51. Ibid. p. 131.

52. Ibid. p. 127.

53. L. Trotsky, *The Permanent Revolution* (London: New Park, 1982), pp. 161–254.

54. Beetham, *Max Weber and The Theory of Modern Politics*, p. 161.

55. Max Weber, *The Russian Revolution* (Cambridge: Polity, 1995), pp. 103–4.

56. Mommsen, *Max Weber and German Politics*, p. 88.

57. Ibid p. 88.

58. Weber 'The National State and Economic Policy', p. 207.

59. Mommsen, 'Robert Michels and Max Weber', p. 125.

60. Mommsen, *Max Weber and German Politics*, p. 122.

61. Ibid p. 112.

62. Sturmer, *The German Empire*, p. 51.

63. Max Weber, 'Socialism' in *Political Writings*, p. 288.

64. G. Lukács, *The Destruction of Reason* (London: Merlin Press, 1980), p. 608.

65. A. Giddens, *Politics and Sociology in the Thought of Max Weber* (London: Macmillan, 1972), p. 9.

3 THE SPIRIT OF CAPITALISM

1. Quoted in G. Therborn, *Science, Class and Society* (London: New Left Books, 1976), p. 306.

2. W. Sombart, *The Jews and Modern Capitalism* (Glencoe: Free Press, 1951).
3. W. Mommsen, *Max Weber and German Politics* (Chicago: University of Chicago Press, 1984), p. 13.
4. Marianne Weber, *Max Weber: A Biography*, (New York: John Wiley, 1975), p. 298.
5. Ibid. p. 299.
6. E. Said, *Orientalism* (Harmondsworth: Penguin, 1978), p. 1.
7. Max Weber, *The Protestant Ethic and the Spirit of Capitalism* (New York: Charles Scribner's Sons, 1976), p. 17.
8. Ibid.
9. Ibid.
10. T. Friedman, *The Lexus and the Olive Tree* (New York: Farrar, Strauss and Giroux, 2000), p. 464.
11. Weber, *The Protestant Ethic*, p. 21.
12. Ibid. pp. 30–1.
13. Ibid. p. 38.
14. Ibid. p. 49.
15. Ibid. p. 53.
16. Ibid. pp. 61–2.
17. Ibid. p. 111.
18. Ibid. p. 117.
19. Ibid. p. 121.
20. Ibid. p. 171.
21. Ibid. p. 172.
22. Ibid. p. 177.
23. Ibid. p. 166.
24. Ibid. p. 166.
25. Max Weber, 'The Protestant Sects and the Sprit of Capitalism' in H.H. Gerth and C.W. Mills, *From Max Weber: Essays in Sociology* (London: Routledge and Kegan Paul, 1948), p. 305.
26. Ibid. p. 313.
27. Weber, *The Protestant Ethic*, p. 55.
28. Ibid. p. 183.
29. A. Giddens, 'Marx, Weber and the Development of Capitalism' *Sociology* Vol. 4, No. 4, 1970, p. 303.
30. Weber, *The Protestant Ethic*, p. 90.
31. T. Parsons, *The Structure of Social Action* (Glencoe: Free Press, 1949), p. 533.
32. G. Kolko, 'A Critique of Max Weber's Philosophy of History' *Ethics* Vol. 70, No. 1, 1959, pp. 1–20.
33. See E. Fischoff 'The Protestant Ethic and the Spirit of Capitalism: The History of a Controversy', *Social Research* Vol. 2, No. 1, 1944, pp. 53–77 for some of this type of criticisms.
34. H. Heller, *The Conquest of Poverty: The Calvinist Revolt in 16ᵗʰ Century France* (Leiden: Brill, 1986), p. 70.
35. C. Scott Dixon, 'Narratives of the German Reformation' in *The German Reformation* (Oxford: Blackwell, 1999), p. 2.

36. G. Strauss, *Manifestations of Discontent in Germany on the Eve of the Reformation* (Bloomington: Indiana University Press, 1971), p. ix.

37. P. Blicke, 'Reformation and the Communal Spirit' in Dixon, *The German Reformation*, p. 139.

38. T.A. Brady, 'The Reformation of the Common Man 1521–1524' in Dixon, *The German Reformation*, p. 96.

39. 'Treaty of the Erfurt Town Council with the Clergy, 29 July 1521' in P. Johnston and B. Scribner (eds), *The Reformation in Germany and Switzerland* (Cambridge: Cambridge University Press, 1993), p. 38.

40. C. Hill, 'Protestantism and the Rise of Capitalism', in E.J. Fischer (ed.), *Essays in Economic and Social History of Tudor and Stuart England* (Cambridge: Cambridge University Press, 1961), p. 35–6.

41. P.C. Walker, 'Capitalism and Reformation', in B. Turner, *Max Weber: Critical Responses Vol. 3* (London: Routledge, 1999), p. 224. Walker's article was published in the *Economic History Review* Vol. 8, No. 1, 1937, pp. 1–19.

42. A. Hyma, 'Calvinism and Capitalism in the Netherlands 1555–1700' *Journal of Modern History* Vol. 10, 1938, pp. 321–43.

43. C. George and K. George, 'Protestantism and Capitalism in Pre-Revolutionary England' *Church History*, Vol. 27, 1958, pp. 351–71.

44. C. Hill, *The World Turned Upside Down* (Harmondsworth: Penguin, 1975), pp. 50–6.

45. R.H. Tawney, *Religion and the Rise of Capitalism* (New York: Mentor Books, 1954), p. 99.

46. Quoted in C. Harman, *A People's History of the World* (London: Bookmarks, 1999), p. 188.

47. G. Kolko, 'Max Weber on America: Theory and Evidence' in G.H. Nadel (ed.), *Studies in the Philosophy of History* (New York: Harper and Row, 1965), p. 193.

48. Ibid. p 139.

49. H.M. Robertson, *The Rise of Economic Individualism* (Cambridge: Cambridge University Press, 1935), p. 15.

50. See M. Dobb, *Studies in the Development of Capitalism*, (London: Routledge and Kegan Paul, 1963), Chapter 4.

51. Hill, 'Protestantism and the Rise of Capitalism', p. 36.

52. G. Lukács, *The Destruction of Reason* (London: Merlin Press, 1980), p. 606.

53. Weber, *The Protestant Ethic*, p. 68.

54. Ibid. p. 68.

55. K. Marx, *Capital Vol. 1* (Harmondsworth: Penguin, 1976) p. 895.

56. See P. Linebough, *The London Hanged: Crime and Civil Society in the 18th Century* (Harmondsworth: Penguin, 1991).

57. See E.P. Thompson, 'Time Discipline and Industrial Capitalism' *Past and Present* Vol. 38, No. 1 1967, pp. 56–97.

4 WHY DIDN'T ASIA DEVELOP

1. Quoted in A. Toussaint, *The History of the Indian Ocean* (London: Routledge and Kegan Paul, 1966), p. 150.

2. H. Gerth and D. Martindale, 'Prefatory Note' to Max Weber, *The Religion of India* (New York: Free Press, 1958), p. v.
3. Max Weber, *Economy and Society Vol. 1*, (Berkeley: University of California Press, 1978), p. 552.
4. Ibid. p. 552.
5. Ibid. p. 553.
6. Ibid. p. 553.
7. Ibid. p. 556.
8. Weber, *The Religion of India*, p. 4.
9. Ibid. p. 4.
10. Ibid. p. 38.
11. Ibid. p. 60.
12. Ibid. p. 119.
13. Ibid. p. 120.
14. Ibid. p. 121.
15. Ibid. p. 122.
16. Ibid. p. 122.
17. Ibid. p. 16.
18. Ibid. p. 104.
19. Ibid. p. 11.
20. Ibid. p. 331.
21. Ibid. p. 336.
22. W. Rostow, *The Stages of Economic Growth: A Non-Communist Manifesto* (Cambridge: Cambridge University Press, 1971).
23. Ibid. p. 28.
24. N.B. Dirks, *Castes of Mind: Colonialism and the Making of Modern India* (Princeton: Princeton University Press, 2001), p. 50.
25. Quoted in T. Metcalf, *Ideologies of the Raj* (Cambridge: Cambridge University Press, 1994), p. 86.
26. Weber, *The Religion of India*, p. 124.
27. Ibid., p. 337.
28. Ibid p. 325.
29. Ibid p. 341.
30. Ibid.
31. L. Dumont, *Religion, Politics and History in India* (Paris: Mouton, 1970), p. 47.
32. Quoted in G. Raheja, 'India: Caste, Kinship and Dominance Reconsidered' *Annual Review of Anthropology* Vol. 17, 1988 p. 498.
33. S. Schaar, 'Orientalism at the Service of Imperialism' *Race and Class* Vol. 21, No. 1, 1979, pp. 67–80.
34. R. Inden, 'Orientalist Constructions of India' *Modern Asian Studies* Vol. 20, No. 3, 1986, p. 403.
35. S. Pollock, 'Deep Orientalism? Notes on Sanskrit and Power beyond Raj' in C.A. Breckenridge and P. Van der Veer, *Orientalism and Post-Colonial Predicament* (Philadelphia: University of Pennsylvania Press, 1993), p. 82.
36. A. Abdel-Malek, 'Orientalism in Crisis' *Diogenes* No. 44, Winter 1963, pp. 104–12.

37. K. Gillion, *Almedabad: A Study in Indian Urban History* (Berkeley: University of California Press, 1968).
38. C.A. Bayley, 'Indian Merchants in a "Traditional Setting": Benares, 1780–1830' in C. Dewey and R.C. Hopkins (eds), *The Imperial Impact: Studies in the Economic History of Africa and India* (London: Athlone Press, 1978), pp. 192–3.
39. M.N. Pearson, *Merchants and Rulers in Gujarat* (Berkeley: University of California Press, 1976).
40. T. Raychaudhuri and I. Habib 'Foreign Trade' in *The Cambridge Economic History of India Vol. 1 1200–1750* (Cambridge: Cambridge University Press, 1982) pp. 382–433.
41. S. Malik, *Understanding Indian Civilization* (Simla: Indian Institute for Advanced Studies, 1975), Chapter 7.
42. G.R. Madan, *Western Sociologists on Indian Society* (London: Routledge and Kegan Paul, 1979), p. 125.
43. Raychaudhuri and Habib, 'Foreign Trade', p. 395.
44. D. Rothermind, *An Economic History of India* (London: Croom Helm, 1988), p. 16.
45. A.K. Bagchi 'Foreign Capital and Economic Development in India: A Schematic View' in K. Gough and H. Sharn, *Imperialism and Revolution in South East Asia* (New York: Monthly Review Press, 1973), p. 46.
46. Rothermind, *Economic History*, p. 32–3.
47. M. Davis, *Late Victorian Holocausts* (London: Verso, 2001), p. 312.
48. Metcalf, *Ideologies of the Raj*, p. 134.
49. Dirks, *Castes of Mind*, p. 5.
50. Ibid. p. 177.
51. N.B. Dirks, *The Hollow Crown, Ethnohistory of an Indian Kingdom* (Cambridge: Cambridge University Press, 1987).
52. Quoted in Dirks, *Castes of Mind*, p. 211.
53. See B.S. Cohn, 'Notes on the History of the Study of Indian Society and Culture' in M. Singer, B.S. Cohn, *Structure and Change in Indian Society* (Chicago: Aldine, 1968), pp. 3–28.
54. Max Weber, *The Religion of China* (New York: Free Press, 1951), p.14.
55. Ibid. p. 26.
56. Ibid. p. 91.
57. Ibid. p. 27.
58. Ibid. p. 55.
59. Ibid. pp. 61–2.
60. Ibid. p. 114.
61. Ibid. p. 121.
62. Ibid. p. 132.
63. Ibid. p. 142.
64. Ibid. p. 231.
65. Ibid. p. 231.
66. Ibid. p. 231.
67. Ibid. p. 232.
68. Ibid. p. 124.
69. Ibid. p. 125.
70. Ibid. p. 127.

71. W. Rodzinski, *The Walled Kingdom* (London: Fontana, 1984), p. 148.
72. J.A.G. Roberts, *China: Prehistory to the Nineteenth Century* (Stroud, Gloucestershire: Sutton Publishing, 1996), p. 192.
73. J. Gernet, *A History of Chinese Civilization* (Cambridge: Cambridge University Press, 1982) pp. 437–8.
74. P.B. Ebrey, *Family and Property in Sung China: Yuan Ts'ai's Precepts for Social Life* (Princeton: Princeton University Press, 1984), p. 129.
75. F. Wakeman, 'China and the Seventeenth Century Crisis' *Late Imperial China* Vol. 7, No. 1, June 1986, pp. 1–26.
76. Weber, *The Religion of China*, p. 219.
77. Rodzinski, *The Walled Kingdom*, p. 188.
78. Weber, *The Religion of China*, p. 247.

5 METHODOLOGY

1. See F. Ringer, *Max Weber's Methodology* (Cambridge: Massachusetts: Harvard University Press, 1997), Chapter 1.
2. See F. Ringer, *Decline of German Mandarins: The German Academic Community 1890–1933* (Hanover, New Hampshire: Wesleyan University Press, 1990).
3. See N. Bukharin, *The Economic Theory of the Leisure Class* (New York: Augustus M. Kelly, 1970).
4. Quoted in P. Razzell, 'The Protestant Ethic and the Spirit of Capitalism: A Natural Scientific Critique' *British Journal of Sociology* Vol. 28, No. 1, 1997, pp. 17–37.
5. Max Weber, *Economy and Society Vol. 1* (Berkeley: University of California Press, 1978) p. 4.
6. Ibid.
7. Max Weber, *The Methodology of the Social Sciences* (New York: Free Press, 1949) p. 76.
8. Max Weber, 'Science as a Vocation' in H.H. Gerth and C.W. Mills (eds), *From Max Weber: Essays in Sociology* (London: Routledge and Kegan Paul, 1948), p. 147.
9. Weber, *The Methodology of The Social Sciences*, pp. 17–18.
10. Max Weber, *Roscher and Knies: The Logical Problems of Historical Economics* (New York: Free Press 1975), p. 129.
11. Ibid. p. 125.
12. Weber, *The Methodology of the Social Sciences*, p. 60.
13. Ibid. p. 55.
14. W. Mommsen, *Max Weber and German Politics 1890–1920* (Chicago: University of Chicago Press, 1984), p. 8.
15. Max Weber, *On Universities: The Power of the State and the Dignity of the Academic Calling in Imperial Germany* (Chicago: University of Chicago Press, 1974), p. 20.
16. Ibid. p. 22.
17. A. Gouldner, *For Sociology* (London: Allen Lane, 1973), p. 9.
18. Weber, *The Methodology of the Social Sciences*, p. 72.
19. Ibid. p. 22.

20. Ibid. p. 24.
21. Ibid. p. 84.
22. T. Burger, *Max Weber's Theory of Concept Formation: History, Laws and Ideal Types* (Durham: Duke University Press, 1976).
23. Quoted in Bukharin, *The Economic Theory of the Leisure Class*, p. 41.
24. Weber, *Economy and Society Vol. 1*, p. 9.
25. Weber, *The Methodology of the Social Sciences*, p. 90.
26. Weber, *The Methodology of the Social Sciences*, p. 92.
27. Ibid. p. 106.
28. Weber, *Economy and Society*, p. 25.
29. Ringer, *Max Weber's Methodology*, p. 97
30. Max Weber, *Critique of Stammler* (New York: Free Press, 1977), p. 111.
31. Ringer, *Max Weber's Methodology*, p. 98.
32. P. Hirst, *Social Evolution and Sociological Categories* (London: Allen and Unwin, 1976), p. 62.
33. Quoted in F. Parkin, *Max Weber* (Chichester: Ellis Horwood, 1982), p. 23.
34. G. Lukács, 'Max Weber and German Sociology' *Economy and Society*, Vol. 1, 1972, pp. 386–98.
35. G. Lukács, *The Destruction of Reason* (London, Merlin Press, 1980), p. 612.
36. Ibid. p. 613.

6 CLASS, STATUS AND PARTY

1. J. Westergaard, 'Class in Britain since 1979: Facts, Theories and Ideologies' in D. Lee and B. Turner (eds), *Conflicts about Class: Debating Inequality in Late Industrialism* (London: Longman, 1996), pp. 141–58.
2. R.E Pahl, 'Is the Emperor Naked? Some Questions on the Adequacy of Sociological Theory in Urban and Regional Research', *International Journal of Urban and Regional Research* Vol. 13, No. 4, p. 710.
3. R.J. Holton and B. Turner, *Max Weber on Economy and Society* (London: Routledge, 1989), p. 194.
4. J. Pakulski and M. Waters, *The Death of Class* (London: Sage, 1996), p. 4.
5. Max Weber, *Economy and Society Vol. 2* (Berkeley: University of California Press, 1978), p. 729–30.
6. F. Parkin, *Max Weber* (London: Routledge, 1988), p. 90.
7. Weber, *Economy and Society Vol. 2*, p. 926.
8. Ibid. p. 927.
9. Ibid. p. 927.
10. Ibid. p. 927.
11. Ibid. p. 927.
12. Ibid. p. 928.
13. For a useful summary, see N.R.E. Fisher, *Slavery in Classical Greece* (Bristol: Bristol Classical Press, 2001), Chapter 4.
14. G de Ste Croix, *The Class Struggle in the Ancient Greek World* (London: Duckworth, 1981), p. 40.

15. Weber, *Economy and Society Vol. 1*, p. 302.
16. Weber, *Economy and Society Vol. 2*, p. 931.
17. See S. Lash and J. Urry, *The End of Organised Capitalism* (Cambridge: Polity, 1987).
18. Max Weber, 'The Stock Exchange' in W. Runciman, *Selections in Translation* (Cambridge: Cambridge University Press, 1978).
19. Weber, *Economy and Society Vol. 1*, p. 302.
20. Parkin, *Max Weber*, p. 94.
21. C. Brennan, *Max Weber on Power and Social Stratification: An Interpretation and Critique* (Aldershot: Ashgate, 1997), p. 144.
22. Weber, *Economy and Society Vol. 2*, p. 930.
23. Ibid. p. 936.
24. F. Parkin, *The Marxist Theory of Class: A Bourgeois Critique* (London: Tavistock, 1979), p. 45.
25. Weber, *Economy and Society Vol. 1*, p. 306.
26. Max Weber, 'The Social Psychology of World Religions' in H.H. Gerth and C.W. Mills (eds), *From Max Weber: Essays in Sociology* (London: Routledge and Kegan Paul, 1948), p. 301.
27. Max Weber, 'Socialism' in Runciman, *Selections in Translation*, p. 258.
28. O.C. Cox, 'Max Weber on Social Stratification: A Critique' *American Sociological Review* Vol. 15, 1950, p. 242.
29. Weber, *Economy and Society Vol. 2*, p. 932.
30. Ibid. p. 932.
31. Ibid. pp. 933–4.
32. Ibid. p. 391.
33. Weber, *Economy and Society Vol. 1*, p. 391.
34. Ibid. p. 391.
35. Ibid. p. 392.
36. Ibid. p. 391.
37. Ibid. p. 388.
38. Max Weber, *Ancient Judaism* (New York: Free Press, 1952), p. 417.
39. Weber, *Economy and Society Vol. 1*, p. 388.
40. Parkin, *Max Weber*, p. 90.
41. Weber, *Economy and Society Vol. 2*, p. 939.
42. Max Weber, 'Parliament and Government in Germany' in *Political Writings* (Cambridge: Cambridge University Press, 1994), p. 152.
43. Weber, *Economy and Society Vol. 2*, p. 927.
44. See B. Jones, 'Max Weber and the Concept of Social Class' *The Sociological Review* Vol. 23, No. 4, 1975, pp. 729–59.
45. K. Davis and W. Moore, 'Some Principles of Stratification' in R. Bendix and S.M. Lipset (eds), *Class, Status and Power* (London: Routledge and Kegan Paul, 1967) p. 48.
46. R. Bendix, 'Social Stratification and Political Power' in Bendix and Lipset, *Class, Status and Power.*
47. D. Lockwood, *The Blackcoated Worker* (Oxford:Clarendon, 1989) p. 218.
48. J.H. Goldthorpe, D. Lockwood, F. Bechhofer and J. Platt, *The Affluent Worker: Industrial Attitudes and Behaviour;* and *The Affluent Worker: Political Attitudes and Behaviour* (Cambridge: Cambridge University Press, 1968).

Also *The Affluent Worker in the Class Structure* (Cambridge: Cambridge University Press, 1969).

49. F. Parkin, *Class Inequality and Political Order: Social Stratification in Capitalist and Communist Countries* (St Albans: Paladin, 1972).

50. J.H. Goldthorpe, *Social Mobility and Class Structure in Modern Britain* (Oxford: Oxford University Press, 1980).

51. J.H. Goldthorpe and G. Marshall, 'The Promising Future of Class Analysis: A Response to Recent Critiques' *Sociology* Vol. 26, No. 3, 1992 pp. 381–400.

52. Quoted in H. Braverman, *Labour and Monopoly Capital: The Degradation of Work in the Twentieth Century* (New York: Monthly Review Press, 1974), p. 294.

53. D. Gluckstein, *The Nazis, Capitalism and the Working Class* (London: Bookmarks, 1999), p. 85.

54. Braverman, *Labour and Monopoly Capital*, p. 353.

55. European Foundation, European Industrial Relations Observatory, *Annual Review 2000* (Dublin, European Foundation, 2000), p. 34.

56. N. Klein, *No Logo* (London: Flamingo, 2000).

57. E.O. Wright, *Classes* (London: Verso, 1985), Chapter 2.

7 DOMINATION AND BUREAUCRACY

1. F. Nietzsche, *The Will to Power* (New York: Vintage, 1968), p. 550.

2. F. Nietzsche, *Beyond Good and Evil* (Harmondsworth: Penguin, 1973), p. 173.

3. F. Nietzsche, *Untimely Meditations* (Cambridge, Cambridge University Press, 1983), p. 111.

4. W. Mommsen, *The Age of Bureaucracy* (Oxford: Blackwell, 1974), p. 7.

5. Quoted in W. Mommsen, *Max Weber and German Politics* (Chicago: University of Chicago Press, 1984), p. 394.

6. Max Weber, *Economy and Society Vol. 2* (Berkeley: University of California Press, 1978), p. 904.

7. Weber, *Economy and Society Vol. 1*, p. 54.

8. V.I. Lenin, 'State and Revolution' in *On the Dictatorship of the Proletariat* (Moscow: Progress Publishers, 1976), p. 37.

9. Weber, *Economy and Society Vol. 1*, p. 53.

10. C. Brennan, *Max Weber on Power and Stratification: An Interpretation and Critique* (Aldershot: Ashgate, 1997), pp. 72–3.

11. Weber, *Economy and Society Vol. 1*, p. 53.

12. Weber, *Economy and Society Vol. 2*, p. 946.

13. Ibid.

14. F. Parkin, *Max Weber* (London: Routledge, 1988), p. 77.

15. See N. Abercrombie, S. Hill and B. Turner, *The Dominant Ideology Thesis* (London: Allen and Unwin, 1980).

16. Weber, *Economy and Society Vol. 2*, p. 954.

17. N. Luhmann, *The Differentiation of Society* (New York: Columbia University Press, 1982), p. 23.

18. Brennan, *Max Weber on Power and Social Stratification*, p. 277.

19. Weber, *Economy and Society Vol. 1*, p. 228.
20. Ibid. p. 227.
21. Weber, *Economy and Society Vol. 2*, p. 1008.
22. Ibid. p. 1078.
23. R. Bendix, *Max Weber: An Intellectual Portrait* (London: Heinemann, 1960), p. 364.
24. B. Turner, *For Weber: Essays on the Sociology of Fate* (London: Sage, 1996), p. 315.
25. Max Weber, *General Economic History* (New Brunswick: Transaction Books, 1981), p. 28.
26. Ibid p. 31.
27. Ibid p. 49.
28. Weber, *Economy and Society Vol. 2*, p. 1007.
29. Max Weber 'The National State and Economic Policy' in K. Tribe (ed.), *Reading Weber* (London: Routledge, 1989), p. 199.
30. R. Brenner, 'Agrarian Class Structure and Economic Development in Pre-Industrial Europe' *Past and Present* No. 70, February 1976, pp. 30–74.
31. See T.H. Aston and C.H.E. Philpin (eds) *The Brenner Debate: Agrarian Class Structure and Economic Development in Pre-Industrial Europe* (Cambridge: Cambridge University Press, 1985).
32. H.H. Gerth and C.W. Mills, 'Introduction: The Man and His Work' in *From Max Weber* (London: Routledge and Kegan Paul, 1948), p. 52.
33. Bendix, *Max Weber*, p. 303.
34. Weber, *Economy and Society Vol. 1*, p. 242.
35. Ibid. p. 244.
36. Weber, *Economy and Society Vol. 2*, p. 1114.
37. Weber, *Economy and Society Vol. 1*, p. 243.
38. Weber, *Economy and Society Vol. 2*, p. 1113.
39. Ibid. p. 1116.
40. W.G. Runciman, *A Critique of Max Weber's Philosophy of Social Science* (Cambridge: Cambridge University Press, 1972), p. 5.
41. Weber, *Economy and Society Vol. 2*, p. 1120.
42. Weber, *Economy and Society Vol. 1*, p. 246.
43. Weber, *Economy and Society Vol. 2*, p. 1141.
44. Ibid. p. 1147.
45. Gerth and Mills, 'Introduction' in *From Max Weber*, p. 53.
46. For an account of De Valera's power base, see K. Allen, *Fianna Fail and Irish Labour: 1926–Present* (London: Pluto, 1997).
47. See I. Kershaw, *Hitler 1889–1936 Hubris* (Harmondsworth: Penguin, 1998), Chapter 2.
48. L. Trotsky, *The History of the Russian Revolution Vol. 1* (London: Victor Gollancz, 1932), Chapter 15.
49. Weber, *Economy and Society Vol. 2*, p. 1118.
50. Ibid. p. 980.
51. Weber, *Economy and Society Vol. 1*, p. 219.
52. Weber, *Economy and Society Vol. 2*, p. 983.
53. Ibid. p. 959.
54. Ibid. p. 988.

55. A. Gramsci, 'Soviets in Italy' *New Left Review* No. 51, September–October 1968, p. 39.

56. Weber, *Economy and Society Vol.1*, p. 225.

57. Ibid p. 225.

58. Ibid p. 992.

59. Ibid. p. 222.

60. Weber, *Economy and Society Vol. 2*, p. 973.

61. Ibid. p. 974.

62. A. Gouldner, 'On Weber's Analysis of Bureaucratic Rules' in R.K. Merton, A.P. Gray, B. Hockey and H.C. Selvin (eds), *Reader in Bureaucracy* (New York: Free Press, 1952), p. 49.

63. See S. Hill 'The Social Organisation of the Board of Directors', *British Journal of Sociology* Vol. 46, No. 2, 1995, pp. 245–78.

64. C. Friedrich, 'Some Observations on Weber's Analysis of Bureaucracy' in Merton et al. *Reader in Bureaucracy*, p. 31.

65. R.K. Merton, 'Bureaucratic Structure and Personality' in Merton et al. *Reader in Bureaucracy*, p. 365.

66. Ibid. p. 367.

67. H. Kaufman, 'Fear of Bureaucracy: A Raging Pandemic' *Public Administration Review* No. 41, 1981, pp. 5–6.

8 THE FALL AND RISE OF THE WEST

1. Max Weber, *The Protestant Ethnic and the Spirit of Capitalism* (New York: Charles Scribner's Sons, 1958), p 26.

2. See N. Morley, 'Marx and the Failure of Antiquity', *Helios* Vol. 26, No. 2, 1999, pp. 151–64.

3. Marianne Weber, *Max Weber: A Biography* (New York: John Wiley, 1975), p. 114.

4. Quoted in J. Love, *Antiquity and Capitalism: Max Weber and the Sociological Foundations of Roman Civilisation* (London: Routledge, 1991), p. 14.

5. B. Shaw and R. Saller, 'Editor's Introduction' in M.I. Finley, *Economy and Society in Ancient Greece* (Harmondsworth: Penguin, 1981), p. xvii.

6. Max Weber, The Social Causes of the Decay of Ancient Civilization' in *The Agrarian Sociology of Ancient Civilisations* (London: New Left Books, 1976), p. 389.

7. Ibid. p. 391.

8. Ibid. p. 394.

9. Weber, *The Agrarian Sociology of Ancient Civilisations*, p. 55.

10. Ibid. p. 398.

11. Ibid. p. 404.

12. Weber, 'The Social Causes of the Decay of Ancient Civilisation', p. 408.

13. Love, *Antiquity and Capitalism*, pp. 22–3.

14. C. Antoni, *From History to Sociology* (London: Merlin Press, 1962), p.126.

15. K. Marx, *Grundrisse* (Harmondsworth: Penguin, 1973), p. 513 and K. Marx, *Capital Vol. 3* (London: Lawrence and Wishart, 1959) pp. 327 and 787.

16. Weber, *The Agrarian Sociology of Ancient Civilisations*, pp. 43–4.
17. Ibid. p. 48.
18. Ibid. p. 51.
19. Ibid. p. 365.
20. A. Giddens, *Politics and Sociology in the Thought of Max Weber* (London: Macmillan, 1972), p. 36.
21. L. Ray, *Theorizing Classical Sociology* (Buckingham: Open University Press, 1999), p. 184.
22. R. Collins, *Weberian Sociological Theory* (Cambridge: Cambridge University Press, 1986), p. 35.
23. Max Weber, 'The Social Psychology of World Religions' in H.H. Gerth and C.W. Mills, *From Max Weber: Essays in Sociology* (London: Routledge and Kegan Paul, 1948), p. 280.
24. Ibid. p. 287.
25. Ibid. p. 281.
26. M. Mann, *The Sources of Social Power Vol. 2* (Cambridge: Cambridge University Press, 1993), p. 36.
27. Max Weber, *Ancient Judaism* (New York: The Free Press, 1952), p. 4.
28. Quoted in R. Schroeder, *Max Weber and the Sociology of Culture* (London: Sage, 1992), p. 83.
29. Max Weber, *Economy and Society Vol. 2* (Berkeley: University of California Press, 1978), p. 1192.
30. W. Schluchter, *Paradoxes of Modernity: Culture and Conduct in the Theory of Max Weber* (Stanford: Stanford University Press, 1996), Chapter 4.
31. See S. Williams (ed.), *The Gregorian Epoch: Reformation, Revolution, Reaction?* (Lexington, Massachusetts: D.C. Heath, 1964).
32. Weber, *Economy and Society Vol. 2*, p. 1164.
33. Ibid.
34. See P. Brown, 'The Rise and Function of the Holy Man in Late Antiquity' *Journal of Roman Studies* Vol. 61, pp. 80–101. For a specific case of this relationship see T. Urbainczyk, *Theodoret of Cyrrhus*, (Ann Arbor: University of Michigan Press, 2002).
35. Quoted in Schluchter, *Paradoxes of Modernity*, p. 213.
36. Max Weber, 'Religious Rejection of the World and their Directions' in Gerth and Mills, *From Max Weber*, p. 332.
37. R. Bendix, *Max Weber: An Intellectual Portrait* (London: Heinemann, 1960), p. 359.
38. Weber, *Economy and Society Vol. 2*, p. 1099.
39. Ibid. p. 1082.
40. Quoted in Schluchter, *Paradoxes of Modernity*, p. 218.
41. Weber, *Economy and Society Vol. 2*, p. 1239.
42. Max Weber, *General Economic History* (New Brunswick: Transaction Books, 1981), p. 316.
43. Ibid. p. 312.
44. Ibid. p. 313.
45. Ibid. p. 313.
46. Ibid. p. 314.
47. Ibid. p. 337.

48. E.M. Wood, *The Origins of Capitalism: The Longer View* (London: Verso, 2002), p. 17.
49. For a useful account see P. Siegel, *The Meek and the Militant: Religion and Power across the World* (London: Zed, 1987).
50. Weber, 'The Social Psychology of World Religions', p. 289.
51. R. Hilton, *Bond Men Made Free: Medieval Peasant Movements and the English Rising of 1381* (London: Routledge, 1973), p. 103.
52. C. Hill, *The World Turned Upside Down* (Harmondsworth: Penguin, 1975).
53. R. Hilton, 'A Crisis of Feudalism', in T.H. Aston and C.H.E. Philpin (eds), *The Brenner Debate: Agrarian Class Structure and Economic Development in Pre-Industrial Europe* (Cambridge: Cambridge University Press, 1985)
54. Hilton, *Bond Men Made Free*, p. 112.
55. R.B. Dobson (ed.), *The Peasants Revolt of 1381* (Basingstoke: Macmillan, 1983), p. 342.
56. R. Brenner, 'Agrarian Class Structure and Economic Development' in Aston and Philpin *The Brenner Debate*, pp. 10–64.
57. M. Dobb, *Studies in the Development of Capitalism* (London: Routledge and Kegan Paul, 1963), p. 100.
58. Weber, *General Economic History*, p. 300.

9 CAPITALISM, SOCIALISM AND BUREAUCRACY

1. K. Lowith, *Max Weber and Karl Marx* (London: Routledge, 1993), p. 80.
2. R. Collins, *Max Weber: A Skeleton Key*, (London: Sage, 1986), p. 63.
3. Max Weber, *Economy and Society Vol. 1*, (Berkeley: University of California Press, 1978), p.26.
4. Max Weber, 'Science as a Vocation' in H.H. Gerth and C.W. Mills (eds), *From Max Weber: Essays in Sociology* (London: Routledge and Kegan Paul, 1948), p. 139.
5. Weber, *Economy and Society Vol. 1*, p. 68.
6. N. Bukharin, *The Economic Theory of the Leisure Class* (New York: Augustus M. Kelley, 1970), p. 42.
7. P. Hirst, *Social Evolution and Sociological Categories* (London: Allen and Unwin, 1976), p. 95.
8. Bukharin, *The Economic Theory*, p. 52.
9. Weber, *Economy and Society Vol. 1*, p. 93.
10. Ibid. p. 85.
11. Ibid. p. 85.
12. Ibid. p. 85.
13. Ibid. p. 85.
14. Ibid. p. 86.
15. G. Ritzer, *The McDonaldization of Society* (Thousand Oaks: Pine Forge Press, 1993), p. 144.
16. H. Marcuse 'Industrialization and Capitalism' in O. Stammer (ed.), *Max Weber and Sociology Today* (Oxford: Blackwell, 1971), p. 136.
17. See V. Prashad, *Fat Cats and Running Dogs: The Enron Stage of Capitalism* (London: Zed, 2002), Chapter 1.

18. D. Sayer, *Capitalism and Modernity* (London: Routledge, 1991), p. 96.
19. Weber, *Economy and Society Vol. 1*, p. 93.
20. Ibid. p. 108.
21. W. Mommsen, *The Age of Bureaucracy* (Oxford: Blackwell, 1974), p. 66.
22. Quoted in Mommsen, *The Age of Bureaucracy*, p. 66. (Note different translation to *Economy and Society Vol. 1*, p. 108).
23. Weber, *Economy and Society Vol. 1*, p. 137.
24. Ibid. p. 114.
25. Ibid. p. 137–8.
26. Ibid. p. 138.
27. Ibid. p. 150–1.
28. Ibid. p. 30.
29. Ibid. p. 108–9.
30. W. Mommsen, *The Political and Social Theory of Max Weber* (Cambridge: Polity 1989), Chapter 2.
31. Max Weber, *The Russian Revolutions* (Cambridge: Polity, 1995), p. 108.
32. Ibid.
33. T. Cliff, *Lenin Vol. 1* (London: Bookmarks, 1971), pp. 35–6.
34. Weber, *The Russian Revolutions*, p. 109.
35. Ibid. p. 108.
36. Weber, *Economy and Society Vol. 2*, p. 974.
37. Ibid. p. 975.
38. Mommsen, *The Age of Bureaucracy*, p. 106.
39. Max Weber, *Political Writings* (Cambridge: Cambridge University Press, 1994), p. 165.
40. See R. Michels, *Political Parties: A Study in the Oligarchial Tendencies in Modern Democracy* (New York: Free Press, 1968).
41. Weber, *Political Writings*, p. 154.
42. Ibid. p. 190.
43. Ibid. p. 190.
44. Ibid. p. 159–60.
45. Ibid. p. 161.
46. Ibid. p. 174.
47. Ibid. p. 156.
48. D. Beetham, *Bureaucracy* (Milton Keynes: Open University Press, 1987), p. 58.
49. Weber, *Political Writings*, p. 157.
50. Ibid. p. 157.
51. Ibid. p. 158.
52. Quoted in L. Ray *Theorizing Classical Sociology* (Buckingham: Open University Press, 1999), p. 187.
53. Sayer, *Capitalism and Modernity*, p. 154.
54. K. Marx 'The Critique of Hegel's Doctrine of the State' in *Early Writings* (Harmondsworth: Penguin, 1974), p. 107.
55. K. Marx, 'The Civil War in France' in *The First International and After Political Writings Vol. 3* (Harmondsworth: Penguin, 1974), p. 212.
56. V.I. Lenin, 'State and Revolution' in *On the Dictatorship of the Proletariat* (Moscow: Progress Publishers, 1976) p. 65.
57. Quoted in M. Albrow, *Bureaucracy* (London: Macmillan, 1970), p. 59.

58. Weber, *Economy and Society Vol. 2*, p. 989.
59. Weber, *The Russian Revolutions*, pp. 244 and 252.
60. See for example T. Cliff, *State Capitalism in Russia,* (London: Bookmarks, 1988).
61. E. Mandel, *Power and Money: A Marxist Theory of Bureaucracy* (London: Verso, 1992), p. 13.
62. A. Gramsci, 'Soviets in Italy' *New Left Review* No. 51, September–October 1968, p. 41.
63. H. Braverman, *Labour and Monopoly Capital: The Degradation of Work in the Twentieth Century* (New York: Monthly Review Press, 1974).
64. L. Trotsky, *The Revolution Betrayed* (London: New Park, 1967), p. 112.
65. Mandel, *Power and Money*, p. 204.

10 WAR AND REVOLUTION

1. R. Chickering, *Imperial Germany and the Great War, 1914–1918* (Cambridge: Cambridge University Press, 1998), p. 15.
2. F.L. Carsten, *War against War* (London: Batsford Academic and Educational Ltd, 1982), p. 14.
3. Marianne Weber, *Max Weber: A Biography* (New York: John Wiley, 1975), pp. 521–2.
4. Ibid. p. 531.
5. Chickering, *Imperial Germany and the Great War*, p. 1.
6. Weber, *Max Weber*, p. 581.
7. G. Hardach, *The First World War* (Berkeley: University of California Press, 1977), p. 56.
8. H.U. Wehler, *The German Empire 1871–1918* (Lemington Spa: Berg, 1985), p. 205.
9. C. Harman, *The Lost Revolution* (London: Bookmarks, 1982), p. 29.
10. G. Mann, *The History of Germany since 1789* (Harmondsworth: Penguin, 1988), p. 510.
11. Ibid. p. 515.
12. W. Mommsen, *Max Weber and German Politics 1890–1920* (Chicago, University of Chicago Press, 1984), p. 196.
13. Ibid. p. 233.
14. Ibid. p. 235.
15. Ibid. p. 194.
16. Ibid. p. 256.
17. Ibid. p. 205–6.
18. Ibid. p. 207.
19. Ibid. p. 312.
20. J.P. Mayer, *Max Weber and German Politics: A Study in Political Sociology* (London: Faber, 1944), p. 82.
21. C. Harman, *A People's History of the World* (London: Bookmarks, 1999), p. 412.
22. Max Weber, *The Russian Revolutions* (Cambridge: Polity, 1995), p. 252.
23. Ibid. p. 255.

24. D. Beetham, *Max Weber and the Theory of Modern Politics* (London: Allen and Unwin, 1974), p. 201.
25. Mommsen, *Max Weber and German Politics*, p. 277.
26. Ibid. p. 279.
27. Ibid. p. 273.
28. Ibid. p. 294.
29. Weber, *Max Weber*, p. 627.
30. Mommsen, *Max Weber and German Politics*, p. 296.
31. Ibid. p. 296.
32. Ibid. p. 297.
33. Ibid.
34. Weber, *Max Weber*, p. 633.
35. Mommsen, *Max Weber and German Politics*, p. 314.
36. Ibid. p. 300.
37. Ibid. p 305.
38. Weber, *Max Weber*, p. 642.
39. Mommsen, *Max Weber and German Politics*, p. 326.
40. Weber, *Max Weber*, p. 648.
41. Ibid. p. 673.
42. Ibid. p. 672.
43. Max Weber, *Political Writings* (Cambridge: Cambridge University Press, 1994), p. 272.
44. Ibid. p. 273.
45. Ibid. p. 274.
46. Ibid. p. 274.
47. Ibid. p. 281.
48. Edward Mortimer, 'Global Gloom' *Financial Times*, 25 March 1998.
49. Weber, *Political Writings*, p. 292.
50. Ibid. p. 302.
51. Ibid. p. 361.
52. Ibid. p. 359–60.
53. Ibid. p. 360.
54. Quoted in Beetham, *Max Weber and the Theory of Modern Politics*, p. 237.
55. Mommsen, *Max Weber and German Politics*, pp. 395–6.
56. Beethham, *Max Weber and the Theory of Modern Politics*, p. 234.
57. Ibid. p. 234.
58. Max Weber, 'Politics as a Vocation' in *Political Writings*, p. 351.
59. Quoted in Beetham, *Max Weber and the Theory of Modern Politics*, p. 231.
60. Ibid. p. 236.
61. Weber, *Max Weber*, p. 653.
62. Mommsen, *Weber and German Politics*, p. 401.
63. H. Marcuse, 'Industrialization and Capitalism' in O. Stammer, *Max Weber and Sociology Today* (Oxford: Blackwell, 1971), p. 146.

11 CONCLUSION

1. A. MacIntyre, *After Virtue* (Notre Dame: University of Notre Dame Press, 1981), p. 108.
2. M. Lowy, *Georg Lukács – From Romanticism to Bolshevism* (London: New Left Books, 1979), pp. 37–43 and pp.122–3.
3. G. Lukács, *History and Class Consciousness* (London: Merlin Press, 1971), p. 96.
4. D. Kellner, 'Critical Theory, Max Weber and the Dialectics of Domination', in R. Antonio and R. Glassman (eds), *A Weber–Marx Dialogue* (Lawrence: Kansas University Press, 1985).
5. Max Weber, *Ancient Judaism* (New York: Free Press, 1952), p. 344.
6. Ibid. p. 344.
7. S. Kalberg, 'Max Weber' in G. Ritzer, *Blackwell Companion to Major Social Theorists* (Oxford: Blackwell, 2000), p. 151.
8. Max Weber, *The Protestant Ethic and the Spirit of Capitalism* (New York: Charles Scribner's Sons, 1958), pp. 30–1.
9. W. Mommsen, *The Age of Bureaucracy* (Oxford: Blackwell, 1974), p. 44.
10. E.O. Wright, 'The Shadow of Exploitation in Weber's Class Analysis', paper from Department of Sociology, University of Wisconsin, Madison, July 2002, p. 35.

Additional Reading

CHAPTER 2

There is a wealth of literature on Max Weber's sociology but, strangely, there are a limited number of biographies. The standard biography is Marianne Weber's, *Max Weber: A Biography* (New York: John Wiley, 1975). Arthur Mitzman's *The Iron Cage: An Historical Interpretation of Max Weber* (New Brunswick: Transaction, 1985) provides an interesting backdrop on the psychological tensions in his life.

Weber's overall political orientation is discussed in a comprehensive manner in Wolfgang Mommsen's *Max Weber and German Politics 1890–1920* (Chicago: Chicago University Press, 1984) David Beetham's *Max Weber and the Theory of Modern Politics* (London: Allen and Unwin, 1974) provides a useful overview. You will also find a good discussion of German society at the time in D. Blackbourn and G. Eley (eds) *The Peculiarities of German History* (Oxford: Oxford University Press, 1984).

CHAPTER 3

There is a vast literature on the Protestant Ethic thesis. *Protestantism and Capitalism* (Boston: Heath 1955) edited by Robert Green is an older, short book which gives a flavour of some of Weber's early critics. Fischoff's article on '*The* Protestant Ethic and the Spirit of Capitalism: The History of a Controversy' *Social Research* Vol. 2, 1944, pp. 53–77 maps out some of the main contours.

A comprehensive defence of Weber's position can be found in Gordon Marshall's *In Search of the Spirit of Capitalism* (London: Hutchinson, 1982). An early but devastating refutation can be found in H.M. Robertson, *The Rise of Economic Individualism* (Cambridge: Cambridge University Press, 1935).

CHAPTER 4

A sympathetic summary of Weber's view on Asia and the West can be found in B. Nelson 'On Orient and Occident in Max Weber' *Social Research* vol. 43, 1976, pp. 114–29. An even more positive endorsement of his argument can be found in D. Gellner, 'Max Weber, Capitalism and the Religion of India' *Sociology* vol. 16, 1982, pp. 526–43.

G.R. Madan, *Western Sociologists on Indian Society* (London: Routledge and Kegan Paul, 1979) gives a good summary of Weber's arguments and raises some critical points. Nicholas Dirk's book, *Castes of Mind* (Princeton: Princeton University Press 2001) barely mentions Weber but it provides an important critique of Western writers who thought they could explain India's underdevelopment through the caste system.

CHAPTER 5

F. Ringer's, *Max Weber's Methodology* (Cambridge, Massachusetts: Harvard University Press, 1997) is probably te best book in this difficult area. For a good overview of the value-free controversy try, M. Root, *Philosophy and Social Science* (Oxford: Blackwell, 1993).

An excellent critique of Weber's value-free form of research can be found in A. Gouldner. 'The Anti-Minotaur: The Myth of Value Free Research' in *For Sociology* (London: Allen Lane, 1973). However, it would be difficult to surpass an early critique of Weber's individualism in G. Lukács, 'Max Weber and German Sociology' *Economy and Society*, Vol. 1, 1972, pp. 386–98.

CHAPTER 6

Frank Parkin probably provides the most lucid exposition of Weber's view on class, status and party in his book *Max Weber* (London: Routledge, 1988). For an interesting discussion on Weber's concept of social class see B. Jones, 'Max Weber and the Concept of Social Class' *Sociological Review* Vol. 23, 1975, pp. 729–59.

A useful introduction to the relevance of Weber for current debates on stratification can be found in R. Crompton, *Class and Stratification: An Introduction to Current Debates* (Cambridge: Polity, 1993).

Brennan's, *Max Weber on Power and Stratification: An Interpretation and Critique* (Aldershot: Ashgate, 1997) gives a careful overview of his ideas and deserves a much wider readership.

CHAPTER 7

R. Bendix, *Max Weber: An Intellectual Portrait*,(London, Heineman, 1960) gives one of the clearest overviews of Weber's sociology of domination. W. Mommsen's *The Political and Social Theory of Max Weber: Collected Essays* (Cambridge: Polity, 1989) provides a stimulating discussion. As does his earlier book, *The Age of Bureaucracy: Perspectives on the Political Sociology of Max Weber* (Oxford: Blackwell, 1974).

Merton's *Reader in Bureaucracy* (New York: Free Press, 1952) contains a number of stimulating articles on the subject. For a trenchant critique of Weber's elitism see P. Hirst, *Social Evolution and Sociological Categories* (London: Allen and Unwin, 1976).

CHAPTER 8

Weber's theory of history is discussed in W. Schluchter, *Paradoxes of Modernity: Culture and Conduct in the Theory of Max Weber* (Stanford: Stanford University Press, 1996). For an alternative account of what constitutes Weber's central question see W. Hennis, *Max Weber: Essays in Reconstruction* (London: Allen and Unwin, 1988). For yet different interpretation from a hugely sympathetic follower, see R. Collins, *Weberian Sociological Theory* (Cambridge: Cambridge University Press, 1986).

For an important critique see the chapter on Weber in A. Callinicos, *Social Theory: A Historical Introduction* (Cambridge: Polity, 1999).

CHAPTER 9

Lowith's, *Max Weber and Karl Marx* (London: Routledge, 1993) is interesting even if it makes too much of the affinity between Weber and Marx. Mommsen's 'Max Weber as a Critic of Marx' *Canadian Journal of Sociology* Vol. 2. 1977, pp. 373–98 brings out the differences much more clearly while presenting a sympathetic account of Weber.

H. Marcuse's 'Industrialization and Capitalism' in O. Stammer's (ed.) *Max Weber and Sociology Today* (Oxford: Blackwell, 1973) provides an important rejoinder. As do the books by Hirst and the article by Lukács already cited above.

CHAPTER 10

The detail about Weber's reaction to the First World War and the subsequent German Revolution can be found in Mommsen's *Max Weber and German Politics* and in Marianne Weber's biography.

Beetham's, *Max Weber and the Theory of Modern Politics* (London: Allen and Unwin, 1974) gives an accurate overview of his outlook.

For an account of the German Revolution written from a left-wing standpoint see C. Harman, *The Lost Revolution* (London: Bookmarks, 1982).

Bibliography

Abdel-Malek, D., 'Orientalism in Crisis' *Diogenes* No. 44, Winter 1963

Abercrombie, N., S. Hill and B. Turner, *The Dominant Ideology Thesis* (London: Allen and Unwin, 1980)

Albrow, M., *Bureaucracy* (London: Macmillan, 1970)

Allen, K., *Fianna Fail and Irish Labour: 1926–present* (London: Pluto, 1997)

Antoni, C., *From History to Sociology* (London: Merlin Press, 1962)

Antonio, R. and R. Glassman (eds), *A Weber–Marx Dialogue* (Lawrence: Kansas University Press, 1985)

Aston, T.H. and C.H.E. Philpin (eds), *The Brenner Debate: Agrarian Class Structure and Economic Development in Pre-Industrial Europe* (Cambridge: Cambridge University Press, 1985)

Bagchi, A.K., 'Foreign Capital and Economic Development in India: A Schematic View' in K. Gough and H. Sharn, *Imperialism and Revolution in South East Asia* (New York: Monthly Review Press, 1973)

Bayley, C., 'Indian Merchants in a "Traditional Setting": Benares, 1780–1830' in C. Dewey and R.C. Hopkins (eds), *The Imperial Impact: Studies in the Economic History of Africa and India* (London: Athlone Press, 1978)

Beetham, D., *Max Weber and the Theory of Modern Politics* (London: Allen and Unwin, 1974)

—— *Bureaucracy* (Milton Keynes: Open University Press, 1987)

Bell, D., *The End of Ideology: On the Exhaustion of Political Ideas in the Fifties* (New York: Free Press, 1960)

Bendix, R., *Max Weber: An Intellectual Portrait* (London: Heinemann, 1960)

Bendix R. and S.M. Lipset, *Class, Status and Power: A Reader in Social Stratification* (London: Routledge and Kegan Paul, 1967)

Berghahn, V., *Imperial Germany 1871–1914* (Oxford: Berghahn Books, 1994)

Bilton, T., K. Bonnet, P. Jones, T. Lawson, D. Skinner, M. Stanworth and A. Webster, *Introducing Sociology* (London: Palgrave, 2002)

Blackbourn, D., *Fontana History of Germany 1780–1918: The Long Nineteenth Century* (London: HarperCollins, 1997)

Bottomore, T., *Sociology and Socialism* (Brighton: Harvester, 1984)

Bourdieu, P., *Acts of Resistance: Against the New Myths of Our Time* (Cambridge: Polity, 1998)

Braverman, H., *Labour and Monopoly Capital: The Degradation of Work in the Twentieth Century* (New York: Monthly Review Press, 1974)

Brennan, C., *Max Weber on Power and Social Stratification: An Interpretation and Critique* (Aldershot: Ashgate, 1997)

Brenner, R., 'Agrarian Class Structure and Economic Development in Pre-Industrial Europe' *Past and Present* No. 70, February 1976

Brown, P., 'The Rise and Function of the Holy Man in Late Antiquity' *Journal of Roman Studies* Vol. 61, pp. 80–101

Bukharin, N., *The Economic Theory of the Leisure Class* (New York: Augustus M. Kelly, 1970)

Burger, T., *Max Weber's Theory of Concept Formation: History, Laws and Ideal Types* (Durham: Duke University Press, 1976)

Carsten, C.L., *War against War* (London: Batsford Academic and Educational Ltd, 1982)

Chickering, R., *Imperial Germany and the Great War, 1914–1918* (Cambridge: Cambridge University Press, 1998)

Cliff, T., *Lenin Vol. 1* (London: Bookmarks, 1971)

—— *State Capitalism in Russia* (London: Bookmarks, 1988)

Cohn, B.S., 'Notes on the History of the Study of Indian Society and Culture' in M. Singer and B.S. Cohn, *Structure and Change in Indian Society* (Chicago: Aldine, 1968)

Cohen, J., L. Hazelbrigg and W. Pope, 'DeParsonizing Weber: A Critique of Parsons' Interpretation of Weber's Sociology' *American Sociological Review* Vol. 40, No. 2, 1975, pp. 229–41

Collins, R., *Max Weber: A Skeleton Key* (London: Sage, 1986)

—— *Weberian Sociological Theory* (Cambridge: Cambridge University Press, 1986)

Cox, O.C., 'Max Weber on Social Stratification: A Critique' *American Sociological Review* Vol. 15, 1950, pp. 236–44

Davis, K. and W. Moore, 'Some Principles of Stratification' in R. Bendix and S.M. Lipset (eds), *Class, Status and Power: A Reader in Social Stratification* (London: Routledge and Kegan Paul, 1967)

Davis, M., *Late Victorian Holocausts* (London: Verso, 2001)

De Ste Croix, G., *The Class Struggle in the Ancient Greek World* (London: Duckworth, 1981)

Dirks, N.B., *The Hollow Crown, Ethnohistory of an Indian Kingdom* (Cambridge: Cambridge University Press, 1987)

—— *Castes of Mind: Colonialism and the Making of Modern India* (Princeton: Princeton University Press, 2001)

Dobb, M., *Studies in the Development of Capitalism* (London: Routledge and Kegan Paul, 1963)

Dobson, R.B. (ed.), *The Peasants Revolt of 1381* (Basingstoke: Macmillan, 1983)

Dumont, L., *Religion, Politics and History in India* (Paris: Mouton, 1970)

Ebrey, P.B., *Family and Property in Sung China: Yuan Ts'ai's Precepts for Social Life* (Princeton: Princeton University Press, 1984)

Eley, G., 'The British Model and the German Road: Re-Thinking the Concept of German History before 1914' in D. Blackbourn and G. Eley (eds), *The Peculiarities of German History* (Oxford: Oxford University Press, 1984)

Falk, W., 'Democracy and Capitalism in Max Weber's Sociology' *Sociological Review* Vol. 27, 1935

Femia, J., 'Civil Society and the Marxist Tradition' in S. Kaviraj and S. Khilnani (eds), *Civil Society: History and Possibilities* (Cambridge: Cambridge University Press, 2001)

Fischoff, E., 'The Protestant Ethic and the Spirit of Capitalism: The History of a Controversy' *Social Research* Vol. 2, No. 1, 1944, pp. 53–77

Fisher, N.R.E., *Slavery in Classical Greece* (Bristol: Bristol Classical Press, 2001)

Friedman, T., *The Lexus and the Olive Tree* (New York: Farrar, Strauss and Giroux, 2000)

George, C. and K. George, 'Protestantism and Capitalism in Pre-Revolutionary England' *Church History* Vol. 27, 1958, pp. 351–71

Gernet, J., *A History of Chinese Civilization* (Cambridge: Cambridge University Press, 1982)

Gerth, H.H. and C.W. Mills, *From Max Weber: Essays in Sociology* (London: Routledge and Kegan Paul, 1948)

Giddens, A., 'Marx, Weber and the Development of Capitalism' *Sociology* Vol. 4, No. 4, 1970, pp. 289–310

—— *Politics and Sociology in the Thought of Max Weber* (London: Macmillan, 1972)

—— *The Third Way: The Renewal of Social Democracy* (Cambridge: Polity, 1998)

Gillion, K., *Almedabad: A Study in Indian Urban History* (Berkeley: University of California Press, 1968)

Gluckstein, D., *The Nazis, Capitalism and the Working Class* (London: Bookmarks, 1999)

Goldthorpe, J.H., *Social Mobility and Class Structure in Modern Britain* (Oxford: Oxford University Press, 1980)

Goldthorpe, J.H. and G. Marshall, 'The Promising Future of Class Analysis: A Response to Recent Critiques' *Sociology* Vol. 26, No. 3, 1992, pp. 381–400

Goldthorpe, J.H., D. Lockwood, F. Bechhofer and J. Platt, *The Affluent Worker: Industrial Attitudes and Behaviour* (Cambridge: Cambridge University Press, 1968)

—— *The Affluent Worker: Political Attitudes and Behaviour* (Cambridge: Cambridge University Press, 1968)

—— *The Affluent Worker in the Class Structure* (Cambridge: Cambridge University Press, 1969)

Gouldner, A., *The Coming Crisis of Western Sociology* (London: Heinemann, 1971)

—— *For Sociology* (London: Allen Lane, 1973)

Gramsci, A., 'Soviets in Italy' *New Left Review* No. 51, September–October 1968

Hamilton, P., *Max Weber, Critical Assessments* (London: Routledge, 1991)

Hardach, G., *The First World War* (Berkeley: University of California Press, 1977)

Harman, C., *The Lost Revolution* (London: Bookmarks, 1982)

—— *A People's History of the World* (London: Bookmarks, 1999)

Heller, H., *The Conquest of Poverty: The Calvinist Revolt in 16th Century France* (Leiden: Brill, 1986)

Hennis, W., *Max Weber, Essays in Reconstruction* (London: Allen and Unwin, 1988)

Hill, C., 'Protestantism and the Rise of Capitalism' in E.J. Fischer (ed.) *Essays in Economic and Social History of Tudor and Stuart England* (Cambridge: Cambridge University Press, 1961)

—— *The World Turned Upside Down* (Harmondsworth: Penguin, 1975)

Hill, S., 'The Social Organisation of the Board of Directors' *British Journal of Sociology* Vol. 46, No. 2, 1995, pp. 245–78

Hilton, R., *Bond Men Made Free: Medieval Peasant Movements and the English Rising of 1381* (London: Routledge, 1973)

Hirst, P., *Social Evolution and Sociological Categories* (London: Allen and Unwin, 1976)

Holton, R.J. and B. Turner, *Max Weber on Economy and Society* (London: Routledge, 1989)

Horowitz, I., *The Decomposition of Sociology* (Oxford: Oxford University Press, 1994)

Hyma, A., 'Calvinism and Capitalism in the Netherlands 1555–1700' *Journal of Modern History* Vol. 10, 1938, pp. 321–43

Inden, R., 'Orientalist Constructions of India' *Modern Asian Studies* Vol. 20, No. 3, 1986

Johnston, P. and B. Scribner (eds), *The Reformation in Germany and Switzerland* (Cambridge: Cambridge University Press, 1993)

Jones, B., 'Max Weber and the Concept of Social Class' *The Sociological Review* Vol. 23, No. 4, 1975, pp. 729–59

Kaesler, D., 'From Academic Outsider to Sociological Mastermind: The Fashioning of the Sociological "Classic" Max Weber', paper delivered to UCD Department of Sociology, 2002

Kalberg, S., 'Max Weber' in G. Ritzer, *Blackwell Companion to Major Social Theorists* (Oxford: Blackwell, 2000)

Kaufman, H., 'Fear of Bureaucracy: A Raging Pandemic' *Public Administration Review* No. 41, 1981

Kershaw, I., *Hitler 1889–1936 Hubris* (Harmondsworth: Penguin, 1998)

Klein, N., *No Logo* (London: Flamingo, 2000)

Kolko, G., 'A Critique of Max Weber's Philosophy of History' *Ethics* Vol. 70, No. 1, 1959, pp. 1–20

—— 'Max Weber on America: Theory and Evidence' in G.H. Nadel (ed.), *Studies in the Philosophy of History* (New York: Harper and Row, 1965)

Lash, S. and J. Urry, *The End of Organised Capitalism* (Cambridge: Polity, 1987)

Lenin, V.I., *On the Dictatorship of the Proletariat* (Moscow: Progress Publishers, 1976)

Linebough, P., *The London Hanged: Crime and Civil Society in the 18th Century* (Harmondsworth: Penguin, 1991)

Lipset, S.M., 'The End of Ideology' in C. Waxman (ed.), *The End of Ideology Debate* (New York: Simon and Schuster, 1969)

Lockwood, D., *The Blackcoated Worker* (Oxford: Clarendon, 1989)

Love, J., *Antiquity and Capitalism: Max Weber and the Sociological Foundations of Roman Civilisation* (London: Routledge, 1991)

Lowith, K., *Max Weber and Karl Marx* (London: Routledge, 1993)

Lowy, M., *Georg Lukács – From Romanticism to Bolshevism* (London: New Left Books, 1979)

Luhmann, N., *The Differentiation of Society* (New York: Columbia University Press, 1982)

Lukács, G., *History and Class Consciousness* (London: Merlin Press, 1971)

—— 'Max Weber and German Sociology' *Economy and Society* Vol. 1, 1972, pp. 377–98

—— *The Destruction of Reason* (London: Merlin Press, 1980)

MacIntyre, A., *After Virtue* (Notre Dame: University of Notre Dame Press, 1981)

MacRae, D., *Weber* (Glasgow: Fontana/Collins, 1974)

Madan, G.R., *Western Sociologists on Indian Society* (London: Routledge and Kegan Paul, 1979)

Malik, S., *Understanding Indian Civilization* (Simla: Indian Institute for Advanced Studies, 1975)

Mandel, E., *Power and Money: A Marxist Theory of Bureaucracy* (London: Verso, 1992)

Mann, G., *The History of Germany since 1789* (Harmondsworth: Penguin, 1974/1988)

Mann, M., *The Sources of Social Power Vol. 2* (Cambridge: Cambridge University Press 1993)

Marcuse, H., 'Industrialization and Capitalism' in O. Stammer (ed.), *Max Weber and Sociology Today* (Oxford: Blackwell, 1971)

Marx, K., *Capital Vol. 3* (London: Lawrence and Wishart, 1959)

—— *Grundrisse* (Harmondsworth: Penguin, 1973)

—— *Early Writings* (Harmondsworth: Penguin, 1974)

—— *The First International and After Political Writings Vol. 3* (Harmondsworth: Penguin, 1974)

—— *Capital Vol. 1* (Harmondsworth: Penguin, 1976)

Marx, K. and F. Engels, *Collected Works Vol. 8* (London: Lawrence and Wishart, 1975)

Mayer, J.P., *Max Weber and German Politics: A Study in Political Sociology* (London: Faber, 1944)

Merton, R., A.P. Gray, B. Hockey and H.C. Selvin (eds), *Reader in Bureaucracy* (New York: Free Press, 1952)

Metcalf, T., *Ideologies of the Raj* (Cambridge: Cambridge University Press, 1994)

Michels, R., *Political Parties: A Study in the Oligarchial Tendencies in Modern Democracy* (New York: Free Press, 1968)

Miller, S. and H. Potthoff, *A History of German Social Democracy* (New York: St Martin's Press, 1986)

Mommsen, W., *The Age of Bureaucracy* (Oxford: Blackwell, 1974)

—— 'Max Weber as a Critic of Marx' *Canadian Journal of Sociology* Vol. 2, 1977, pp. 373–98

—— *Max Weber and German Politics 1890–1920* (Chicago: University of Chicago Press, 1984)

—— *The Political and Social Theory of Max Weber* (Cambridge: Polity, 1989)

Mommsen, W. and J. Osterhammel (eds), *Max Weber and His Contemporaries* (London: Allen and Unwin, 1987)

Morley, N., 'Marx and the Failure of Antiquity', *Helios* Vol. 26, No. 2, 1999, pp. 151–64

Nietzsche, F., *The Will to Power* (New York: Vintage, 1968)

—— *Beyond Good and Evil* (Harmondsworth: Penguin, 1973)

—— *Untimely Meditations* (Cambridge: Cambridge University Press, 1983)

Pahl, R.E., 'Is the Emperor Naked? Some Questions on the Adequacy of Sociological Theory in Urban and Regional Research' *International Journal of Urban and Regional Research* Vol. 13, No. 4, 1989, 709–20

Pakulski, J. and M. Waters, *The Death of Class* (London: Sage, 1996)

Parkin, F., *Class Inequality and Political Order: Social Stratification in Capitalist and Communist Countries* (St Albans: Paladin, 1972)

—— *The Marxist Theory of Class: A Bourgeois Critique* (London: Tavistock, 1979)

—— *Max Weber* (London: Routledge 1988)

Parsons, T., *The Structure of Social Action* (Glencoe: Free Press, 1949)

—— 'The Circumstances of My Encounter with Max Weber' in R. Merton and M.W. Riley (eds), *Sociological Traditions from Generation to Generation: Glimpses of the American Experience* (Norwood: Ablex Publishing, 1980)

Pearson, M.N., *Merchants and Rulers in Gujarat* (Berkeley: University of California Press, 1976)

Pollock, S., 'Deep Orientalism? Notes on Sanskrit and Power beyond Raj' in C.A. Breckenridge and P. Van der Veer, *Orientalism and Post-Colonial Predicament* (Philadelphia: University of Pennsylvania Press, 1993)

Prashad, V., *Fat Cats and Running Dogs: The Enron Stage of Capitalism* (London: Zed, 2002)

Raheja, G., 'India: Caste, Kinship and Dominance Reconsidered' *Annual Review of Anthropology* Vol. 17, 1988, p. 498

Ray, L., *Theorizing Classical Sociology* (Buckingham: Open University Press, 1999)

Raychaudhuri, L. and I. Habib, 'Foreign Trade' in *The Cambridge Economic History of India Vol. 1 1200–1750* (Cambridge: Cambridge University Press, 1982)

Razzell, P., 'The Protesant Ethic and the Spirit of Capitalism: A Natural Scientific Critique' *British Journal of Sociology* Vol. 28, No. 1, 1977, pp. 17–37

Ringer, F., *Decline of German Mandarins: The German Academic Community 1890–1933* (Hanover, New Hampshire: Wesleyan University Press, 1990)

—— *Max Weber's Methodology* (Cambridge, Massachusetts: Harvard University Press, 1997)

Ritzer, G., *The McDonaldization of Society* (Thousand Oaks: Pine Forge Press, 1993)

Roberts, J.A.G., *China: Prehistory to the Nineteenth Century* (Stroud, Gloucestershire: Sutton Publishing, 1996)

Robertson, H.M., *The Rise of Economic Individualism* (Cambridge, Cambridge University Press, 1935)

Rodzinski, W., *The Walled Kingdom* (London: Fontana, 1984)

Rostow, W., *The Stages of Economic Growth: A Non-Communist Manifesto* (Cambridge: Cambridge University Press, 1971)

Roth, G., 'Political Critiques of Max Weber: Some Implications for Political Sociology' *American Sociological Review* Vol. 30, No. 2, 1965, pp. 213–23

Rothermind, D., *An Economic History of India* (London: Croom Helm, 1988)

Runciman, W., *A Critique of Max Weber's Philosophy of Social Science* (Cambridge, Cambridge University Press, 1972)

—— *Selections in Translation* (Cambridge: Cambridge University Press, 1978)

Said, E., *Orientalism* (Harmondsworth: Penguin, 1978)

Sayer, D., *Capitalism and Modernity* (London: Routledge, 1991)

Schaar, S., 'Orientalism at the Service of Imperialism' *Race and Class* Vol. 21, No. 1, 1979, pp. 67–80

Schluchter, W., *Paradoxes of Modernity: Culture and Conduct in the Theory of Max Weber* (Stanford: Stanford University Press, 1996)

Schneider, E.V., 'The Sociology of C. Wright Mills', in J. Alexander, R. Boudron and M. Cherkaoui (eds), *The Classical Tradition in Sociology: The American Tradition* (London: Sage, 1997)

Schroeder, R., *Max Weber and the Sociology of Culture* (London: Sage, 1992)

Schroeder, G. 'Max Weber as Outsider: His Nominal Influence on German Society in the Twenties' *Journal of the History of Behavioural Sciences* Vol. 16, 1980, pp. 317–32

Scott Dixon, C., 'Narratives of the German Reformation' in C. Scott Dixon (ed.), *The German Reformation* (Oxford: Blackwell, 1999)

Seligman, A., *The Idea of Civil Society* (New York: Free Press, 1992)

Shaw, B. and R. Saller, 'Editor's Introduction' in M.I. Finley, *Economy and Society in Ancient Greece* (Harmondsworth: Penguin, 1981)

Sheehan, J., *German Liberalism in the Nineteenth Century* (London: Methuen, 1982)

Shils, E., 'Max Weber and the World since 1920' in W. Mommsen and J. Oesterhammel (eds), *Max Weber and His Contemporaries* (London: Allen and Unwin, 1987)

Siegel, P., *The Meek and the Militant: Religion and Power across the World* (London: Zed, 1987)

Sombart, W., *The Jews and Modern Capitalism* (Glencoe: Free Press, 1951)

Strauss, G., *Manifestations of Discontent in Germany on the Eve of the Reformation* (Bloomington: Indiana University Press, 1971)

Sturmer, M., *The German Empire 1871–1919* (London: Weidenfeld and Nicolson, 2000)

Tawney, R.H., *Religion and the Rise of Capitalism* (New York: Mentor Books, 1954)

Therborn, G., *Science, Class and Society* (London: New Left Books, 1976)

Thompson, E.P., 'Time Discipline and Industrial Capitalism' *Past and Present* Vol. 38, No. 1, 1967, pp. 56–97

Toussaint, A., *The History of the Indian Ocean* (London: Routledge and Kegan Paul, 1966)

Tribe, K., *Reading Weber* (London: Routledge, 1989)

Trotsky, L., *The History of the Russian Revolution* (London: Victor Gollancz, 1932)

—— *The Revolution Betrayed* (London: New Park, 1967)

—— *The Permanent Revolution* (London: New Park, 1982)

—— *Max Weber: Critical Responses Vol. 3* (London: Routledge, 1999)

Turner, B.S., *For Weber: Essays on the Sociology of Fate* (London: Sage, 1996)

—— *The Talcott Parsons Reader* (Oxford: Blackwell, 1999)

Urbainczyk, T., *Theodoret of Cyrrhus* (Ann Arbor: University of Michigan Press, 2002)

Wakeman, F., 'China and the Seventeenth Century Crisis' *Late Imperial China* Vol. 7, No. 1, June 1986, pp. 1–26

Walker, P.C., 'Capitalism and Reformation' *Economic History Review* Vol. 8, No. 1, 1937, pp. 1–19

Weber, Marianne, *Max Weber: A Biography* (New York: John Wiley, 1975)

Weber, Max, *The Methodology of the Social Sciences* (New York: Free Press, 1949)

—— *The Religion of China* (New York: Free Press, 1951)

—— *Ancient Judaism* (New York: Free Press, 1952)

—— *The Religion of India* (New York: Free Press, 1958)

—— *On Universities: The Power of the State and the Dignity of the Academic Calling in Imperial Germany* (Chicago: University of Chicago Press, 1974)

—— *Roscher and Knies: The Logical Problems of Historical Economics* (New York: Free Press, 1975)

—— *The Agrarian Sociology of Ancient Civilisations* (London, New Left Books, 1976)

—— *The Protestant Ethic and the Spirit of Capitalism* (New York: Charles Scribner's Sons, 1958/1976)

—— *Critique of Stammler* (New York: Free Press, 1977)

—— *Economy and Society* (Berkeley: University of California Press, 1978)

—— *General Economic History* (New Brunswick: Transaction Books, 1981)

—— *Political Writings* (Cambridge: Cambridge University Press, 1994)

—— *The Russian Revolutions* (Cambridge: Polity, 1995)

Wehler, H.U., *The German Empire 1871–1918* (Leamington Spa: Berg, 1985)

Westergaard, J., 'Class in Britain since 1979: Facts, Theories and Ideologies' in D. Lee and B. Turner (eds), *Conflicts about Class: Debating Inequality in Late Industrialism* (London: Longman, 1996)

Williams, S. (ed.), *The Gregorian Epoch: Reformation, Revolution, Reaction?* (Lexington, Massachusetts: D.C. Heath, 1964)

Wood, E.M., *The Origins of Capitalism: The Longer View* (London: Verso, 2002)

Wright, E.O., *Classes* (London: Verso, 1985)

—— 'The Shadow of Exploitation in Weber's Class Analysis', paper from Department of Sociology, University of Wisconsin, Madison, July 2002

Index

Compiled by Sue Carlton